HUMAN DEVELOPMENT AND WORKING LIFE

Human Development and Working Life

Work for Welfare

Edited by

HELGE HVID AND PETER HASLE

with

Anette Bilfeldt, Peter Hagedorn-Rasmussen, Elsebeth Hofmeister, Hans Hvenegaard, Michael Søgaard Jørgensen, Christian Kock, Tage Søndergaard Kristensen, Hans Jørgen Limborg, Hanne Meyer-Johansen, Niels Møller, Christel Arendt Nielsen, Martin Nielsen, Peter Olsén, Lars Smith-Hansen, Inger Stauning, Peter Vogelius

Routledge
Taylor & Francis Group
LONDON AND NEW YORK

First published 2003 by Gower Publishing

2 Park Square, Milton Park, Abingdon, Oxon OX14 4RN
711 Third Avenue, New York, NY 10017, USA

Routledge is an imprint of the Taylor & Francis Group, an informa business

First issued in paperback 2016

British Library Cataloguing in Publication Data
Human development and working life : work for welfare
1. Personnel management - Denmark 2. Work - Psychological aspects 3. Management - Employee participation - Denmark
4. Quality of work life - Denmark
I. Hvid, Helge II. Hasle, Peter
658.3'009489

Library of Congress Cataloging-in-Publication Data
Hvid, Helge.
Human development and working life : work for welfare / Helge Hvid and Peter Hasle.
p. cm.
Includes bibliographical references and index.

1. Manpower policy. 2. Human capital. 3. Human capital--Management. I. Hasle, Peter. II. Title.

HD5713.H94 2003
658.3--dc21

2003045233

ISBN 978-0-7546-3419-5 (hbk)
ISBN 978-1-138-25856-3 (pbk)

Contents

Preface

Does development of human resources in working life bring about a good working life, where the work is arranged in accordance with the individual person's qualifications and needs? Does it bring about a working life where the individual gains more influence and where security is created through learning and development? Or does the development of human resources lead to stress, insecurity, expulsion from the labour market, and more divisiveness in society? And how do the collegial and the management/employee relationships develop, when the human resources are developed? These are the questions we intend to address in this book.

The book is a result of the research project SARA (*Social and Welfare Consequences of the Application of Human Resources at Work*). For a number of years, we have studied companies that have made efforts to 'develop its human resources'. In the companies we have followed, the organization has been changed. Demands have been made and opportunities have opened up for the individual and the employee as a whole towards learning on the job, taking responsibility, making decisions, showing loyalty, and becoming involved and creative.

The overall hypothesis of the SARA project is that the ongoing initiatives in the development of the human resources make extensive positive changes possible in working life and in the relationship between work and spare time. But these are opportunities that are not necessarily brought to fruition. The SARA project identifies the pre-conditions that must be present and utilized, if the individual's life quality, the companies' developmental opportunities, and welfare and democracy in society, are to be improved. The SARA project is further presented in the Supplement in the end of the book.

The SARA project has been carried out in a Danish context. The companies that are part of the project are all Danish, and all the researchers involved are Danish. However an international audience may find the project interesting for two reasons:

- Development of human resources in the workplace is in no way just a Danish phenomenon. The issues related to human resource development that Danish companies work with are found worldwide.
- In Denmark, a certain political interest has been present to develop the human resources in the workplace in such a way that both productivity and work conditions would stand to win. This political interest has its roots in a Scandinavian industrial relations tradition. Scandinavia has a tradition for strong trade unions, a high level of organization, an extensive cooperation between the labour market's parties and a strong involvement on the part of the State in social security and in development of work environment, competence, and productivity.

The book thus deals with issues that are common for modern economy all over the world, but here they are enacted in a particular institutional and political framework. The book provides an insight into general problems in working life that are linked to development of the human resources in work, and at the same time, the book inspires action by presenting a particular institutional and political reaction to the issues in question.

All researchers associated with the SARA project have been involved in the making of the book by contributing with papers and by discussing one another's contributions.

Helge Hvid and Peter Hasle have edited all the contributions to provide a cohesive text. The following writers have special responsibility for each of the book's chapters:

Chapter 1: Peter Hasle and Helge Hvid.

Chapter 2: Helge Hvid, Niels Møller, Tage Søndergaard Kristensen and Lars Smith-Hansen. Tage Søndergaard Kristensen and Lars Smith-Hansen are responsible for the questionnaire study.

Chapter 3: Christian Kock, Peter Hagedorn-Rasmussen and Peter Vogelius.

Chapter 4: Hans Hvenegaard, Hans Jørgen Limborg, Niels Møller, Christel Arendt Nielsen and Peter Olsén. The Section 'Development and Solidarity Among the Employees' is primarily based on Niels Møller's and Peter Olsén's research. The Section 'Employee Participation in Development of the Work' is primarily based on Hans Jørgen Limborg's and Hans Hvenegaard's research. The Section 'New Working Life Strategies and the Perception of Risk' is primarily based on Hans Jørgen Limborg's research.

Chapter 5: Anette Bilfeldt, Elsebeth Hofmeister, Michael Søgaard Jørgensen, Hanne Meyer-Johansen, and Inger Stauning. The section 'Employees' Role in the Development of Quality' is primarily based on Michael Søgaard Jørgensen's research. The Section 'Environmental Sustainability and Working Life Development' is primarily based on Hanne Meyer-Johansen's and Inger Stauning's research. The Section 'Quality in Elder Care' is primarily based on Anette Bilfeldt's and Elsebeth Hofmeister's research.

Chapter 6: Helge Hvid and Peter Hasle.

Hanne Rask Sønderborg translated the book.

Acknowledgements

This book is a result of an extraordinary well functioning collaboration between 18 researchers at four research institutions. It has been necessary for all of us to give up some personal priorities in favour of the common project. However, in the end all of us have gained from this project.

Even more important for the success of the project have been the hundreds of employees and managers who have spent hours with us as 'victims' of our interviews or observations and the thousands of employees and managers who have taken the time to fill out questionnaires.

Hanne Rask Sønderborg has done an excellent job in translating the Danish manuscript into English, as has Helle Manscher who has been responsible for the layout. Special thanks also go to professor Tom Whiston, who read the entire manuscript and made many helpful suggestions.

Finally, the Danish Research Agency must be mentioned. Without considerable funding from the agency the whole project would not have been possible.

Chapter 1

Current Work Politics

Work is a concept of central political importance because the scope and the character of work have decisive influence on a number of factors, such as economy, identity, family relations, social security, and education. The very fact that work has such immense political importance means that work in and of itself becomes the object of many political initiatives, and work is shaped within a political process. Certainly, market conditions and technology are also essential to the formation of work, but the specific development of work is shaped in a political process in companies. This political process is influenced by consulting firms and management gurus each championing their own political program on the development of work. Also, the development of work is influenced by the politics pursued by trade unions and employers' associations and by government agencies as well.

The purpose of this book is to contribute to the knowledge about the development of work, and we hope that this knowledge can be conducive for the work politics pursued in companies, by trade unions and employers' associations, and by governmental authorities. The employment policy of the European Union launched at the Amsterdam Summit in 1997 and continued in the so-called Luxemburg Process, could be a frame for such a policy. Here 'adaptability' is a keyword emphasizing the need for adapting modern work organizations to human needs and at the same time create a competitive organization (European Commission 1997 and 2001). The framework is an analysis of the social and welfare consequences of the utilization of human resources at work in Denmark, and the point of departure for the analysis is a discussion of the concept of work politics.

From Work Society to Individualized Work

Never has such a large part of the population in the developed industrial nations worked in the formal money economy. The employment rate has never been higher, and Denmark and Sweden are setting a record in this field. At the same time, leading sociologists and social debaters say that we are moving away from the work society (e.g. Gorz 1999). This view is based on the observation that work does not, to the same degree as earlier, determine how the rest of life will be lived. Previously, the division of the population into various occupations also implied the division into housing forms, life patterns, political affiliation, cultural preferences, etc. That is no longer the case. Income, lifestyle, and political affiliation develop across occupational groups. Work is no longer the fundamental social category that determines all other social relations.

This, however, does not mean that work has less importance in the life of the individual. There is an unprecedented focus on work with its specific qualification requirements, challenges, demands, and strains. Work has become the decisive means to self-fulfilment and identity formation for the population aged between 20 and 60. Interesting work with long working hours has become a privilege that signifies success in life (Bauman 1998). For the unskilled group, however, many working hours are hardly viewed as a privilege. Here it is in many cases more important to get home as fast as possible, from a dull and drudging work that does not hold many opportunities for personal development.

When development of the human resources is at the centre of economic development and survival of companies, the perception of the work of the highly educated stratum is elevated to be of universal validity. The career life style becomes a standard in the public debate about work – a standard for what is normal and desirable. The question is, however, whether the career life style corresponds to the aspirations and opportunities of the great majority of the working population. And it is questionable whether they in fact will be happier and healthier if this is the trend – especially if viewed in a lifelong perspective. Also, one may ask, what initiatives in work policy are necessary to achieve this positive effect? These are the central questions, which the book will seek to answer by analyzing Danish efforts in developing the human resources in work.

The analyses of the book are related to two perspectives on work politics. The first perspective is the current crisis of the welfare state in Western Europe, and in particular, in Scandinavia. Work has been put on the agenda as an important issue by this crisis. The second perspective is grounded in contemporary global development patterns and international competition.

Welfare and Work

Developing the welfare state was the main task for the nations of Western Europe in the second half of the previous century. In the Nordic countries, it was the Social Democratic Party in particular, which put the welfare state on the agenda, and the development demonstrated far into the century that the task was in fact being accomplished. Everybody – or almost everybody – was at work and attained substantially increased incomes. At the same time, the state placed a safety net under the population with opportunities for education, the necessary medical treatment, and a rather fine-meshed social safety net for unemployed people, retirees and others in need. Although many societal problems were far from solved, the Northern European welfare states in particular seemed (about 1970) to be very close to the goal.

Towards the end of the century, however, the welfare state came under two-sided pressure from the economy and politics. In the wake of the Oil Crisis in the 70s, financial problems arose for the welfare state. The expenses continued to grow – the populations' need for welfare and health benefits was apparently insatiable. This was due, in particular to increased unemployment, wear and tear of many workers with subsequent exclusion from the labour market and an increasingly older population. The limit for the tax level seemed to be about reached, and it was increasingly difficult to finance the welfare state. Many countries apparently began to get permanent state deficits. Simultaneously, political problems arose. The labour movement put in a claim for a better work environment and the young people demanded more democracy. Concurrently, there was growing discontent with the rising taxes in parts of the population that, among other things, led to tax-refusal parties in the Scandinavian countries. A growing individualization also led to a perception of the welfare state as a straightjacket with too many rules that curbed the possibilities for the individual. Liberal political parties picked up these signs of dissatisfaction and began to agitate for deregulation and the free play of the individual. The extreme version of this was seen in Thatcherism in the UK. Therefore, it became necessary for those parties and groups who were behind the welfare state (first and foremost the labour movement and political parties such as the Social Democrats) to seek new ways to revitalize it. In so doing, work has, to an increasingly greater extent, taken centre stage.

Previously, the state had merely seen work as a source of income where the main question was one of distribution: How should the cake be divided between employees, employer, and public disbursements? The employment as a source of income was important, the economic growth was important, but the work *per se* and in particular the content of work did not have a high priority.

This situation has changed considerably. The first sign of a new attention to work was the interest in the work environment, which has manifested itself since the beginning of the '70s. The economic growth of the '60s had caused a high increase in the health risks at work, which first led to intense debate in the public sphere, and then to an increase in government intervention. During the '80s and '90s, this attention to work grew, particularly at the prospect of a rising number of retirees and falling number of youths. Both led to a stagnant work force in the following years; the possibility of increasing the employment frequency among women has largely been exhausted in Denmark, and it has therefore become important to safeguard the work force by securing the marginalized wage earners at work or re-introduce the excluded workers force into the labour market. This means that the companies and their way of organizing the work are given a central role in the continued formation of the welfare state. Social policy tends to penetrate the company setting.

It may therefore be said that we are moving away from the welfare state, towards the 'work-fare' state (Jessop 1990, Nielsen 2000). Wolfgang Streck speaks about a re-thinking of European concepts of social solidarity taking place in recent years in Europe, 'where national communities seek to defend their solidarity, less through protection and redistribution than through joint competitive and productive success – through politics, not against markets, but within and with them, gradually replacing protective and re-distributive with competitive and productive solidarity' (Streck 1999 p. 6).

Developing the human resources in working life now becomes an important factor in social politics, because such politics (besides strengthening the companies' ability to compete and strengthening the innovative forces of society) has two social political advantages:

- Increasing employment opportunities for the work force, thereby reducing state disbursements.
- Reducing social risk tied to the work, thus lowering the risk of work-related disease, expulsion from the labour market and strain on family life.

Initiatives to Development of the Work

The European Union launched a work policy in the late 1990s in relation to its employment policy (European Foundation on Social Quality, 2002). The aim of the policy is

> the replacement of hierarchical and rigid structures by more innovative and flexible structures based on high skill, high trust and increased involvement of employees. To reach that goal policy makers are to: develop or adapt policies which support, rather than hinder, fundamental organizational renewal and (..) to strike a productive balance between the interests of business and the interests of workers, balance between flexibility and security throughout Europe (European Commission 1997).

The EU policy for development of work organization is, however, still a policy in its creation. The policy is realized through 'soft instruments' such as inspiration, reporting, research, etc. In 1999, the European Work Organisation Network (EWON) sponsored by the European Commission was established, with the goal of collection and dissemination of experience with new forms of work organizations. As it appears quite clearly from the homepage of EWON many of initiatives are being taken related to the socially responsible development of the work organization (http://europa.eu.int/comm/employment_social/social/workorg/ewon/index_en.htm).

In Scandinavia, a socially responsible development of the work organization was put on the agenda at an early time. In Norway and Sweden, as well as in Denmark there is a long tradition for dealing with development of work from a social and humanistic point of view. Socio-technique was the first big step in this direction. Already in the '60s, Emery and Thorsrud (1976) cunducted experiments on the development of work, with the goal of creating a more interesting and healthy work, which was also competitive. Emery and Thorsrud worked primarily in Norway, but the tradition was carried on in the '70s, in Sweden with experiments in the auto industry (Sandberg 1992), and in Denmark with experiments in the metal industry (Agersnap 1973).

Scandinavia has also been characterized by a well-organized labour movement and the greater part of the work force is organized. On this basis, a labour market system was created, where the two parties (the employers and the labour movement) would regulate wages and working hours through mutual general agreements. In this connection, a cooperative system with shop stewards and work councils, entitled to a certain influence on decisions made in the companies, was also forged. This system is supported by the state with legislation about, among other things, labour law and conciliation. Furthermore, the two parties participate in most types of state regulation of the labour market. This is particularly true for legislation on the work environment, vocational training, work centres, and unemployment benefits (Due et al. 1994). In Denmark, as well as in the other Scandinavian countries, this particular industrial relation system has been utilized to advance productivity development in the companies. Although it certainly did not proceed without conflicts, employers and the labour movement cooperated to introduce productivity-advancing wage systems that became an important part of the introduction of Taylorized work in Denmark after the 2nd World War.

The prerequisites were therefore good for staking on developing the human resources in the Scandinavian countries in the '90s. This development would not only hold a management perspective, but also a bottom-up perspective, so that a better, healthier, and more interesting work for the average wage earner could be created. In Denmark, this opportunity was supported by the strong labour movement and by a relatively anti-authoritarian work culture. Here, the wage earners have, to a greater extent than was the case in other countries, made individual decisions about what they do, without automatically submitting to their foremen (Hofstete 1994). At the same time, the Danish work culture has been characterized by a relatively high job satisfaction and commitment to the job and to the work place (Kompetencerådet 2000, Ingelhard et al. 1998).

The Trades Union Congresses of the Scandinavian countries thus launched a program in the '90s for 'The Developmental Work', which is based on this very perspective. The Danish Government later adopted 'Developmental Work'. The concept was used as guideline for the state's own personnel policy. Simultaneously, the Government launched a program that would help the companies in adopting the ideas of 'Developmental Work'. 'Developmental Work' is a pivotal point of this book, and it is given a more detailed presentation in Chapter 2. 'The Developmental Work' is based on two important assumptions:

- The wage earners want more exciting and challenging work, and this work makes them happier and healthier.
- The companies become more competitive by developing the human resources from a social and humane viewpoint, and the company's management has realized (or can be made to realize) that it is an advantage for the company.

There exists, however, very little documentation for any of these assumptions, and the limited evidence we have is quite contradictory. Thus, desires of more exciting work and greater individual opportunities have been found (Jørgensen et al. 1993), but there are also many stories of resistance towards changes, where the wage earners actively or passively protest against the new types of organization. There are also signs of increased stress (Paoli & Merllie 2001, Borg & Burg 1997), which does not harmonize with better work. On the other hand, there is also no documentation that these types of organization actually succeed in gaining wide recognition in Danish companies. Csonka (2000) thus finds that flexible and human resource oriented companies are less common, than is often assumed in many quarters. There are companies that prefer more top-down oriented models, where the management has more control over the development, and where, perhaps, a fast economic return might also be expected. The companies do not in all cases become more competitive by developing the human resources in work.

Consequently, one can question the approach of 'Developmental Work' in several ways. Does it work in practice? Are the wage earners doing better? And do the companies even want to move in this direction? In the following chapters, we shall look more closely into this; but first, we shall look at another perspective on the development of work – the increased pressure from global competition.

Globalization and Flexibility

The assumption that the trends to globalization implies drastically increased competition is commonly accepted. This is, among other things, caused by free movements of capital, unfettered streams of information, more open commerce with opportunities of trading all over the globe and options (threats) of moving the production to the countries, which is more economically lucrative. In addition, the market of the industrialized nations has reached the saturation point for many mass-produced goods, and more customized products are needed. This development, therefore, demands increased product innovation with a shorter research period, shorter production time, increased marketing, and especially increased price competition. Inter-woven with this, there is new technology, primarily in the form of information technology, which both holds new opportunities and demands more from the companies. Although it is arguable how broadly globalization trends have succeeded (Hirst & Thompson 1996), a perception has spread in society at large that competition is in every way much harder, as a result of the globalization, and that continual rationalizations as well as production and product innovation are necessary. This perception is not only prevailing in those industry and service companies that compete in the global market, but also among the more locally oriented companies and in the public sector. The overall strategy for adapting to the new conditions for competition can be comprised under the concept of flexibility. In industrial companies it means more frequent and shorter duration of product innovation, more product varieties, shorter readjustment period for the production, faster turnover of products, and shorter delivery times. In service production it means faster customer orientation, incessant innovation of new service products, and continuous organizational changes. Both the companies and the management literature have realized, however, that the companies cannot achieve this flexibility, without a flexible work force. The most important task for Human Resource Management (Legge 1995) is therefore to develop flexible employees. Human resource management demands both functional flexibility-skill and will to do various work tasks – and numerical flexibility – flexibility in relation to working hours and conditions of employment – and not either or as Atkinson suggest (1984). We will here re-word functional flexibility to internal flexibility and numerical flexibility to external flexibility. Internal as well as external flexibility, is expected and required of the employees. The internal flexibility demands that the employees:

- Accept responsibility for work they do, and for meeting the requirements
- Make decisions within the given boundaries
- Find creative solutions
- Make the social relations work
- Are capable of performing several diverse work functions.

However, there is also an external flexibility concerning the company's need to utilize the available manpower in the most optimal manner. This implies:

- Flexible working hours – you go home when there is nothing more to do, regardless of whether this means a long or a short work day.

- Flexible conditions of tenure – you are employed when there is work, however short or long a period of time that may be.
- Individual flexible salary – you are paid in accordance with the company's wishes, as stated in an individual agreement. Thus, the company pays each individual in accordance with an estimate of the person's services, importance to the company, loyalty, flexibility, and the like.

The management literature is under the implicit assumption that the development of this flexibility is in the mutual interest of both the company and the employee. The company has an obvious interest in increased employee flexibility, so that it can meet the market's demands on increased flexibility. The reason for the wage-earners interest should be looked for in the increased individualization of modern man. The assumption is that the individuals have a steadily growing need for self-fulfilment through personal decisions and acts, thereby creating an independent identity. People are therefore interested in a work that is autonomous and challenging, just as they also readily partake in a competition for higher wages by delivering more, be it in the form of physical work or loyalty. They also don't mind irregular working hours, which private life will have to adapt to. Also temporary conditions of tenure are accepted, since people are on a continuous search for another job anyway, a job where they will have a better chance of self-fulfilment. To the extent that these assumptions are true, the high degree of organization in the Danish labour movement is also put under pressure. If the wage-earner does well and satisfies his or her needs through individual competition with other wage earners, the wage-earner may not see the need to be a member of a trade union.

With such an *a priori* assumption of mutual interests, management literature has developed a set of various theories and methods that claim increases in competitive power through enhanced flexibility and effectiveness. There is great attention to Human Resource Management (HRM), and to concepts such as Business Process Re-Engineering (BPR), Total Quality Management (TQM), Lean Production, and management-influenced approaches to the educational organization (Jackson 2001).

In this context, it is important to point out that this management literature to a predominant extent is based on a belief, which is presented as a persuasive truth. There is, by and large, no empirical documentation to prove that the various management fads actually yield the economic gains that are being promised. The books hold very persuasive argumentation and a few disparate examples are presented, but there is no documentation that for instance BPR renders the promised gains. On the contrary, BPR supporters themselves refer to the fact that 50–70% of the attempts to introduce this type of management fail (Champy & Hammer 1993). These concepts are given a more detailed analysis in Chapter 3.

The question is, however, whether management literature's assumption that there is a mutual interest in the development of flexibility actually holds water. Do the employees even want this flexibility? Do their lives improve with flexibility?

Flexibility For the Management or For the Employees

From the outset the two parties, companies and wage-earners, have very distinct rationales and wishes as concerns the development of flexibility.

Table 1.1 Flexibility in relation to rationale and wishes

	Rationale	Wish
Company	Economical	Personal flexibility: to adjust the employees to the company's needs
Employees	Determined by need	Company flexibility: that the companies are adjusted to the needs of the employees

After Navrbjerg 1999, p. 38.

Even if the starting point is different the concrete situation may not turn out to be so. The company may have an interest in giving the employees better opportunities for developing loyalty and involvement, and the employees may perceive it as meaningful to contribute to the survival of the company, through a high degree of personal flexibility. But there will also be a fight over the direction of the flexibility. Should it be adjusted to the needs of the management or to the needs of the employees? The outcome of this fight depends to a great extent on how the involvement of the employees takes place, and it also depends on who controls the information streams. Do the employees have real contributory influence, or are they just being informed? Is it management who controls the streams of information, or does the information flow freely in the company?

In practice, one will hardly find the extremes where either, it is the management that totally dominates, or it is the employees who are given free hands to command the development. In particular, the employee-oriented approach is most likely not allowed full play. In Chapter 4, we shall further examine the complexity of these problems, both as to how these approaches actually play out in practice, and as to what it means to the employees.

It is, however, also a commonly held view among decision-makers in both the state and in the labour market organizations, that the introduction of flexibility on the whole is a win-win situation – or could be made to a win-win situation. If flexibility is introduced in the right way both parties are supposed to gain from it. This is the position for the Developmental Work approach of the welfare state and labour movement, as well as for management literature's many bids for enhanced competitive power through flexibility.

There are of course many problems in this understanding, and we shall analyze them more closely in the following chapters. Is this in fact a win-win situation, or is it rather a win and lose situation for both parties, in which there will always be losses connected to the gains achieved? And, in particular, we shall focus on which conditions are critical for the company development to yield the greatest possible gains for the wage earners, when it comes to achieving a more satisfactory and healthy work as well as better living conditions.

The Product and the Content of the Work

The content and the result of the work are, by and large, absent in literature on socio-technique and human resource management. The content and the result of the work in the form of a product (including a service output) have, on the whole, been taken for granted. It has however turned out to be too narrow an approach, because the employees are engaged in what they do. They need meaning in their work. That is why employees care about the quality of the product and about the societal meaning of the product. They consider whether is it useful for society and what it means to the environment. In the opposite, the experience of meaninglessness in work carries mental strain along with risk of neurosis and burnout (Isaksen 2000).

This understanding is reflected in the concept 'The Developmental Work', where pride in work and the societal value of the product play important roles. The company management and the management consultants have gradually also discovered the importance of the employees in this context.

From the management point of view, systematic quality management has obtained a solid footing as the keyword for development of both market and production. In the beginning, the ISO-9000 standards were dominant, although companies only partly implemented the standards without getting the certificate. Later, the ISO system was expanded with ISO-14001, which is an environmental management standard. Other environmental management systems are also manifest, such as the European system EMAS. These quality and environmental management systems rest on an instrumental and bureaucratic philosophy. Important elements are clear goals, placement of responsibility, development of formalized procedures, extended registration, and control. Quality and environmental management has therefore, in many cases contributed to making the work more Tayloristic in character, with more fixed routines and greater control.

It turned out, however, that it is difficult to make quality and environmental systems work, if the employees do not have a certain understanding of the systems. The systems work the best, if the employees are actually engaged in issues of quality and environment. Many companies have therefore made an effort to communicate quality awareness to the employees, and in many cases total quality management (TQM) has become a more popular approach, since it emphasizes the necessity to include the employees in quality development. Accordingly, a number of attempts to include employees in environmental improvements have been made in Denmark (Le Blansch & Lorentzen 1996).

This opens up potentially new perspectives for the work. The horizons under which work is performed, widens. The customers, the users, and the environment become more present, not just with the individual, but also in the systems and procedures that are in effect in the company. The individual must not only meet the company's demands in accordance with the company's own horizon. He or she must also relate to the demands of customers, users, and environmental organizations.

Thus, the individual is not only a wage earner, who does as told. The individual also becomes a producer, who reflects on what is being produced, and who consciously participates in the development of society, through work.

Still, the fact that quality and user consideration has played an important role for the employees, is no news. The artisan's whole identity has been linked to the quality of the products he made. In welfare work, the quality for the users – the children, the elderly, or the sick – is present in the work every day. Also in routine and heavily monitored work, the primary meaning of the work has been tied to the quality of the product that the individual was contributing to produce.

The new element of quality development and environmental improvements is, however, that now a verbalization and systematization of quality and environment is taking place, and this may also politicise the area. In the companies, quality and environment become politicized sectors. Both in the companies and in the labour market, it becomes a political issue of how quality and environment should be governed, and how much influence the employees should have on these issues. In this way, new relations between work and everyday life are developed, and new relations are created between labour market organizations, environmentalists, and user organizations. In Chapter 5 we shall look more closely at the dynamics in the companies, when the new orientation towards quality and environment is introduced.

Working life Development as a Political Process

As it appears from the above, the development in working life may be viewed from several different angles, where different actors influence working life, each with their specific interests. Three groupings in particular stand out: the political participants behind the welfare state, who are envisioning opportunities to develop working life in a direction that will secure the survival of the welfare state, wage earners and their organizations that are seeking to secure an interesting, stimulating, and healthy work, and the management of the companies and their management consultant that are trying to involve the employees in the continued survival and development of the company.

Therefore it becomes important to point out that the development in working life is the result of a political process, which does not have a given outcome (Dawson et al. 2000). It is not indefinable globalization, or the concepts of the management consultants, that automatically creates a certain structure of work; it is various actors attempting to influence the development, and the result will show how large or small the actors influences have been, dependent upon political power and ability. This is not only true for societal politics (legislation, state subsidies, etc.), but also in the individual company, where the management and the employee must engage in a political play with one another and the surroundings, about the development of work. It is therefore possible to influence the development, and it is also possible to influence work in certain directions. It is this opportunity to influence the development of work and, in particular, to steer it in a direction of more humane work, which is discussed in various ways in the rest of the book.

Chapter 2

Developmental Work

Introduction

Developmental Work is flexible and quality-oriented. There is a sound and healthy work environment and autonomous, empowered, and organized employees. Developmental Work is a vision, a strategy, and it is also a concept for development of production and work.

- Developmental Work is a vision about work that results in human development of competent, autonomous, and empowered employees, who create the basis for a sustainable wealth production through advanced democracy in the work place.
- Developmental Work is at the same time a strategy for development of production and work, which is based on the organized collaboration between labour and management. In this collaboration, management implements some of its interests related to flexibility and quality, and labour also implements some of its interests in good working conditions. Such cooperation always involves compromises, and the strategy will therefore never fully implement the vision. Nevertheless, the vision is important as a guide to the strategy.
- Finally, Developmental Work is becoming a concept that comprises a number of recommendations on the organization of the work in accordance with the vision and the strategy.

In Denmark, the concept of developmental work has in the last ten years been an important reference point for a broad, open discussion concerning hopes, opportunities, and experiences in relation to work and working life. As a visionary concept, Developmental Work has played a part in establishing new discussions and relations between firms, researchers, consultants, and organizations in the labour market.

In this chapter, we shall briefly outline the Developmental Work concept's roots in the Scandinavian work political tradition and work life research. We shall briefly review the 10–year old history of Developmental Work. We shall present the Developmental Work vision and confront it with the realities, both as can be read from survey data from the SARA project, as they are presented in qualitatively oriented evaluations and case studies.

In Chapter 4, the social dynamics that are involved in implementing the Developmental Work strategy in companies, shall be further examined on the basis of the SARA project's qualitative case analyses.

Historical Roots of Developmental Work

The three Scandinavian countries we are focusing on are all characterized by highly organized labour markets with a high degree of co-operation between trade unions and employers both on the general level and in the companies. In the post war period, a unique relation was established between trade unions, employers' associations, and the growing welfare state: employers obtained labour market stability and a collaborative labour force in a period of heavy rationalization. The unions achieved a common wage policy at the labour market level and influence at company level, in return for acceptance and active involvement in rationalizing the industry. The welfare state secured economic growth and increased tax income in return for support to the labour market institutions and support to rationalization of the industry.

Norway and Sweden

In the Scandinavian collaborative strategy after World War II, it was the Tayloristic rationalization that was at the centre; however in Norway, an alternative to Taylorism arose in the beginning of the 1960s: the socio-technical cooperative experiments. The socio-technical principles were presented as an alternative to the Tayloristic principles and, notably, as usable in mass-producing companies. A number of experiments were carried out to replace Taylorism with multi-skilled jobs and teamwork. These experiments were led by Thorsrud and Emery (Thorsrud 1970, Emery et al. 1976). In Sweden, the most well known example is the Volvo experiment with semi-autonomous teams in the car industry (Berggren 1993).

The socio-technical approach did not spread widely in Scandinavian industry at that time. The companies were more inspired by scientific management than by the socio-technical approach, and this marked the industrial relations. Co-determinism in relation to technology, work, and organization was on the agenda, but still, employment and wages were the core elements of the industrial relations. However, the critique of Taylorism survived, and the ideas of the socio-technical approach and co-determination became core elements of Developmental Work, as it is practised today.

In the 1970s, the socio-technical approach was criticized for not focusing on the unequal power relations in the companies. As a supplement to the socio-technical approach, a technology policy was developed up through the '70s and the '80s, which was aimed at strengthening the position of the employees in the cooperation on development of technology and organization. The basic idea was that an equitable cooperation between employers and employees on the development of technology and organization, presupposes a build-up of skill resources on the part of the employees, based on knowledge and action competency (Sandberg 1992).

This philosophy was supported by a number of legislative initiatives. In the Scandinavian countries, laws were passed in the seventies, which gave employees democratic rights at the company level. The most far-reaching law was the Swedish Act on the Joint Regulation of Working Life (Medbestämmandelagen) from 1977.

In the 1980s, new threats to the Scandinavian labour market model arose. The neo-liberal turn, the introduction of new flexible production systems, and new information technology reduced the sufficiency of the traditional labour market regulation. The first trade union to realize this was the Swedish Metalworkers Union (Metallindustriarbetareförbundet 1985, LO 1991b). The union explicitly rejected the strategies being pursued by capital, which would lead to a polarisation on the shop floor and in society at large. To secure welfare, the trade unions must change the traditional common wage politics towards common work politics, which on the one hand could secure the competitiveness of the industry under post-Fordist conditions, and, on the other hand, could secure solidarity and social security.

However, the trade union did not only formulate a common work policy with the intention of avoiding expulsion and polarization; it also saw the development from a societal perspective:

> Only an industry that can take seriously people's resources and be developed to promote a cleaner environment and improved social welfare can provide...good jobs. Our union and political work aims to reach this goal. Common work policy is our means (Metallindustriarbetareförbundet, 1989:8, translated in Mahon, 1991).

In continuation of the Developmental Work strategy, The Swedish Working Fund (the LOM program) was established in 1990. It ran until 1995. It granted 10 billion Swedish crowns to work place development, and it created 25.000 projects. More than half of the Swedish labour market was affected by this program initiative. The purpose of the program was to support change and improvements of working life. In the course of the period, there was a shift of focus from safety and health to the connection between productivity, organizational development, and health. About half of the program's funds were spent on projects on socio-technical work organizational development (Gustavsen et al. 1996).

In Norway, 'The Enterprise Development 2000 program' was started in 1995 (Gustavsen 2000). The idea of the program is to establish 'development coalitions' consisting of networks of companies tied to networks of researchers. These coalitions will contribute to facilitate an enterprise development in the individual company that creates a productivity development, based on development and improvement of the work environment. There are about 60 companies and 30 researchers connected to this development program.

Since 1991, the economic and political climate has changed radically in Sweden, and in the nineties the Swedish labour market policies have been focused on unemployment and business development (Kjellberg 2001: 355). So let us turn to Denmark and study the story of Developmental Work there.

The Developmental Work in Denmark

In Denmark, the concept of Developmental Work was introduced with two debate books in 1990 and in 1992 (Hvid 1990, Hvid & Møller 1992) and also with an presentation for Danish TUC congress 1991 (LO 1991a), heavily inspired by Sweden. In this congress presentation, it was argued that new organizational principles, new technology, and in particular new values and attitudes to work among the Danish TUC (LO) members, made a renewal of the union strategies necessary.

But Developmental Work was more than a new company-oriented policy for organizational renewal. The Danish TUC, LO's original definition of Developmental Work linked Developmental Work to the individual, the work place, the product, the environment, 'the whole life', and to societal development;.

> Developmental Work is work that constantly contributes to a positive development of the individual, the work place, and the society in which we live. A trade union policy in favour of Developmental Work includes development of the job, the product, the environment and 'the whole life'. Thus, Developmental Work is not a steady stage to be reached, but a goal we continuously strive for (LO, 1991a).

Developmental Work was thus from the start expressed as a visionary concept, which should be capable of politicizing work. The intention was to open up arenas in the companies and in society, where work and its development could be a political concern. The labour movement could here play an active role, along with the environmental organizations, consumer associations, and others.

In the beginning of the 1990s, Developmental Work became a point of reference for a new strategic orientation in labour organizations. It was a strategy, where labour politics shifted from having its centre of gravity in market relations – salary and work time – towards the work and its quality. It was a strategy where common wage politics were replaced by common labour politics, with equal distribution of developmental opportunities. It was a strategy that should have given labour organizations a voice in the development of flexible, quality oriented organizations, and a strategy that views the new management principles, not just as a threat, but also as an opportunity.

Starting as The Danish TUC (LO) politics, the Developmental Work strategy gradually became a strategy for development of production and work in the companies. In particular, the concept has gained widespread recognition in the public work places (Finansministeriet, 1994), but also many private companies are oriented towards Developmental Work.

Various public funds assisted the diffusion of Developmental Work into Danish companies. One fund was established on the basis of which public work places could apply for money for Developmental Work projects. Another, larger fund named 'Better Work Life and Increased Growth' distributed funds to both private and public companies, and was functioning 1996–99. The fund was allocated 105 mio. Dkr over a four year period to support projects that could improve both the flexibility and competitive development of the companies, and at the same time improve the work environment for the employees, reduce the risk of expulsion, and improve the relationship between work and family life.

With this fund, the State became involved in a very sensitive area: the organizational life of the company, in areas that traditionally are part of the employers' prerogatives to management. The fund is therefore presented as an offer, and the full autonomy of the companies is maintained. However, funding a project required that it was carried out in cooperation between the management of the company and the representatives of the employees, and also that the companies participate in an evaluation of the projects (Arbejdsmarkedsstyrelsen 2001a). Approximately 200 companies have received funding from this pool.

The evaluation showed that it was possible to develop work and work organization, which both led to increased growth and a better working life. The results supported the assumption of both human resource development and Developmental Work that the employees possess unused resources, and that release of those resources by increased employee involvement and more interesting job tasks will improve the working life as well as competitiveness.

The lesson learned with respect to the changing processes was, among other things, that it was important to involve the employees in the process, but also that it was necessary to develop management and managers in connection with the changes. The ability to listen to and involve the employees is not given to the managers. Developmental Work often implies comprehensive changes in management.

To receive a subsidy, the projects were required to have support in the work councils. However the projects were mostly initiated by the management and were generally management-dominated. In the project implementation, there has often been a considerable employee influence, typically by affected workers being involved in project groups. Shop stewards and safety representatives have often been involved in the development of the projects. However, the trade unions outside the companies have not played a significant role in supporting the change process in the companies. The trade unions seem still to have a limited contact with the members who partake in the developmental projects.

The fund 'towards better working life and increased growth' had, well attuned to Developmental Work strategy, also a broader societal goal. The pool was thus intended to support projects aimed at creating a better connection between working life and family life and securing equality between the sexes. The evaluation shows that there were only a very few projects that involved a family or equality perspective (www.arbejdsliv.dk). It seems to be very difficult for the companies to carry out change projects that unite various and heterogeneous goals.

The fund 'towards better working life and increased growth' has only supported a limited number of companies in their change process. There is no doubt, however, that a much larger number of Danish companies have gained inspiration from the ideas that Developmental Work concept is based on. In some cases, so to speak, without knowing that what they did had a name. Thus, it is rather few companies who have committed to Developmental Work as a 'concept'.

If the ideas of Developmental Work should survive, it has been necessary to institutionalize Developmental Work in the industrial relations. This institutionalizing hasn't been perfect, but Developmental Work concept has been central to the political development of work in the 1990s. The concept has established new discussions on cooperative relations between companies, researchers, consultants, and organizations in the labour market. Developmental Work has inspired new perceptions of links in working life between education, organizational development, and work environment, and discussions of employees' participation in the development of the companies have been opened, for instance in the environmental area. The political interest that has existed around the Developmental Work concept is reflected in a very large number of publications on Developmental Work, up through the 1990s (cf. the literature overview in www.saraweb.dk).

The driving forces behind the strategy have been the labour movement, initiatives from public employers, and also programs in a governmental context. The working life researchers and parts of the consulting world have also played an important role, by creating attention to the idea and to the current conclusions made over the 10–year period.

In particular the Danish TUC has spent many resources on marketing Developmental Work. Many interesting and creative tools have been produced for use in work places that wished to put Developmental Work on the agenda, and shop stewards have been trained in implementation of Developmental Work projects. This has meant that the labour movement has been acquainted with philosophies and tools that normally belong in the world of management, on its own terms.

With Developmental Work, the labour movement invited cooperation on the implementation of modern production methods and organizational forms. It is, however, a cooperation that moves into areas that the employers for more than a hundred years have had a monopoly on: organization and management. This is probably why the private employers' associations have been evasive, when called on to make Developmental Work a common strategy for the labour market's parties.

The employers have not directly counteracted Developmental Work, but they have not given Developmental Work their active support, even though the two parties have interests in the development of work. The employers' associations have, in the same period, worked with projects parallel to Developmental Work. The concepts of the learning organization have been especially promoted. The labour movement has thus not succeeded in forming agreements with the employers' associations that could create a more solid platform for the Developmental Work strategy.

Developmental Work's missing anchoring to the system of collective agreements has made it more difficult to get Developmental Work adopted in the established system of industrial relations. But the Developmental Work concept and the Developmental Work philosophy lives on, and a number of institutional changes are made in the labour market that support the development towards Developmental Work. Some of these are:

- Decentralization of the system of collective agreements, but under centrally set norms.
- Development of the decentralizing effort in the work environment area, among other things, by assessing the work place and certification of the companies work environment.
- Vocational training programs aimed at the commitment of the employees in the development of the production.
- An action plan against repetitive work, coordinated by the State and the labour market organizations (Hasle & Møller 2001).

Working Life Research in the Scandinavian Countries as an Inspiration for Developmental Work

Developmental Work takes two essential points of reference from working life research and practice: the socio-technical approach and the psychosocial factors at work. The socio-technical tradition has, to a great extent contributed with tools to the development of organization and work. The Swedish-American tradition for studies of the psychosocial factors at work has contributed with arguments to discontinue the Tayloristic and Fordist principles, by showing that they could pose a health hazard. At the same time, this tradition has focused on those conditions of work that should be promoted, in order to create healthy work places.

The Socio-Technical Approach

The Norwegian cooperation experiments that began in 1961 took place in close collaboration between the labour market's organizations, companies, and working life researchers. In the beginning, researchers from the Tavistock Institute of Human Relations in London participated. The activities were financed by LO and the Norwegian Employers Association. Later, the Norwegian Government contributed to the funding. The socio-technical theory became in many ways epoch-making for the philosophy of a specific Scandinavian alternative to Taylorism. Even though the socio-technical approach idea did not attain extensive practical recognition in the companies in the '60s and '70s (Björkman & Lundquist 1981: 339), the scientific communication of results and ideas in Norway, and later in the two other Scandinavian countries mentioned, resulted in the socio-technical concept for work organization becoming commonly known, as an alternative to Taylorism and mass production.

The cornerstone of the socio-technical theory is the idea of optimising or harmonizing the technical system with the social system. The right form of a socio-technical system, is a form that takes the technical-economic and the social demands into consideration.

The technical-economic demands are about increased productivity. Only much later was the flexibility demand added. The social system also had demands that were defined by the researchers. The so-called psychological job demands were listed. They summed up the need-based research and how far it had come at the present time. It had, however, a weak scientific basis.

With the socio-technical approach, control is replaced with autonomy, fragmentation is replaced with whole-ness and variation in the work and apathy with involvement and meaning. The goal of the socio-technical approach was to create autonomy and competency in the work. The Scandinavian socio-technical approach has in recent decades moved from a design-oriented approach towards a participation-oriented approach. This reorientation has had a strong voice in Bjørn Gustavsen (1992). Here, the assumption that the socio-technical approach shall prescribe how the work should be, is rejected. The companies must, on the contrary, formulate for themselves their own needs and establish their own development, but they must do so in a committed and democratic way. This made it important to create time and space for the employees' involvement in the development of new forms of organization, and the free and binding dialogue became the crucial principle of the new socio-technical approach.

The question as to what extent the socio-technical approach has been documented and is valid, is a controversial issue (Skorstad 1999: 140). However, there is no doubt that the merit of the socio-technical approach is that it has created production concepts, using intelligible terms that have been frequently used in the continued development of work in the Scandinavian countries.

In the socio-technical approach's vision of work, the competent and autonomous producer is clearly at the forefront. Furthermore, the socio-technical approach created a model for a committed cooperation between the organizations, the companies, and the researchers on the development of work that has been continued in the collaboration between researchers and labour movement about the Developmental Work.

The Swedish-American Tradition for Research in Psychosocial Work Environment

In 1979, the American Robert Karasek presented the Demand-Control Model in an article in Administrative Science Quarterly (Karasek 1979). The article comprised both a presentation of the Demand-Control Model, and a number of empirical analyses of the correlation between job strain and health. The Demand-Control Model (Figure 1) operates with two dimensions: psychological job demands and job control (or decision latitude). The psychological demands in the work are first and foremost quantitative demands, such as high speed, large workload, and intensive time pressure. Decision latitude has two sub-dimensions, which are decision authority (influence on the worker's own work) and skill discretion (opportunities to develop through the work). There is often – but not always – a high association between these two sub-dimensions. In connection with the presentation of the model, Karasek proposed two main hypotheses: 1. The combination of high demands and low influence results in a 'high strain' situation. This means that employees, who are exposed to this combination in their work, may expect to develop stress, low job satisfaction, psycho-somatic symptoms, mental health problems, and in the long term, chronic disorders, such as cardiovascular diseases. Individuals with low demands and high control may inversely be expected to have the best wellbeing and health. 2. The combination of high demands and high control ('the active jobs') gives occasion for personal growth and learning in connection with work. Individuals with this type of job will develop a competency that makes them able to master problems and challenges in work, as well as outside. Inversely, individuals in 'passive jobs' will develop passivity and 'learned helplessness'. In continuation of this hypothesis, one can expect that individuals with 'active jobs' will be best at following health advice, such as quitting smoking, staying ahead in the information age, etc. People with active jobs will also be most active in their spare time and in societal life, for instance with political activity in societies, parental work, etc.

The Demand-Control Model has in the period 1980–2000 been the dominant model in research on the correlation between the psychosocial work environment and health. The model was soon utilized in a long line of effective Swedish studies of high quality, and, in the course of a few years, it also became utilized by researchers in North- and South America, Europe, Japan, and Australia. While taking point of reference in the model, it was shown that high job strain is not only related to mental health, but also to absence, industrial accidents, consumption of medicine, disorders of the locomotive system, hospital admissions, cardiovascular diseases, and total mortality (Schnall et al 1994, Kristensen 1996, Karasek &

Theorell 1990). Combined, the job strain research composed the first comprehensive international demonstration that a 'soft area' such as psychosocial work environment has great impact on a number of 'hard' problems, such as cardiovascular diseases, accidents and death. In doing so, this research contributed greatly to render this problem area visible, which had earlier appeared as a 'luxury problem', without the same gravity as the 'real' work environmental problems, such as chemical substances, dust, and noise.

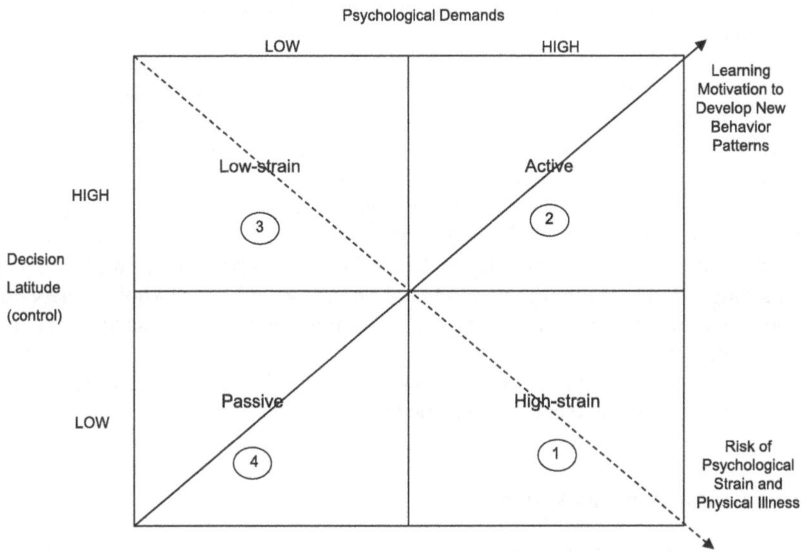

Figure 2.1 Karasek's Demand-Control Model

An American with an unorthodox interdisciplinary background and a highly developed capability for academic innovations developed the Demand-Control Model. However, it was in Scandinavia the model first found its concretization in practical working life. From the mid 1970s the Demand-Control Model was an important part of the change oriented Scandinavian working life research. This research was heavily involved in the change of work and in the development of new regulations in the labour market. Betil Gardell and his co-researchers were the most profound figures in this research tradition (Gardell 1977 & 1991).

Gardell represented, in his own person the combination of engaged researcher and politically active individual that has been characteristic for the whole tradition around the research in Developmental Work (Johnson & Johansson 1991). The central element of Gardell's philosophy was that the organization of work – not the employees – had to be changed, if a serious attempt had to be made to reduce alienation and mental health problems, while simultaneously encouraging motivation, work pleasure, and personal growth. The following quotation sums up the important elements of Gardell's theory:

> This research makes it sufficiently clear that industrial production systems can be organized in a way that is incompatible with the broadened concept of health and safety and with the social goals of a democratic working life. Among the critical factors in technology and organizational design special emphasis is laid on workers lack of control of pace and working methods, severely impoverished job content and socially isolated jobs. It is shown first that these conditions lead to stress in both a physiological and a psychological sense and to different signs of ill health. Second, that people cope with these conditions by non-participation and by holding back of human resources (Gardell in Johnson & Johansson, 1991, p. 9–10).

Both the socio-technical tradition and the Scandinavian research tradition within psychosocial work environment have been strongly influenced by an extensive cooperation between the labour movement and the researchers. Especially in Sweden, this cooperation has been strong, where the Social Democracy in the entire period (1970–2000) has had a strong standing. The country has been characterized by a strong egalitarian and democratic ideology that has had a great impact on the attitudes to contributory influence and democracy in the workplace. In addition, in Sweden there has been a strong belief that through research and rational reforms, the whole society could develop in a more humanistic direction. Such a combination of a humanistic, egalitarian, and democratic ideology, a large labour party, and a belief in progressive reforms, carried out by a strong public sector, has had a very solid standing in Sweden, Norway and Denmark have to some extent developed a similar tradition.

Developmental Work as Vision

Developmental Work is based on visions that are fostered in this Scandinavian tradition and which have adapted to the new changes of work especially in the last decade, characterized by flexibility, decentralization, and individualization. The vision has never become, and probably never will become a reality, but the vision plays an active role as a point of orientation for the many Developmental Work inspired projects. The vision is rarely formulated coherently, but it works by repeating or referring to previously formulated ideas, histories, and experiences. The Developmental Work vision thus draws on three sources:

- The Scandinavian socio-technical approach that has fostered a vision of a productive work, which takes equal consideration to the human system and the technical system. Work is performed by autonomous employees, who have a big say in their work.
- The Scandinavian tradition of democracy in the work place that has created a vision on companies, that are led by a coalition of diverse interests and view points, and where the employees have high control *over* the work.
- Finally, the Developmental Work vision has taken inspiration from the great interest of the 1990s in the creation of common values through dialogue.

Developmental Work therefore holds a vision of free and open dialogues, as a basis for development of values and attitudes in the company.

With reference to these three sources, we shall present the Developmental Work vision (see also Hvid & Møller 2001). It is divided in three parts:

- the vision of the productive work;
- the vision of work, interests, and politics;
- the vision of values developed in free dialogue.

The Vision of Productive Work

As already mentioned the Developmental Work vision of productive work is to a high degree, based on the experiences of the socio-technical approach. The vision is, however, also further developed in the State initiatives of the 1980s and 1990s; to combine increased flexibility and a better working life, which we have briefly described above. On this background three fundamental principles of the vision can be outlined.

The First Principle: The work is developmental for the individual employee, work-wise as well as personally. The work must be organized in such a way that the demands and expectations of the work are adapted to the individual. The individual employee carries out many diverse functions. In doing so, the work becomes more alternating and developmental, and concurrently, the company becomes more functionally flexible and re-adjustable. The developmental opportunities in the work are created by the employee's participation in the production and product innovation, in the interpretation of the customers' demands, and in general in their orientation towards reflection on the entire company and its development. It implies that the boundaries in the company are broken down between departments, between hierarchical strata, and between professions.

The Second Principle: The work is collectively organized. This means that the individual worker is part of a producer collective that is transparent to him/her, and where the employees are commonly responsible for coordination and execution of the group's tasks. Organization, management, and execution of the work is the group's common responsibility, and the group enjoys full competency and freedom to develop and rationalize the organization and execution of the work. This means that it is the work group that has the ownership of the work organization – not management or the owners of buildings and technology. Within the framework, set by the goals of the production of the company, the productive work is owned by those, who execute the work. This is true for both the daily work arrangement and for the development of the organization and the production. The ownership is most clearly expressed in the fact that it is the employees themselves, who head the development of new forms of work organization. From this point of view, the employees not only 'own' their own individual manpower, but also the collective manpower and organization. This does not imply that the group should refrain from drawing on external consulting and knowledge from leaders and consultants. It means that the development takes place with the starting point in the group's own experiences. Just as the Developmental Work-ideal of productive work implies that the individual worker is independent and competent, this also goes for the group.

The Third Principle: The usefulness of the work to the surrounding world is clearly present. The external relations of the group to the company and to society are equally important as the internal organization. The group has both the right to and the responsibility of maintaining the external relations to 'the surrounding world'. Both the individual worker and the group are as close to the customer as possible. The work is organized in such a way that the customer can influence the work process and interact with those executing the work. The customer is completely visible to the employee, and the customer contact is a learning process for both parties. The ideal productive work commands a breakdown of the boundaries between the company and its surrounding world. The ideal is that the group directs its activities on the basis of a common understanding of the task and of the usefulness the task holds for others (customer, client, etc.).

In this vision, the work is not governed by external factors such as wage systems, regulations, and supervision, but by the meaning of the work. The meaning of the work evolves in the interaction between, on the one hand, the individual and the group's development of their productive skills, on the other, experiences with performing tasks for other actors inside and outside the workplace. The productive work is based on competent, independent (autonomous), and responsible workers, who develop the work themselves, thus innovating and maintaining their ownership to the productive work and its collective organization.

The Developmental Work vision holds as many, or maybe more productive potentials, than the vision of Taylorism, where work is a continuation of the machinery system, or than modern management concepts' vision of management-run flexibility (Appelbaum 2000). Here performance and flexibility will be grounded in a commitment among the employee's growing out of other experiences, values and will. Resources used on management and control will be minimized. High flexibility will be based in stable social relations.

Implementing these productive potentials, however, presupposes a high degree of trust and mutual respect, which cannot solely be developed in the production, but to a great extent must involve interest protection and the setting of rights and duties that relate to the second part of the vision (see below). Likewise, implementing the productive potentials in the Developmental Work vision presupposes a culture and certain values that support this production, which relates to the third part of the vision (see below).

To the work environment, the vision of productive work carries the risk that the individual is urged to make a bigger effort than is recommendable from a health perspective, precisely because it involves responsibility and meaningfulness as motivating factors. There is, so to speak, no stricter employer, than oneself, or the customer or the colleague. The implementation of the vision of productive work can easily lead to a huge workload, responsibility, stress, and too many challenges. These negative consequences can only be reduced through strong interest protection, that secure social support in daily work, create visible norms of workload, working hours and training and which create supportive rules for protection of family life and spare time activities from work overload.

The Vision of Work, Interests, and Politics

The Developmental Work vision of work and interest is a continuation of two main trajectories in more than a hundred years of trade union and democratic struggle in the labour market. The first trajectory comprises experiences with trade union protection of workers' interests with emphasis on collective action, collective negotiation, and collective agreements. The second trajectory comprises experiences with an almost equally long struggle for democratizing the companies, after the parliamentary democracy with universal suffrage was gained (Christensen & Westenholz 1999, Christensen & Westenholz 1997).

The first trajectory, which Westenholz and Christensen call 'collective negotiation', is very much alive in Denmark and in the Scandinavian countries, with more than 80% of the wage earners organized in the labour movement, with a significant trade union stronghold at the national as well as at company level, and with collective agreements in place as the dominant form of control of the labour market.

The second trajectory, Westenholtz and Christensen call 'co-leadership among "citizens" in the company'. The democratic visions that have been carried forward in this trajectory are far from being implemented. However, the trajectory has materialized itself through an extensive cooperation in the companies, in work councils, in safety committees, and in more informal fora in connection with these committees. In addition, the employees have a legal right to elect representatives to the board of directors in private companies, and thereby participate in strategic decision-making.

In recent decades, the second trajectory 'co-leadership' has won more impasses. This is, among other things, visible in the changed role that the shop stewards have been given as part of the strategic development of the company. It is also in this second trajectory, the philosophy of Developmental Work is rooted. However, the Developmental Work vision cannot be implemented without the first trajectory, the 'collective negotiation' also operating.

The vision of protection of interests is characterized by three principles, where the first principle is rooted in the 'co-leadership trajectory', and the two other principles are rooted in the trajectory of 'collective negotiations':

First Principle: Co-Leadership. In Developmental Work, there is a vision of politicizing work. The employees should not only have a say, when it comes to wage and work conditions. There should be arenas in the companies, where the production task, resource consumption, investments, strategy, and societal role become a political concern to the employees, in principle to the same extent as it is to the management of the company. Here the employees should play an active role, as citizens of the company.

The idea that the employees shall be enabled to protect the company's interests is not as utopian as some might think. In many of the companies studied in the SARA project, shop stewards play a crucial role in the management of the companies. In the larger private companies, the board of directors include employee representatives. The primary task is to protect holistic-oriented company interests, and within this framework the representatives seek to protect employee interests (Christensen & Westenholz 1999).

Even in a developed company democracy, there are narrow limits as to which decisions can be made. Also, the Developmental Work companies must honor the obligations to the owners, society, and customers in the same manner as in traditional companies. The difference is that in the Developmental Work company, there is a broader forum to weigh the various interests among equally legitimate parties.

Second Principle: Collective Rights, Adapted to the Local Situation. If employees are to take part in a real dialogue concerning the development of work and their company, it is a requirement that they can maintain and improve their rights concerning job security, payment, and working hours. Also, they must have the right to access information and to get involved in influencing the decision-making process.

An important Developmental Work criterion is a strengthening of employees' rights at the same time as the centralized rules and regulations, which exist concerning wages, working environment, manning, should be made less detailed. Actually, there is a trend within Danish labour market regulation (like in many other countries) in the direction of less detailed and more flexible rules. Likewise, there is a trend towards making rights more procedure-oriented, in relation to deciding pay, further education, and work place assessment (Due et al. 1993a, 1993b).

Third Principle: Representation of the 'Common Good'. Precisely because the employees are included in the management and responsibility of the company it is essential that there are bodies and individuals in the company; who take care of society's expectations of the company, for instance as concerns work environment and health, ethnic and gender equality, room for people with reduced work capacity (the social responsibility of the company), environment, and sustainability. This task, can in a great extent be performed by the shop stewards of the companies.

The ideal Developmental Work company is characterized by democratic decision-making processes regarding the development of the company. However, one can hardly call the company democratic, because also the ideal Developmental Work company is subject to high external control on the part of the share-holders, the customers, the legislation, etc.

The Vision of Values Developed in Free Dialogue

Working life is full of discussions about what is good and bad. What is or should be the meaning of work and the use of resources. Values are not constructed in the same formalized and goal rational way as the system of production and the system of politics. Values develop out of the actors' relation to, and meaning about production and politics, but include (potentially at least) all the values that people have.

The traditional values have, in many companies, been placed under pressure in recent years. There is a strong pressure for change coming from the firm's production and political systems. Flexibility, new production concepts, the development of human resources, project organization, and market demands all put the old values under stress. There is also a trend towards individualism that makes it difficult to maintain traditional values. At the same time, personal responsibility, self- management, and personal commitment are all central elements in the new values, which are being created.

The ideal principle for the construction of the Developmental Work value system is the idea of a free and open dialogue in the company, on all matters concerning the company and the work. In particular the contemporary Norwegian tradition of the socio-technical approach has developed theories and practices in this area. [See for instance Gustavsen et al. (1996) and Pålshaugen (1999), who speak of the internal public sphere of an organization.]

There are three principles for the development of values in free dialogue:

First Principle: Diversity is accepted. In the ideal Developmental Work company, diversity is accepted and it is used in the development of work. It is accepted that some find their identity and meaning by involving themselves in the company's development, whilst others perhaps find their identity in the professions and yet others in their life outside work. It is accepted that work gives different meanings depending on one's personality, previous experience and phase of life. Young people entering the labour market will often have a different attitude towards work than the middle aged, who have settled with the company as the cornerstone of their working life. The groups of older employees, who are in the process of leaving the labour market, will perhaps have a more retrospective attitude toward work. The demands and expectations, which are set individually or to groups of employees, must fit into the culture these employees create. It must be accepted that the culture of the company will only change slowly, and that changes in company culture are a collective matter, and not just an issue for the management.

Second Principle: Open dialogue. The ideal Developmental Work value system is characterized by the acceptance of differences of opinion, changing alliances and conflicts. But these conflicts do not develop to an open fight; they are handled in an open dialogue characterized by equality in the conversation, active listening, and acceptance of different opinions (See Pålshaugen 1999 on details about dialogue in workplaces).

Third Principle: Responsibility. Within a Developmental Work company, the employees have responsibilities, both regarding the production and the politics. This implies having a broad discussion about problems and opportunities for development in both production and interest systems. Constructive drafts on how the organization and production could develop are part of everyday informal dialogue.

The development of attitudes and values are an important dynamic force, both for the development of the productive work and for the development of political and interest protection. These three elements: the acceptance of diversity, open dialogue, and responsibility are the building blocks of an ideal model for value development in the Developmental Work company.

The Developmental Work vision is alive in many different forms of practice. The Developmental Work vision has functioned as an often not very precisely formulated point of focus for a long line of various work political actors:

cooperation-oriented managers, trade union representatives and consultants, working with work environment, education, and organizational changes.

The vision is, however, unlikely to ever be fully implemented because of the limitations set by the established technology, asymmetrical power relations, the rigid demands from the market, and the division of employees in various professions and interest groups. But even if the vision cannot be fully implemented, any work place can move in the direction of the vision. In the following section, we shall see what in fact happens to the work, when it moves in the direction of Developmental Work.

Developmental Work in Reality. Does Developmental Work Represent Social and Welfare Progress?

The vision differs from reality. This is not surprising. One can, however, be close to or further away from the vision. The central question is, whether the advantages to the employees, promised by the vision are obtained as it gets closer to fulfilment. We shall examine this in the next three chapters. First, we shall present the results from a cross-sectional study of the companies that is included in the SARA project. In these companies, people have very diversified work conditions. To some, the work is close to the Developmental Work vision, to others it is far away. Employing survey data, we shall analyse the social and welfare consequences, and examine if the work is closer to or farther away from the vision of Developmental Work. In the next section (2.6.), we shall examine what happens to companies that are making a conscious effort to move in the direction of Developmental Work.

In the SARA project, the social and welfare consequences of Developmental Work have been analyzed through collection and analysis of survey data that comprise 3,010 employees from 71 work places. For the analysis of these survey data, four scales have been developed in order to measure the degree of Developmental Work for the respondents. These Developmental Work scales are related to profession and level of education, skills, job satisfaction and psychological well-being and health.

We have chosen to draw up more than just one scale for Developmental Work, because as it appears from the above, Developmental Work is a composite concept, which contains elements at several levels, from the job of the individual to the entire labour market. The Developmental Work concept has been separated into four sub-scales:

1. Developmental Work, such as it is experienced by the individual employee (*Individual Developmental Work*) .
2. Developmental Work understood as a management concept, where the employees are involved and acknowledged in a range of different important areas (*Developmental Work Management*).
3. Developmental Work as a model for co-determination and representation through the formal bodies in the work place (work council, safety committee, a.o.) (*Developmental Work Representation*).

4. Developmental Work understood as a concept where consideration is taken to the surrounding environment and to broad societal conditions, such as holding jobs, integration of immigrants, expulsion, etc (*Developmental Work Society*).

The four scales do not express the Developmental Work vision as it was presented above, rather, they relate to it. Scales 1 and 2 thus relate to the Developmental Work vision of the productive work, and scales 3 and 4 relate to the Developmental Work vision of interests and politics. It has not been possible for us to make a scale that links to the vision of free dialogue.

On the Construction of the Four Developmental Work Scales

The four Developmental Work scales were constructed on the basis of the existing questionnaire data in the following way:

1. Individual Developmental Work: The scale includes four elements of the individual's own work. Each of these elements is measured by utilizing scales that include more questions: 1. Influence on the work (7 questions). 2. Developmental opportunities in the work (4 questions). 3. Meaning in the work (4 questions). 4. Degree of autonomy in the work (3 questions). Total 18 questions.
2. Developmental Work Management: The scale includes three subscales, where each scale is based on several questions: 1. Information from management (2 questions). 2. Social support from management (2 questions). 3. Management quality (4 questions). Total 8 questions.
3. Developmental Work Representation: The scale is based on three questions: Do you have influence on major changes in the work place through your shop steward? Do you have influence on major changes in the work place through your safety representative? How often can you receive support from your shop steward?
4. Developmental Work Society: This scale is based on four questions that involve the following issues: Whether the company is environmentally aware and does much to improve the natural environment? Whether the company does much to improve the work environment? Whether the company does much for the work place to be socially accountable? Whether the company is family-friendly?

As it appears, the two upper scales are based on several other scales, which again are based on a number of questions that have been used in the questionnaires of the SARA project. The two lower scales are on the other hand based directly on specific questions. In all cases, we have given the specific questions/scales the same weight, and the utilized answer categories have likewise been given the same weight. An example may illuminate the utilized method: The question 'Do you have an opportunity to learn something new through your work?' has four answer categories: 'Often, sometimes, rarely, never/almost never'. These four answers have been given the score 100; 66,6; 33,3 and 0. This score is, along with the score from the other three questions, included in the scale for 'Developmental Opportunities in the Work'. The total score of the scale equals the average score of the four questions, and thus they go from 0 to 100 for all respondents. If a person has responded to at least half of the questions of a scale, these are utilized for the computation of the scale value. If a respondent on the other hand has responded to less than half of the questions, this person is classified as 'missing'. This means that all the utilized scales of the SARA project go from 0 to 100 and can be immediately interpreted, since for instance a high level of Individual Developmental Work a high value on this scale, while a low level of Individual Developmental Work indicates a low value.

In the following analyses, we shall include all four measures for Developmental Work, but in particular concentrate on the dimension, which from the outset is assumed to have the most importance to the individual employee, that is Individual Developmental Work. As is evident from the above, this dimension is very close to the concept of control or decision latitude in Karasek's terminology.

Who has Developmental Work?

It is clear that the scope of Developmental Work must be assumed to vary considerably among various jobs in the labour market. The concept has especially been aimed at jobs with low influence, low developmental opportunities, and little freedom in the work, which includes assembly line work, piecework, or passive supervision work. In Table 2.1, we see the average scale values of the dimension Individual Developmental Work for the most frequently occurring jobs in the SARA project.

Table 2.1 Average points of the scale for Developmental Work in various jobs of the SARA study*

Job title	N	Points
Managers of small companies	30	89.0
Leading officials	22	85.7
Head nurses, midwives	56	82.5
Engineers	60	82.2
Physical therapists	42	80.6
Social workers	30	78.2
Technicians	88	76.0
Metal workers	71	73.3
Nursing home assistants	556	72.0
Navvies and sewerage workers	108	66.7
Chefs, sandwich maids	92	64.0
Nursery workers	45	63.8
Unskilled workers in the medical industry	199	61.4
Cleaning and kitchen assistants	299	60.9
Unskilled workers in bookbinding businesses	37	60.8
Unskilled workers in the lumber industry	103	59.6

* Only homogenous jobs with at least 20 respondents have been included in the table.

As it appears from the table, the average values for Individual Developmental Work vary from 59 to 89 points for the most commonly occurring jobs in the SARA project. The unskilled jobs have the lowest values (59 to 67 points), while the skilled are placed in the interval 64–74, and jobs, that require mid-level education, have 76–83 points. Finally, leading officials and managers, who typically are academics, are placed in the area 85–90 points. Thus it seems that the scale for Individual Developmental Work to a great extent mirrors the existing hierarchy in the labour market. Table 2.1 may be viewed as a validation of the scale for Individual Developmental Work, since by utilizing this dimension, a number of problems have been identified, each of which characterizes unskilled work.

In Table 2.2 the four utilized goals for Developmental Work are compared with the occupational training of the respondents. Doing this reveals an interesting pattern, since there is a clear association between the length of the qualifying education and the level of Individual Developmental Work, which indeed reconciles with Table 2.1. On the other hand, with regard to Developmental Work Representation and Developmental Work Society, the picture is inverted, albeit less significantly so: Here, it is the respondents with the lowest occupational training, who score the highest. The workers with little education thus work in companies where societal considerations are shown, and where the employees are represented through elected colleagues, whereas for the highly educated it is their own work that can be characterized as being developmental. The pattern is particularly significant for academics, since these respondents have a very low score for Developmental Work Representation, and a high score for Individual Developmental Work. Already here, we can detect the contours of one of the challenging issues, in connection with Developmental Work, as a labour union strategy: it seems that Developmental Work holds a contradiction. The groups, who have a personal work situation that may be characterized as developmental, have at the same time little contact with the formal representative system, which the labour movement traditionally has considered crucially important. One could ask, whether the labour movement by employing this strategy, is sawing off the branch on which it is sitting? We shall return to this question at the end of the chapter.

Table 2.2 Association between occupational training and the utilized goals of Developmental Work

	Education					
	None	Skilled	-3 ys.	3–4ys.	Acad.	p
Individual Developmental Work	64.9	68.8	71.4	76.6	82.2	***
Developmental Work Management	57.5	54.5	57.5	58.7	64.2	NS
Developmental Work Representation	39.9	37.8	29.6	30.8	24.0	**
Developmental Work Society	54.7	54.4	48.6	40.8	54.6	**

** p01 *** p<0.001; NS: non-significant. Spearman correlations.

We shall complete this chapter with Figure 2.1, which illustrates the associations we have looked at in this chapter, displayed in one single figure. The figure shows the association between the respondents' social-economic status (SES) and the score for Individual Developmental Work. Looking at the figure, we see two distinct hierarchies. Among blue-collar workers the skilled workers have evidently higher value on the scale than the unskilled, that have the lowest value of all. Among white-collar workers, a similar hierarchy is noticed, with the lower status officials at the bottom (67.7 points) and leading officials at the top with 85.7 points. Viewed from a social class perspective, the Developmental Work strategy may thus be viewed as a strategy that seeks to extend the work conditions of the upper classes to the rest of society. Here it is, however, important to remember that the comprehensive strategy for Developmental Work does not only include the individual component, but rather seeks to change the entire concept of working life.

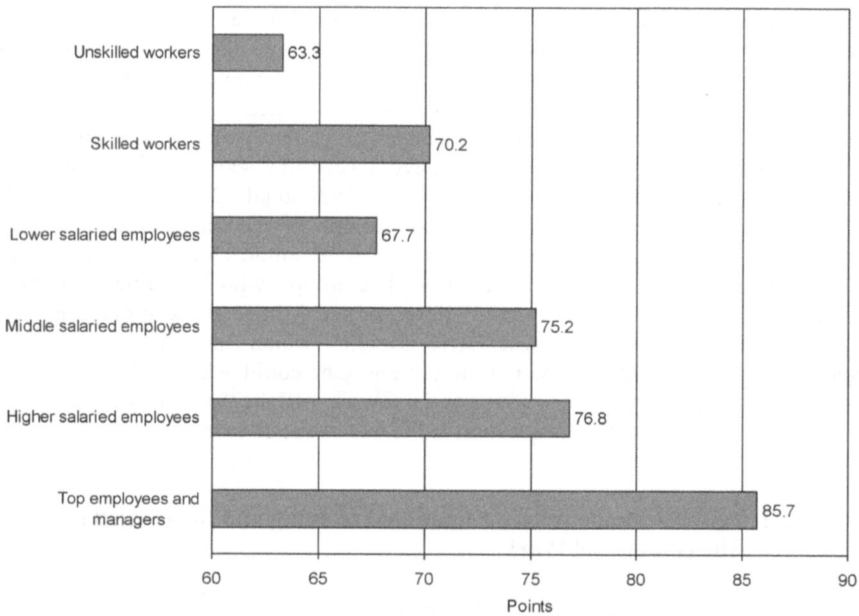

Figure 2.1 The correlation between socio- economic status and the degree of individual Developmental Work

Developmental Work and the Skills of the Employees

In the SARA questionnaire, the respondents were asked the following question: 'What abilities and skills do you need for the everyday work you are doing?'. It was possible to check 16 different types of skills, ranging from physical strength to resolution. The most frequently checked categories were cooperative skills (88.5%) and independence (78.9%). The lowest frequencies were dexterity (25.4%), perseverance (35.7%) and accuracy (39.6%). A large majority of the respondents ticked a high number of diverse skills.

The skills were distributed into four groups: autonomy, cooperation, accuracy, and physicality. Below, the skills are indicated that were included in each of the four groups:

Autonomy Skills: Knowledge of the work task:

- Ability to get good ideas
- Occupational skill-level and experience
- Independence
- Resolution
- Ability to learn something new

Cooperative Skills:

- Ability to cooperate
- Ability to be subordinate
- Willingness to be flexible

Accuracy Skills:

- Dexterity
- Accuracy
- Ability to concentrate

Physical Skills:

- Speed
- Physical strength
- Perseverance

For each of the four groups, a scale variable from 0 to 100 was applied, as for the other scales in the SARA project.[1]

In the literature on technological evolution, organization of work, and skills of the employees, one finds that the transition from artisan to mechanized work usually is accompanied by deskilling, which involves a reduced need for professional skills and for those skills we call autonomy skills. On the other hand, there is a need for a number of process-independent skills, such as speed, dexterity, accuracy, and power of concentration. It is a central part of Developmental Work that there is a need for a

1 The four groups of qualifications were identified through factor analyses and confirmed through tests for internal reliability. One question – 'routine' – turned out to fall outside this pattern, since it did not load on any of the four scales.

broad spectrum of human skills in each job, and in particular the need for autonomy skills and cooperative skills. Inversely, it is expected that there will be less of a need for physical skills and for accuracy skills. It appears from Table 2.3 that most of these hypotheses are confirmed, since the level of Individual Developmental Work is clearly associated with autonomy skills and cooperative skills. Similarly, we see a clear negative association between Individual Developmental Work and physical skills, but contrary to our expectations, it turns out that there is a positive association between Individual Developmental Work and accuracy skills.

Table 2.3 The association between various goals for Developmental Work and the need for skills in the work

	Autonomy	Accuracy	Physique	Coop.
Individual DW	***	***	*** 1)	***
DW Management	***	*	** 1)	***
DW Society	NS	**	*** 1)	NS
DW Representation	NS	**	NS	NS

* $p<0.05$; ** $p<0.01$; *** $p<0.001$; NS: non-significant. Spearman correlations.
1) Inverted association: The more Developmental Work, the less need for skills.

In Table 2.4, we get a more detailed picture of the upper row in Table 2.3 in order to study more closely the obvious associations between Individual Developmental Work and the need for diverse skills in the work. It is clear from looking at Table 2.4 that Individual Developmental Work, in particular is strongly associated with autonomy skills, since the quarter of the respondents that have the lowest level of Individual Developmental Work, on average have a need for about 46% of the stated autonomy skills, while the group with the highest level of Individual Developmental Work on average have a need for as much as 80% of the stated skills. As regards the other skills, the associations are surely also statistically significant however, they appear to be much weaker. Thus we can conclude that Individual Developmental Work is related to the need for a broader spectrum of skills, and specifically a number of skills that can be assumed to be developmental for the employee, such as knowledge, excellence, independence, and the ability to learn something new. This finding corresponds completely to the ideas and hypotheses that were the driving force for Gardell and his colleagues. If we look at Karasek's model, we therefore notice that the dimension Individual Developmental Work in the SARA project corresponds with the theoretical assumptions that make the foundation of the activity diagonal (from passive to active work). These findings re-open an issue that is often raised, when Developmental Work is discussed in work places and in the labour movement. Is it thinkable that Developmental Work to some people with limited intellectual resources and personal capacity may be too demanding and difficult? Will increased influence and many developmental opportunities be a threat to those people, rather than a challenge? What opportunities are there in the information society, based on Developmental Work, for those people who primarily want to and are able to use their *physical* abilities and skills?

Table 2.4 The association between Individual Developmental Work and skill needs in the work

Level of Individual DW 1)				
	Lowest	Under	Over medium	Highest medium
Autonomy skills	46.2	62.7	70.9	80.1
Cooperation skills	61.5	68.2	67.5	68.9
Accuracy skills	32.4	37.2	41.8	45.2
Physical skills	47.6	45.8	44.9	40.8
Skills total	48.6	56.0	59.2	62.0
N	746	746	748	747

* The population is distributed on four equally sized groups of the scale for Individual Developmental Work.

Developmental Work and Job Satisfaction

In the SARA project, we have measured job satisfaction by posing eight questions on various aspects of the respondents' jobs, which previously have been utilized in the British study Whitehall II (Marmot et al. 1991). The questions were as follows:

How satisfied are you with the following:

- Your normal wage?
- Your prospects in the work?
- The people you work with?
- The physical work environment?
- The way your department is managed?
- The way your abilities are being used?
- The challenges and skills involved in your work?
- Your job as a whole, everything considered?

A factor analysis showed that the first question had no connection to the others. Therefore a scale was made for job satisfaction, where all the questions, except the question on wage, were included with equal weight. The respondents were clearly most satisfied with the people they worked with (33% were 'very satisfied'), while the least were satisfied with prospects (9% 'very satisfied') and the physical work environment (10% very satisfied).

It is obvious that the whole philosophy of Developmental Work is based on the fundamental assumption that people with Developmental Work are more satisfied with their work, than are people without it. Thus, we expected to find a strong association between Developmental Work and job satisfaction, and in addition, that there would be a clearer association between job satisfaction and Individual Developmental Work, than was the case with the other measures for Developmental Work.

Again, our hypotheses were only partly confirmed, which is shown in Table 2.5 below. We found the expected clear association between Individual Developmental Work and job satisfaction. As shown, the average score for the 25%, who had the highest level of *Individual Developmental Work*, was 73.3 against 53.9 in the group with the lowest Individual Developmental Work. Still, there was an even clearer association between Developmental Work Management and job satisfaction (scores from 50.9 to 74.7), which is immediately surprising. Moreover, there is also a very strong association between Developmental Work Society and job satisfaction, which also was unexpected. The only one of the four measures that shows a weak association with job satisfaction is Developmental Work Representation. There are thus two clear results here: Firstly, that high quality in management is connected to very high job satisfaction with the employees, and secondly, that there is no particularly strong association between the formal interest protection through cooperative bodies and job satisfaction. The last result contradicts the labour movement's own self-knowledge, where precisely the protection of the employees' interests through elected representatives is supposed to be an important tool to obtain well being and satisfaction in the job. But it is also possible that representation is only needed when job satisfaction and participation is low.

Table 2.5 Associations between the four types of Developmental Work and average scores for satisfaction in the work

	Level of Developmental Work				
	Lowest medium	Under medium	Over medium	Highest medium	p
Individual Developmental Work	53.9	62.0	65.4	73.3	***
Developmental Work Management	50.9	61.7	67.2	74.7	***
Developmental Work Representation	63.6	64.6	65.2	69.3	***
Developmental Work Society	56.7	64.0	69.2	72.9	***
Share of the Four Groups, app.		25%	25%	25%	25%

*** $p<0.001$.

Developmental Work, Psychological Well-Being, and Health

In the questionnaire study, it was possible to compare the level of Developmental Work with psychological well-being and health, since the questionnaire included a universally recognized set of questions, on the basis of which seven different scales can be constructed. These give information on the following health-related conditions: general health, vitality, mental health, behavioural stress, somatic stress, emotional stress, cognitive stress. A further outline of the data basis is given in the framework on the following page.

In the SARA project, we had an expectation that we would find a positive association between Developmental Work and psychological well-being and health, with the strongest association between Individual Developmental Work and health. This hypothesis turned out to be only partly supported. As presented in Table 2.6, there is a strong association between Individual Developmental Work and General Health and Mental Health, and a weaker one with significant association between Individual Developmental Work and behavioural stress and somatic stress. We find, however, a considerably stronger association between Developmental Work Society and health, where there is a strong significant association for 6 of the 7 health measures. On the other hand, the association between Developmental Work Management and health is very poor. Here, we only find a significant association regarding emotional stress, which compared to the clear association between Developmental Work Management and satisfaction, is surprising. Finally, a surprising lack of association is found between Developmental Work Representation and health. To be represented in a satisfactory way through elected representatives, turned out to have no association at all to health or well being.

Table 2.6 Multiple regression analyses of different measures of Developmental Work on the seven measures of health and wellbeing

	Health measure						
	General Health	Vitality	Mental Health	Behavi-oural Stress	Somatic Stress	Emo-tional Stress	Cognitive Stress
Individual D.W.	***		***	*	*		
D.W. Management					*		
D.W. Representation							

Gender, age and socio-economic status were also included in the multivariate analyses.
*** p<0.001; ** p<0.01; * p<0.05. Remaining associations were non-significant.

The scales for health and well being are presented in the frame on the following page.

In the SARA project, health and mental well being have been measured, using seven different scales. Three of these scales are from Short Form 36 (SF-36), which is a questionnaire with 36 questions that are frequently utilized in many countries for measuring health status (Ware et al, 1993). These three scales are General Health, Vitality and Mental Health. The first of these scales measures the person's general self-perceived health, the second measures the dimension of fatigue-energy, while the third measures mental well-being. The other four scales are developed by Setterlind (Setterlind 1995) and they include Behavioural Stress, Somatic Stress, Emotional Stress, and Cognitive Stress. These scales measure various types of stress symptoms, since stress is generally defined, as an individual condition that is characterized by the combination of high arousal and displeasure. Below, a typical question from each of the seven scales is shown.

General Health: In general, would you say your health is: excellent – very good – good – fair – poor?
Vitality: During the past four weeks: – did you feel tired?
Mental Health: During the past four weeks: – have you felt so down in the dumps that nothing could cheer you up?
Behavioral Stress: I have lacked initiative.
Somatic Stress: I have been short of breath.
Emotional Stress: I have had sleeping problems.
Cognitive Stress: I have had difficulties in making decisions.

Later analyses have shown that the scales for Mental Health and Emotional Stress measure largely the same, while the other scales seem to cover different sides of a person's health and well being. We had a basic hypothesis in connection with the SARA project: that Developmental Work in general would be linked to better health and well-being. We expected in particular, that Individual Developmental Work and Developmental Work Management would be positively associated with good health. The bivariate analyses showed a tremendously clear picture: there was non-significant association between Developmental Work Representation and the utilized scales. For the other three measures of Developmental Work, we found, on the contrary, high-significant associations ($p<0.001$) for all seven scales. We typically found 5–20 points difference between the 25% with the lowest Developmental Work and the 25% with the highest Developmental Work.

Since all three measures of Developmental Work displayed heavy association with the health measures in bivariate analyses, we performed a number of supplementary multivariate linear regression analyses with each of the seven health measures as dependent variable (Table 2.6). In these analyses, we furthermore included gender, age, and SES as potential confounders These multivariate analyses showed a surprising pattern, since Developmental Work Society had association with six of the seven health measures (the only exception was behavioural stress), when control was performed for the other factors. On the other hand, Developmental Work Management turned out to be only associated with emotional stress ($p<0.05$), and not with the other six scales. Individual Developmental Work was associated with four of the seven health measures, which is also somewhat less than expected. With regard to Developmental Work Representation, the result from the bivariate analyses was confirmed, since this measure of Developmental Work was not associated with even a single one of the utilized health measures.

Discussion and Conclusion of the Questionnaire Results

Our analyses have had some clear and to some extent unexpected results, which gives occasion for reflection on Developmental Work as a union strategy. In our analyses, we have placed the main emphasis on the component that we have called Individual Developmental Work, but we have also included the other three components of the Developmental Work concept, and this has rendered a considerably more varied picture of the situation around Developmental Work.

The main emphasis has been placed on the dimension individual DW, since it is the positive effects of the development of the individual's work, that has dominated both research and discussion in the field. We could initially see that there is a very heavy association between professional education and SES on the one hand, and the presence of Individual Developmental Work on the other. The higher education and status, the higher the level of Individual Developmental Work. This part of the Developmental Work strategy is thus aimed at extending those work conditions, which are now in place for large parts of the best educated, to also cover low status wage earners who, to a great extent are identical with the traditional Trade union members.

This strategy raises a number of questions that we shall briefly mention here. First of all, one may fear that the Developmental Work strategy will be followed by an increase in the demands to the employees regarding cognitive and social skills, which may create a risk for exclusion of employees, who today have jobs with little influence and developmental opportunities. One often meets this discussion in the work places, where a number of the employees doing routine work protest the plans of Developmental Work, because they see it as much too demanding and threatening. This argument may be said to have a certain support in our analyses of qualification demands in connection with Individual Developmental Work. These analyses clearly show that there is a need for considerably more qualifications (in particular regarding cooperation, autonomy, professional knowledge, and the ability to learn something new). Faced with these demands, many prefer to just 'do their work'.

It has sometimes been argued that this resistance is a resistance to change, rather than a resistance to Developmental Work. An often-occurring observation has been that 'everybody wants development, but nobody wants changes'. As far as we know, there is not much research-based knowledge on this matter.

It is interesting to see that two of the other dimensions of Developmental Work – Developmental Work Society and Developmental Work Representation – expose the opposite association with SES. With these dimensions, it is the lowest status strata that have the highest level of Developmental Work. These findings could give rise to a hypothesis that the traditional structures of the employees' organization and the societal effort of the companies will have a tendency to disappear over time, as the individualized form of Developmental Work gains a foothold.

The analyses of the associations between various measures of Developmental Work on the one hand, and job satisfaction and health on the other, render a positive picture for three of the Developmental Work dimensions. Meanwhile, the fourth dimension – Developmental Work Representation – is not associated with even a single one of these potentially positive effects. Here, it must be pointed out that a sectional study such as this is not well suited to show causality. This is particularly problematic, when the 'causes' as well as the 'effects' are measured by the use of questionnaires, where there will be a tendency toward information bias (Kristensen 1996).

However, one may say that a missing association in a sectional study as this – such as we have seen in connection with Developmental Work Representation – is a very strong indicator that in a prospective analysis, one will also not be able to find any association. So far, we can conclude that people who score high for various dimensions related to Developmental Work, are also more satisfied with their work and in addition have a better health and mental well being. These findings correspond with the previously mentioned findings in connection with Karasek's Demand-Control Model, where in particular the control dimension has turned out to be a good predictor of health problems, absence, low well-being, etc. (Marmot et al. 1991, Kristensen 1999).

All in all, it thus seems that the concept of Developmental Work advances job satisfaction and the usage of a broader set of skills in the work. In doing so, there is a clear potential for the individual to learn and develop through work and thereby strengthen his or her personal competency. However, it seems that essential sides of the Developmental Work concept are in opposition to the traditional organization in the work place, where influence is exerted through the elected representatives in the formal bodies. This dilemma is further widened by the fact that exactly the dimension Developmental Work Representation – as the only one of the four examined components – is not positively associated with satisfaction or health. One may therefore pose the question: must the labour movement surrender its traditional position to further the life quality of the members? And: In doing so, will the labour movement set the stage for an individualization of the work conditions and their regulation, which potentially removes the labour movement from the arena, because nobody feels in need of it? And finally: Has the labour movement launched a strategy for Developmental Work, which will contribute to weaken the link between the labour movement and its own members?

Vision, Strategy and Concept

As pointed out in the beginning of this chapter the Developmental Work is also a vision for the development of working life, a strategy to maintain organized collaboration between labour and management, and a concept to organize the work.

The vision is based on the Scandinavian working life tradition, with roots in organized, stable and collaborative industrial relations, and in the last thirty years developed into a vision of work as the source for a human development of competent, autonomous, and empowered employees, who create a basis for a sustainable wealth production through advanced democracy in the work place.

However, the vision of Developmental Work is not the only existing vision for work and its development. Also in Denmark, there is a strong promotion of new management concepts, which are built on a completely different set of visions and historical traditions. Only a small part of both the private businesses and the public sector move clearly in the direction of Developmental Work. However the vision is alive, and it does influence the development of work, also in companies implementing 'total quality management', 'business process engineering', and other modern concepts to improve productivity through organizational and human development. This is further elaborated in Chapter 3.

Developmental Work is a strategy to maintain organized industrial relations in an era where business is engaged in extended flexibility, human resource development, decentralization, downsizing, and individualized relations between management and labour. The strategy of the Developmental Work is to make organized labour and empowered employees important actors in decentralized development of the flexibility and human resources.

Whether the strategy has succeeded it is too early to say; but at least it has until now not appeared as a fiasco. The institutions of the labour market have been sustained and continued. More than 80% of the wage earners are members of trade unions. The greater part of the labour market is covered by collective agreements, and increasingly so up through the 1990s. There has not been the same differentiation in wages and income in Denmark and the other Scandinavian countries, as has been the case in most of the highly developed industrialized countries (Larsson 1999).

It is, however, too early to declare the patient well. In most Developmental Work projects, the labour movement only plays a minor role. In addition, the significance of collective interest protection is apparently reduced the more work becomes characterized by Developmental Work. In the survey, we find no positive association between interest representation strength and the quality of the work environment. This may be due to the fact that interest representation tends to be strongest where it is most needed – which is exactly where the work environment and the wages are worst.

Many of the possible negative aspects of Developmental Work, as mentioned above, could be prevented by stronger interest protection. For instance, it thus seems to be the case that marginalization of employees associated with Developmental Work is reduced where the employee representatives are strongly involved in the change process (Teknologisk Institut 2000). However, the process in direction of Developmental Work is hard to plan and triggers a number of new conflicts and dilemmas. These conflicts and dilemmas in Developmental Work will be further elaborated in chapter 5.

Developmental Work was originally formulated as a strategy, which not only had the company as its developmental horizon, but which also related to the social and environmental development in society. In the most Developmental Work projects, the societal perspectives are, however, quite absent. The horizon of the projects is solely that of the company and its development. There exists however, some potential for breaking the company horizon, which will be further elaborated in Chapter 5.

Several tools are created to realize the concept of Developmental Work. They draw intensively on tools from other concepts to develop organization and human resources. The concept of Developmental Work does, however, see the employees as subjects in the development of the company, and not just as objects for managerial manipulation, and it includes the collective organizations at company level. The tools of the concept are, however, too instrumental to be further examined here.

Chapter 3

New Management and Working Life – the Forced Marriage

Management concepts, often spiced with information technology, seem to be setting the agenda for a large part of modern working life. These management concepts prescribe the development of organization and work, they are intended for the management, and they represent a different set of ideas for the future of working life, than does the Developmental Work approach.

Whereas developmental work takes its starting point in the development of welfare, in the companies as well as in society, (cf. Chapter 2), management concepts are missing the welfare dimensions. This is also true when it comes to working conditions, development of qualifications, and co-determination. However, opportunities do exist for setting welfare dimensions in connection with the concepts' visions of organization, technology, and workflow, when it comes to the practical use of management concepts. These opportunities may become available in the long journey from the first ideas of management researchers, or consultants, to a fully fledged concept that precedes the final introduction of the concepts in the workplaces. So even if new management concepts and welfare are an odd couple, something valuable may still emerge from combining the different starting points. At any rate, the management concepts are here to stay, and a welfare-oriented work policy cannot ignore the management concepts. Occasionally, good things do happen from forced marriages.

If one reads a typical presentation of a management concept, the management concept is presented as a practically oriented theory that presents past experiences in an abstract and general manner. A typical concept contains a diagnosis of problems in the company's management, and it offers suggestions for how to solve them. Also, the concept contains methods for analysis, as well as suggestions for procedures to follow, in order to make the change. More implicitly, it is based on a certain philosophy of people and companies.

In studies on the management concepts, one may, however, find different definitions and understandings. Generally speaking, management concepts are conceived in three different ways: researchers of neo-institutional orientation view the management concepts, as standard prescriptions. Others see the concepts as more or less pure knowledge. And finally, we maintain that the management concepts should be viewed as political programmes.

A number of authors of neo-institutional orientation take an interest in the rhetoric of the concepts, and they see the popularity of the concepts as trends, succeeding one another (Abrahamson 1996, Meyer 1996, Benders & Bijsterveld 2000, Furusten 1999). The management concepts are largely understood as stable theory that becomes popular for a period of time and after a while loses its attraction. Those who view the concept as stable theory share this perception with those who view the management concept as almost neutral knowledge that holds rational and common sense solutions (Van Veen, & Sanders 1997).

We understand changes (e.g. implementation of a management concept in an organization) as political processes (Hagedorn-Rasmussen 2000). Our approach is based on a combination of organisational theory on political processes in organizations (Pfeffer 1981, Pettigrew 1973, Knights & Murray 1994), and recent sociology of knowledge and science (Latour 1987, Callon 1987 and 1991, Grint 1995). Taking this starting point, we see management concepts as socially constructed political programmes that hold intentions of change. The political programme unfolds in interaction with its context in a political process. In the political process, alliances are established between actors (called coalitions) in an active interaction with the content of the political programme. There are some actors, who are in a 'driver-role'. This is particularly true for the management consultant firms that make their living from product development of new management concepts. The actors inside and outside the companies get involved in the coalitions and are simultaneously changing the political programme. This process is characterized by emergence; it does not occur in any predictable way. The political programme may contain more or less direct reference to working life and welfare.

In this chapter the consequences of the management concepts for working life and welfare are discussed from two points of view. Firstly, we look at a number of management concepts. What do they tell about themselves and are there any relations to welfare? Secondly we look into details of Business Process Re-engineering; how has it developed and how has it been implemented in Denmark. This is presented through two case stories.

Management Concepts Without Welfare – Humans as Means of Production, the Company as a Goal?

The company as a goal and the employees as means! Are the intentions in management concepts such as Business Process Re-engineering, Total Quality Management, The Learning Organization and Human Resource Management really that harsh? Is it really true that these management concepts all classify a person as a variable, to be adjusted in order to gain increased revenue for shareholders and investors? These are the central questions, and we examine whether people play a role as an end in themselves, or whether they are merely a means to something else. Is there room for welfare dimensions when implementing management concepts?

Welfare is linked to society. Welfare implies society's ability to create social safety, health, developmental opportunities, and influence for the individual. In Denmark and most other industrialized countries lack of welfare is more or less effectively compensated by a government-based welfare system consisting of a social security system, health care system, educational system, etc. but both the welfare and the lack of welfare are created in everyday life. Working life plays a decisive role in development of welfare. The companies are under a certain pressure to develop the welfare dimensions of working life. The employees may exert pressure in this direction. The trade unions may push for it, and the Government may put a certain amount of pressure on the companies to accommodate welfare. And finally, the customers may in some cases also put a certain pressure on the companies to develop the welfare dimensions of working life.

The management concepts do not, as a starting point, have objectives that involve welfare. Their perspective and interest rest with the business opportunities for the company. It is thus of interest to examine, whether the management concepts as political programmes have a content that harm the welfare dimensions of working life, or whether there are also elements in management concepts that have the potential for increasing welfare in the work.

Four welfare perspectives are used for the evaluation of the management concepts:

An Economic Perspective. The work force is an important economic factor in the company. It has considerable welfare implications as to how the management concepts define and understand this factor. It has welfare implications, whether the work force is seen as an instrumental product factor, bought by the company to perform certain tasks, or whether the work force is seen as a subjective factor, able to learn and develop itself for the benefit of the individual person, the production, and the company.

An Organizational Perspective. The organizational perspective has two dimensions: How do the management concepts intend to organize the proposed changes? And what is the more permanent organizational design that the management concept proposes? For both of these dimensions, it has great impact on welfare, whether the employees have influence and how the employees participate in making changes.

The Work Environment Perspective. Health and safety and employment security in work can be strongly influenced by the changes that are carried out by initiating the management concepts. The management concepts may therefore be evaluated on the basis of what work environmental deteriorations and what potential work environmental improvements the concepts imply.

Responsibility Towards the Society as a Perspective. In the public discourse in Denmark and the EU, the companies are increasingly held socially responsible for the integration of people with reduced work ability, the elderly, the young, women, and people from underprivileged ethnic groups. Likewise, the company is made responsible for the employees' family to thrive, while the work is being performed. Finally, the company is made responsible for the products to contribute to the development of welfare in the society. Can the management concepts in any way contribute to the development of the companies' societal responsibility, or will they marginalize and maybe suppress this responsibility?

These perspectives are used for a brief welfare examination of eight selected management concepts which are currently in use with regards to evaluating their welfare potential. Each concept is briefly described with focus on the primary goal for the concept, the inherent philosophy of people and organizations. The most important means that the concept suggests, are also described. The presentation is based on Buhl et al. (2001). Each of these concepts has different variants but to clarify the content, we have made use of the artifice to describe an 'average variant' of each concept.

Business Process Re-engineering (BPR) is distinguished by its focus on customers and on business processes. Business Process Re-engineering has been associated with radical efforts, where IT often plays an important part as the 'pile driver' for extensive restructuring. Some consider BPR a rehabilitation of the leadership initiative, as a sort of counterbalance to the more soft TQM. BPR evolved in the U.S. in a period of depression, and the concept was launched as a radical means to solving a crisis in American companies. BPR's template for a company is an information system with a number of information flows. There are rarely put words on competencies, employee influence, and work relations.

Total Quality Management (TQM) has a long history which, among other things, can be traced back to statistical control methods and systematic approaches to quality control. In this context, quality assurance has been technically oriented towards process improvements in companies. The TQM concept itself emerged from a culture theoretical approach and at a time, where Quality of Working Life played a major role in the U.S. A few dimensions were added, which opened up the possibility that TQM could include work conditions and employee influence.

Customer Relationship Management (CRM) aims at building long-term relations between customer and company, thereby adding value to the company and the customer through the opportunity of adjusting the products to the customers. It includes examination of the companies customer needs, market evaluation, preparing a market introduction, market communication, sales and customer service. CRM is based on a number of processes and (IT) systems that, among other things, are intended to accumulate knowledge about the customers and support a customer-oriented marketing strategy.

Companies are considered as harmony-oriented, and the employees must be mobilized either with IT or with education in order to sell better. CRM is often practiced with IT as the primary element, and the organization is seen as a system of information flows that need to be made more effective by use of IT systems. The employees may contribute with knowledge, but they do not have any independent role to play. Qualifications must be improved and attitudes of the employees must be worked on to support the CRM change. Thus, there is the opportunity for (further) qualification of some employee groups, but it is a competency development that stays in close proximity to the company, and it may have side effects in tying the employees to the company. Working conditions are not mentioned as an issue.

Supply Chain Management (SCM) is a process focusing on the supplier of raw materials, sales people and customers in order to achieve an integrated material flow from supplier to end-user. Reorganization of sub-contractors and the set-up of framework agreements with the remaining contractors, are central means of the strategy. The focus is on the material-flow from the suppliers of raw materials, through the organization, and on to the customer. The flow that receives attention is the physical flow of materials, as opposed to BPR that focuses on the economy and the flow of information.

Some consultants view SCM as a technical system, while others point out that it implies new forms of management and that involvement of people are required. In order to work, the concept must have an element of communication, trust, and contracts. Cooperation across the companies means that the management cannot use the usual power tools. In addition to these elements, SCM can be quite unilaterally focused on material flow, and there is rarely any advanced concept of the human factor. It means that there is no language on work conditions, competencies and participatory influence.

The Learning Organization (LO) is aimed at the organization's ability to learn. It is carried out through delegating management, adjusting organization and technology, and by focusing on learning in the job and through education. Coaching, i.e. a supportive managerial role, group work and improved communication, can be key efforts. Knowledge and learning are central elements, and they are to varying degrees linked to skill and competency development among the organization's members and in the organization as a whole. Often focus is on individual learning and knowledge. There is, however, also quite a lot of focus on the leadership role and thus on training of leaders. Typically, there is room for employee participation, while working conditions rarely get attention.

Knowledge Management (KM) focuses on the management of the company's production of knowledge. The main idea is to let the company's employees and managers develop and share the necessary knowledge as effectively as possible. Knowledge Management overlaps partly with the Learning Organization, dependent on which approach is used. KM is typically facilitated by technology, which is used for storing knowledge (information), knowledge distribution and the search for knowledge. Similar to the Learning Organization, there can in Knowledge Management be a strong focus on the individual person and his or her opportunities for acquiring and passing on knowledge. Knowledge Management is dominated by a resource perspective where people are seen as a productive resource to be utilized in the best possible way. Again, there is an opportunity especially for high-resource employees to participate in shaping the practical implementation, but there is no language on working conditions.

Enterprise Resource Planning (ERP) are IT-control systems aimed at creation of overview and coordination of the various activities of the organization. The purpose of the ERP systems is to coordinate different processes, activities, and functions. The systems integrate the entire business processes of the company, and at the same time contain functionality of specific areas, such as economy management and storage management. Therefore, ERP is often also used in connection with BPR projects. People are a resource managed by a few dimensions inserted in the system. The company is seen as a series of information flows, and unless the company is focused on setting up the system in a decentralized manner, a standard ERP acquisition will contribute to centralization. Competency development is usually taking place with a strong focus on the employees who use the systems the most. Furthermore the training often focuses on cementing existing tasks. There is no focus on working conditions or employee participation.

Human Resource Management (HRM) is an umbrella for a number of different variations of concepts focusing on development of the human resources. Emphasis is put on development of joint visions and objectives and success is evaluated in relation to these whereas detailed measurements and norms as seen in other concepts play a lesser role. Important elements are breaking down hierarchies and creating fewer job categories in connection with team building. There is a tendency to move from collective settlement of salary and working conditions towards multi-dimensional and individual contracts. At the same time, HRM intends to create increased involvement and motivation by binding the employees closer to the company. By dissemination of knowledge of visions and objectives, the company culture also plays a significant role. The intention is that the company and employees become closely connected. Working conditions are occasionally involved in this concept.

The various management concepts focus on different parts of the company and will typically affect different personnel groups in the company. The figure below shows what personnel groups are primarily affected by each management concept.

Affected department/ Concept	All	Finance	Sales	Purchase	Construction	Mid-level Managers Planning	Produc-tion	Storage	Distri-bution and service
BPR			X	X		X	X	X	X
TQM				X		X	X		
CRM			X						X
SCM				X		X		X	
LO	X				X		X		
KM					X				
ERP	X	X	X	X		X	X	X	X
HRM	X	X	X	X	X	X	X	X	X

Figure 3.1 Personal groups affected by different management concepts

Buhl, Hansen & Koch 2001.

The Concepts and the Welfare Rationales

In the following, we discuss the relations between concepts and the four welfare perspectives.

The Economic Perspective: The Company as a Goal. The concepts are for the most part sold by consultants on results, linked to economy. It is characteristic, however, that the concepts relate selectively to economy, and they often define their own economic measurements. This is for instance the case for Knowledge Management and the Learning Organization. Both of them seek to establish an economy that views knowledge as the central asset of a company.

Furthermore it is characteristic that it is the individual company, and implicitly the management of the individual company, that constitutes the target group of the concepts. There are, however, some concepts, which also look at the interplay between different companies (Business Process Re-engineering and Supply Chain Management).

The economic rationale is also shown in the concepts' philosophy of human beings. In a discourse analysis of literature on a number of concepts including The Learning Organization, Human Resource Management and Total Quality Management, Poul N. Dahl (1999:55–56) reaches the conclusion that the person is made into an object and is viewed as harmony-seeking and rational in his or her actions. Likewise, the concepts are viewed as rational tools that can contribute to the most sensible way to reach the organization's goal. Conflicts of interest and individual differences are neglected, or as Dahl says,

> People are viewed as having no biography and no history. There is no consideration for the fact that a person has different needs at different times in his or her life, or for the fact that life history, socialization, and social background play into how the needs are shaped and create a person's horizon (Dahl 1999: 55).

The Organizational Perspective. The Management Concepts, Competency Development and Employee Participation. The management concepts treat, to varying degrees, the employees as actors in the change processes. As a main rule, however, the concepts include various techniques for employee involvement. These techniques are constructed in such a way that the employees are typically objectified. The employees are treated as objects that can render knowledge to be used for restructuring and changing. The employees are a means to obtain previously decided goals for the organisation. Business Process Re-engineering is a particularly clear example.

In contrast to the objectivization is a form of influence in which the employees participate in shaping goals and adjusting means. This form would require exchange of views and dialogue at many levels and in many fora in the company. For employee influence to become a reality, it usually presupposes a collective representation of the employees, as a counterbalance against the management dominance of power and insight that are characteristic for most organizations. In Denmark, employees are secured a certain level on influence by election of shop stewards and safety representatives and through formal collective representation in works council and safety committees, but the management concepts are characterized by a detachment of this form of representation (Buhl 2000, s. 108). Neither cooperative committees nor employee representatives are mentioned in the management concepts.

Competency development is part of most concepts as a tool for change. By introducing Enterprise Resource Planning, for example, large groups of employees must first be trained. This training, however, often involves cementing of the existing work organization. It is usually the core work force, meaning the work force that cannot easily be replaced with other workers in the labour market, that receives priority in training activities. In the company, the core work force has most often already received valuable and long-term competency development (Storey 1992). With the management concepts, this group is given an additional raise. The result is often an even greater distance between the core employees on the one hand, and the ones who are more easily replaceable, on the other. Training can then lead to marginalizsation, thereby ultimately weakening the welfare dimension.

The Work Environment Perspective. The work environment and the working conditions are almost never directly mentioned in the rhetoric of the management concepts. In this respect, the concepts are in fundamental opposition to established ideas of control of health risks though company planning. See for instance the OSHA 18000 standard for occupational health and safety management systems. It is emphasizing that consideration for the work environment must be integrated at all levels of the company. Although the work environment is not mentioned in the concepts, they can nevertheless have considerable consequences for the development of the work environment. The concepts function as a basis for changes in technology and organization and will, as such, have an impact on the work environment. Business Process Re-engineering is an example of how the changes may have both positive and negative consequences for the work environment. Thus, there are elements in the BPR strategy that point to a Tayloristic philosophy: the work must be mapped and restructured according to a rational logic. But there are also elements that can lead to improvements of the work environment, as presented in Champy & Hammers's (1994) discussion of BPR. The most important results of a BPR process are, according to Champy and Hammer personnel reduction, faster turnover, more effective business processes, process-oriented IT and IT management. But at the same time, they describe a series of visions for the work, after the BPR process has been completed out:

- multi-dimensional jobs that are not narrowly function-oriented;
- process groups;
- from outside control to personal authority in the work;
- measure and reward on the basis of results instead of activity;
- promotion on the basis of competencies, rather than performance;
- changes in culture, including 'the customer pays my salary';
- a new kind of manager: from superior to consultant.

Similar examples are found in concepts such as Knowledge Management, the Learning Organization, and Customer Relationship Management.

Societal Responsibility as a Perspective. A broader welfare rationale does not play any role in the concepts. The underlying understanding is that what is good for the companies, is also good for society. Important issues such as social responsibility and an accommodating labour market are too far-reaching to appeal to the rationales of the management concepts.

It is well-known, however, that in a situation where there is a lack of manpower, the companies have an interest in presenting a more social profile, in order to attract manpower. When the social responsibility of the companies rests on a rational micro-economic argumentation it is initially the internal labour market that stands to win compared to openess towards the external labour market. The knowledge that the employees already possess is so valuable that the company has an interest in tying them closer to the company (Ibsen 1999). The economic rationale determines, at the same time, that the social responsibility will primarily target the core work force. The consequence is therefore often a larger distance between core work force and the other employees. This pushes the welfare perspective even further away.

Discussion

It is not surprising that the previous outline of selected management concepts demonstrates that their primary goal and starting point is business development of the company. In the evaluation of the management concepts' welfare perspectives, we may, however, place each concept on a continuum that spans from a narrow efficiency and productivity focus, to personal development in the working life. The continuum rests on the observation that each concept is found in many variants, and that there exists a long and politically formative transformation from idea to practice. There is no certain connection between, on the one side, ideas in the form of intentions and objectives that the individual management concepts describe, and on the other, practice as created when the management concepts are implemented in the companies. In the table below, a number of positive and negative potentials for the welfare development are presented for each management concept.

TQM, for example, has quality as its core concept, and many techniques have been developed to improve quality. The practice of these techniques is based on an interpretation of the concept of quality. If quality circles are practiced with a focus of creating a culture to encourage permanent improvement in order to reduce costs and create increased productivity; issues of welfare and improved work conditions risk being given secondary priority – and maybe none at all. If quality circles, on the other hand, are practiced with the intention to create coherent work processes that may induce increased competency development for the employees, the concept opens up for a development of work, with a number of welfare improvements to follow.

Concept replaces concept, and each of them poses a risk to the employees. There exists a danger that the work will be intensified, resulting in physical as well as mental hazards, and groups of employees could potentially become marginalized and expelled. The concepts thus contain a number of negative potentials related to the welfare development of the work. This is reinforced by the social dynamics that the management concepts are a part of. The concepts are sold by consultants, introduced by managers, and practiced in companies, as the answer to badly understood complex conditions and rapid changes. But in reality, the concepts are not completely determined before introduction to the company. They are bent and negotiated in complex political processes. The inherent structure that is laid down in the concept does, however, contribute to directing the change processes. A pro-active and conscious formation during the long transformation process may open possibilities for inclusion of welfare dimensions. This, however, requires some powerful strategies by the political actors in the company. In the following, we shall take a closer look at the political formation of the concepts based on the experience from the introduction of Business Process Re-engineering into Denmark.

Humans as Goal	Interpretation	Concept and Core Concept	Interpretation	Humans as Means
Association between quality of work and performance	Integration of work practice and quality considerations	TQM Quality	Statistical effectiveness and productivity	Technical rationality
Increased integration between competencies and processes	Restructuring of the work processes to support the skill-level	BPR Value	Rationalizing time and productivity	Technical rationality
Development of space for learning General competency development	Learning with experience-based practice as a starting point	DLO Learning	Narrow cognitive approach in close proximity to the company	Learning as a technical ability that can be measured. Technical rationality
Personal growth	Knowledge as a capacity that develops individually and collectively	Knowledge Management Knowledge	Knowledge as tools that can be accumulated in data-warehouses. Knowledge as economy	Reinforcement of the company's 'knowledge bank'
Developing relations with customers	Sales with a human face	CRM Customer Relation	Optimization of sales processes	Human relations instrumentali-zed
Developing work tasks with support from IT	Support of work processes and developmental opportunities	ERP Data Control	Rationalization of work processes – of time and productivity	The all-controlled human machine
Knowledge expansion	Development of the human resources	HRM Human Resources	Exploitation of the human resources	'Human' as an economic factor. Technical rationality
Employee Influence Presupposed			The Concept as Tool for Experts	

Figure 3.2 Humanization or instrumentalization in management concepts

The Continuum of Change

When new management concepts are introduced, it often gives the impression that if you want to make it, you must get on the train right away. If you don't, it will be too late.

In this chapter, we shall use Business Process Re-engineering (BPR) to describe the journey from where the concept was first fostered until it dissolved. This train set off in the U.S. at the end of the 1980s. It was first introduced to Danish companies about 1990. It is probably fair to say that the BPR wave reached its climax in 1995. But as we are writing (2001), there are still BPR projects under way. So even if the train is moving, the train is long, and you can get on in many places along the way. But as time goes by, the destination of the train becomes more uncertain.

The SARA study of the BPR journey has revealed some of the dynamics that characterize a management concepts' passage through time: globally, regionally, and in the companies. When introducing management concepts, there are long time spans between ideas, plans, projects, and the final implementation that has consequences for working conditions. In this prolonged process from idea to reality, the management concept becomes entangled in what we here call 'the continuum of change', where the changes are never finalized, and where no stable 'after-state' is established, in which a final evaluation of the results of the management concept can take place.

In the transformational journey of the concepts, working conditions become directly and indirectly issues that continue to affect the welfare dimensions of working life. We shall present this relationship by analyzing the development of BPR in three more or less merged contexts: the U.S, Denmark, and two Danish companies, and we shall evaluate the consequences for three welfare dimensions: working conditions, competency, and employee influence.

The BPR in the USA

Business Process Re-engineering aims at a radical restructuring (re-engineering) of the company's business processes in order to strengthen the cross-cutting processes that are valuable for the customer. This definition comes close to Davenport and Hammer's definitions from 1990 (Davenport & Short 1990, Hammer 1990). Later, an abundance of variants have developed; however they all have 'shared goods' from the definition above.

Early observers went out of their way to show that BPR did not contain anything particularly new.

BPR was just considered a new bundle of old theories, concepts and solutions related to a specific perception of problems (Grint 1995, Earl 1994, Burke & Peppard 1995). Some of the BPR core philosophy and rhetoric was developed in the MIT research programme 'Management in the 90s', carried out in 1984–1989. Other parts were developed in cooperation between consulting firms, such as Index and their customers. Davenport has since then described the environment in which Re-engineering and Re-design emerged as a 'soup' where no single person can take credit for inventing the concept (Davenport 1994a).

In 1990, Davenport & Short (1990) and Hammer (1990) published articles on how to use information technology for transforming business processes. Davenport and Short called their concept Business Process Redesign, while Hammer in 1990 used Re-engineering. Davenport recalls:

> and then about a month or so before the article [the 1990–article Ed.] was going to be published, I ran into Mike Hammer, who said he was writing an article on the same thing. It was totally independent work (Davenport 1994a).

Two different versions of BPR were thus articulated in 1990: Davenport's and Hammer's. Michael Hammer was a computer science professor at MIT (Kleiner 1995). He left MIT and started his co-operation with James Champy from Index, a Cambridge based technology consulting company. Champy and Hammer became known as the main promoters of BPR. In their early versions of BPR, welfare dimensions were almost absent. Cutting costs and restructuring were central in Re-engineering up through 1990. Davenport's approach was, however, less radical and more open to welfare dimensions.

A BPR wave rose in the U.S. that had a support structure consisting of management consultants such as Ernst & Young, central periodicals (Harvard Business Review, Sloan Management Review), major firms (Ford, Texas Instruments), professional associations (Council of Logistics Management, APICS), book publishers, business schools and universities. The number of titles that included BPR rose explosively in American management literature. When the wave crested, Champy and Hammer, in 1993, published the book 'Re-engineering the Corporation'.

The original visionary thinking on Re-design and Re-engineering were transformed and modified into neat packaged consultant methods, like Price Waterhouse's 'Change Integration' and Ernst & Young's 'Fusion'. These methods were gradually developed and fine-tuned to the customers and they became a body of practical experiences.

When Champy and Hammer wrote the book 'Re-engineering the Corporation' in 1993, they could actually look back and draw on a great deal of practical experience from consulting work, rather than an academic production (which strengthened their argumentation by drawing on examples; the book was stuffed with small case stories). A parallel case was Davenport's 1993 book on 'Process Innovation'; it drew on Ernst & Young's experience. The Champy and Hammer book became a bestseller and was translated into fourteen languages, including Danish.

Champy and Hammers' book clearly presents a full-fleshed concept, including a number of more or less constructed enterprise examples. While the book is rather detailed, it does not compare to the management consultant concepts that have detailed descriptions of procedures for a BPR-project. So, on the one hand, the book contributed to the acceleration of the social movement, and, on the other, it added unintentionally to a vague content by avoiding detailed prescription and evaluation. Part of this is also the handling of the welfare dimensions. Champy and Hammer described the new organisational forms and implied that they would improve working life, including competencies. Employee participation was not seen as a tool, however.

A Gartner Group 1995 analysis of BPR (Digrius 1995) presented a variety of consulting concepts and abilities. Gartner Group employed four dimensions of consultant capabilities: IT planning, organizational design, analysis of business processes, and the integration of these three primary categories. Among seventeen leading edge companies, they found common strength in the analysis of business process, but a significant variety in the other capabilities. A Gartner Group 1996 analysis noted:

The fragmented BPR tool market continues to grow in terms of new vendors, links, alliances and partnerships (Kleinberg 1996).

The development and multiplicity of concepts was one of several trends. And the core philosophy developed too. Digrius/Gartner (1995) as well as Hammer (1995) pointed out that companies in a growth situation would adopt BPR (which was coined second generation BPR). Champy (1995) and Digrius focused on the soft side of enterprises; organizational design culture, values etc. Cross-company processes came more into focus. In general, an opening for welfare issues could also be detected in these later versions.

BPR in Denmark – a Cascade of Variants

The spread of BPR, was a process of many actors, with some of them operating across sectors and actor networks, whereas others acted locally. The story of BPR is thus multiple and possibly different for different actors. Despite prevalent beliefs in transparency between enterprises and sectors, it turned out that disparate parallel processes were going on. The two figures below communicate some of the written material that came out of the process (discussed in Heusinkveld et al. 2000). A number of Danish actors are observing primarily the US and secondarily the international debate on BPR. The multinational consulting firms located in Denmark are supported with information on new concepts, as a part of an internal process. The Danish-based local consulting agencies, unions, universities and the technological service network rely on public processes like international conferences, business journals, or visits to universities in the U.S.

The early explicit BPR implementations in enterprises located in Denmark progressed from about 1991. The international companies such as Price Waterhouse, Andersen Consulting, IBM, and Ernst & Young were active. Two consultants from IBM wrote the first public article in November 1991 on BPR. In the following period from 1992 to 1994, a number of consulting agencies began to make use of the concept in enterprise cases. They all referred to their own cases as seminal. The publishing of Sant & Hviid's book and the translation of the Champy & Hammer books marked the beginning of a public wave where a form af synergy between the different consultants, enterprises and the semi-public arenas began to develop, supported by books, articles and seminars.

Every now and then when visiting managers and customers, they had bought the Sant & Hviid book and wanted to hear my opinion (Consultant on the situation in 1994).

The Sant & Hviid book was followed by five other books on BPR in Danish. Articles were published in the professional press and rearticulate specific communities of practices, such as the engineering management community. The articles demonstrate disparate views on how to understand BPR.

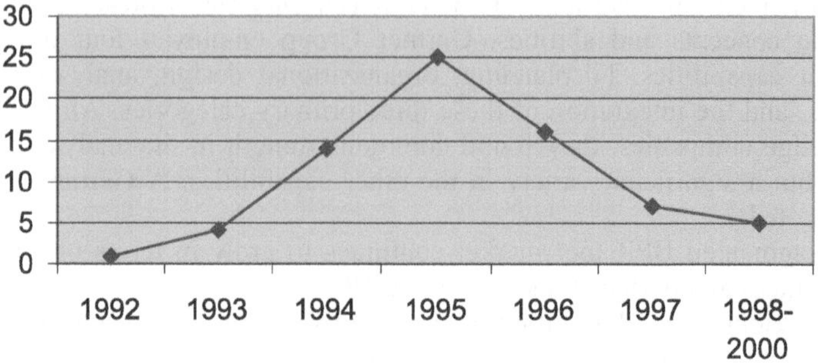

Figure 3.3 Publishing year of Danish Articles on BPR

By the end of 1994 and throughout 1995, there was at least one conference on BPR per month. The typical agenda was a consultant presentation of BPR followed by an enterprise presenting practical experience. Often the presentation was made by one of the consultant's clients, and the seminars had a clear market purpose for the consultant and his concept. A consultant such as Sant & Bendix presented mainly manufacturing enterprises as cases, whereas other consulting agencies would use cases from the service sector or the public sector. These early presentations served to re-constitute the consultants profile and correspondence with certain sectors. Cases from the public sector seemed to emerge a little later, mainly from 1995 and 1996.

Sant & Bendix and their cases seemed to obtain a crosscutting role as templates of BPR. The core competency is manufacturing engineering and management, but their work with BPR became known in a wider management context. One explanation why Sant & Bendix obtained this credibility could be found in their past status, as a Danish consulting agency, with a strong local/national network. The fact that Sant & Bendix actually merged with Cooper & Lybrand a.1990, made it possible for them to develop BPR concepts and methods in a positive direction. But their public profile continued to have a strong local bias. They managed to stay international and balance it with local orientation.

In January 1997, the SARA project did a snowballing of actors promoting BPR in Denmark. A small group of consultants had some broad recognition; Ernst & Young, Promentor, Sant & Bendix, Andersen Consulting, PA Consulting and Price Waterhouse. While the list of others, recognised only by a few, continued to grow (such as consultants, publishers, associations, enterprises), more than fifty actors were identified, when the snowballing was halted.

Fewer public functions were held after 1996, but in the same period, a considerable portfolio of on-going enterprise projects was available. Head of Department Carsten Bogh of the Danish Technological Institute claimed in January 1996, that 70 BPR-projects were currently going on in Denmark, and that 30 of them were finished. He also foresaw an increase in projects (Teknik&Data 1996). From 1995 onwards, it was a clear that the IT players, such as Enterprise Resource Planning-vendors, were the ones, who most strongly promoted BPR. Thus, there was a tendency of BPR to become a phase in an IT implementation project, whereas the purely organizational versions did badly.

An employee oriented concept was developed with public funding presented by the Danish Technological Institute which is a semi-Governmental organization aimed at industry support. It was based on employee participation with a management group as the steering committee. This variant was used in 3–4 Danish companies, and it must be compared to the more than 100 BPR projects in Denmark in the same period.

The vast majority of enterprise cases published and communicated in the period 1992–97 were success stories (about 50). Examples of failures were rare, even when informal information was included, despite the often communicated failure rate at 50–70 % (Champy & Hammer 1993).

Case 1: BPR and Enterprise Resource Planning at a Production Company – a failed project

Olsen is the pseudonym of a manufacturing network owned by a multinational corporation, organized as part of a Scandinavian division. In Denmark the manufacturing network consists of three factories, a net of sales offices and a distribution system. Olsen is characterized by high volume production of discrete products. The management coalition that adopted Enterprise Resource Planning (ERP) and BPR as their political programme was predominantly embedded in the production departments.

The case study follows and discusses the experience of the coalition of managers and employees, which over a period of five years tried to implement an ERP-system and BPR. While the ERP element is strongly flagged and communicated in the enterprise and to the outer world, the BPR element is somewhat discrete and occasionally occurs in technical disguise. The coalition that promoted the ERP and BPR programme is called the management coalition below.

Context. Olsen enjoys enhanced turnover and a virtually dominant position in their field over the five years of our case study. The management coalition does not put particular emphasis on traditional interpretations of the market and competition. A central orientation point for the early parts of the process is the IT-strategy of the division, which the management coalition wants to outmanoeuvre.

The IT strategy of the division points to a particular platform and ERP application, which the management coalition distrusts.

Cooperation with the ERP-supplier and consultants does not develop into an integrated coalition. Consultants are substituted several times. Internally, sales and administration successfully argue that the customers' demands must be met, which leads to an increase in variants and components to be processed in the enterprise.

Industrial relations in Olsen are characterized by high trust. Shop stewards and production management cooperate closely throughout the five-year period. However, there are occasions where the employees on the shop floor exercise different forms of resistance, even towards the shop stewards.

Process. The process started as a management coalition to develop a substitution for the existing manufacturing control system (a Manufacturing Resource Planning II system). Over the first months, an understanding of the required ERP system was developed with a clear ambition of BPR, supported by IT-integration. After half a year, the management coalition chose a system and a supplier.

The process proceeded with a number of unforeseen ruptures and barriers: The company was sold, consultants were deemed incapable of counselling the enterprise and were replaced. Internal project managers were replaced as well. Some internal actors resisted the process. Performance problems were mounting and led to the process that ultimately stopped the project. However, in other periods of the process preparation work and problem solving developed in a rather silent way.

The process is described in the table below. The perspective revolves around the ERP and BPR, promoting the formation of a coalition and actors. The time scale is half a year and 1/1 means first half year of the first year. Main event points to the critical juncture in the process for this particular period.

Content of the Political Programme: BPR. Diverse series of perspectives have been articulated over time. Sales and production competed for resources and power. But other players such as alternating IT-managers, the financial manager, as well as the CEO and the shop stewards, also played roles over time. The first BPR idea that was adopted by Olsen, originates from the external discourse in the mid-nineties. It may be called BPR 1, and it consists of the following:

Product configuration → sales → order communication → order database → production planning

The coalition, which, as mentioned above, consisted of managers in the production, did not use the BPR concept in public, although the vision was clear. One reason is that they faced the possibility of resistance; if BPR's cost-cutting and employee-redundant rhetoric became too visible by the shop floor workers. Another reason is that the arrangement of the order handling process aligns and mediates the interaction between sales representatives, order handlers, production planners and others. The management coalition speculated that if this process is rearranged, the tactics for selling the BPR-idea must be more carefully planned, since the coalition did not have full support from the CEO and other high level management.

The first consultants did not flag BPR directly, but they organized a process of planning control concepts that clearly enforced the cross-cutting perspective.

The process developed into competing ideas regarding the launching of counter programmes and parallel programmes. This is true for larger and decisive elements, such as sales, a sector that wanted to maintain status quo. And it is true for smaller elements, such as deciding who should performs tasks in the new processes. The second BPR-programme is the result of this soup. In BPR 2, the structure would evolve from the crosscutting process:

Lorry route plan → assembly plan → master production schedule → planning → executing operations → lorries

The enterprise and the production areas were characterized by several, sometimes even numerous competing ongoing change projects. Any project coalition therefore had to struggle to maintain the position that their project enjoyed. The ERP and BPR projects were no exception in this respect.

Year	Main event	Management Coalition promoting ERP & BPR	Neutral actors	Actors with competing position
1/1	Choice of IT-supplier	Project group Manager of Production	CEO Production Employees, IT-manager	Owner Group; IT and Division Management
2/1	Sold to new group	Same + ERP Supplier Two Management Consultants	Sales and Finance Production Employees	Division-Management / Owner
1/2	Analysis of business processes	Project Group, Manager of Production Two Management Consultants Finance	Sales Top Management Shop Floor-Employees	Same
2/2	Application of investment	Project Group Manager of Production IT-Manager Division Management	Rep. For Sales Production Employees	-
1/3	Negotiations of contract Configuring of ERP	New Project Group Manager of Production IT-Suppliers Rep. for Finance	Same	-
2/3	Configuring of ERP BPR forgotten? Piecemeal BPR	Re-Structured Project group, IT-Supplier, Finance	Same	-
1/4	Ready for implementing, but performance problems BPR rearticulated	Same	Same	Teams in production coalition active
2/4	Searching solutions for performance problems	Project Group New Consultants Production Employees	Rep. For Sales	Same
1/5	Same	Project Group New Consultants IT-Manager	Same	Attempt to Convene ERP and teams
2/5	Project halted Pause	Coalition dismantled, and later reorganized	Same	Same

Figure 3.4 The political process of BPR in a manufacturing company

The figure above shows that it occurred twice that other political programmes have been competing directly with ERP and BPR. In the first phase, the competitor was the IT strategy of the owner group, and in the last phase it was the 'teams in production' strategy of shop stewards and others coalitions.

Analysis of Strategies In the first phase, the ERP-promoting coalition within the enterprise had the following political programme:

- Enhanced scope of future integrated IT solutions, ambitions of ERP.
- A Danish supplier organization with international strength (to tackle the owner group).
- A shop floor/assembly control system.
- IT integrated handling of the sales order process (BPR 1).
- The system from the one chosen by the owner group.

This was in direct contrast to the strategy of the owner group. The owner group had developed an IT-strategy, with a specific hardware platform and a specific (American) ERP system. The ERP coalition at Olsen wanted to avoid this platform and the related ERP-system, mainly because of previous experiences with the ERP supplier organization in Denmark. Welfare dimensions were almost absent in these strategic considerations. However, the enterprise did carry out a piece of strategy work in parallel to the process of changing ERP, and in this process, work environment is mentioned as a value dimension for the enterprise, whereas competency and participation are not mentioned.

In the last two years, additional political programmes were competing:

- A development of teams in production, with some autonomy for the workers and a reduction of the traditional role of the first line manager. This programme has a rather clear 'improvement of the working life' dimension.
- An ERP-implementation coalition, which aimed at technical solutions for product development, but also used the BPR 2 concept. A part of this solution focuses on competency development for IT-personnel.

The process started with a management coalition that was deliberately formed as a small group. The initial block diagram of central elements and a two-page list of desired features of the technology constituted the coalition's political programme. The block diagram clearly stated the IT-integration ambition, using IT to realize a cross-cutting process from sales offices to production planning. When the production-based coalition proposed two possible systems, the sales department backed out. Later, after choosing one particular system, the coalition tried to include the actors from accounting and sales again, this time with new presentations, demonstrating features of the software, especially the finance modules and the product configuration. The finance and sales actors were faced with a fully developed offer of software for their departments, something that clearly strengthened the position of the coalition, compared to the early block diagram models. But the endeavour still failed; sales, accounting, and part of senior management dissented; and it became necessary for the coalition to restrict the implementation of the system strongly, by cutting out the accounting and the sales modules.

The political programme thus failed to provide a 'social glue effect' in the beginning of the process. It took several years to establish a wider scope for the IT solution and a broader supporting coalition. In the third year of the process, the management coalition signed a contract with a hardware vendor, a software vendor and an implementation consultant. Three major projects were initiated: First, configuring the basic system, including logistics and finance. Second, and scheduled slightly later, the configuration of an assembly control system. Third, the sales system, scheduled significantly later. The project was organized in work groups under the three projects, and it involved approximately six permanent full-time staff and about twenty others from the organization. The project group selected the main modules and reference model to adopt. The workgroups under the first and second project started configuring the software. Throughout the work of the groups, a number of micro-political decisions were made on user profiles, needed customization, etc. A year later, a partial configuration, as result of the first sub-project was finalized, and Olsen started preparing for implementation. Training, information and a full test were scheduled. The training programme was extensive and involved large groups of employees from administrative areas of the company. Information was communicated in an newsletter to all employees. The test, however, revealed serious performance problems. The implementation had to be halted, although the entire organization had been aligned by the training and information activities.

As a part of the BPR 2 strategy, ERP facilities were configured, in order to facilitate a control and scheduling system of the assembly process. To support this, exact timing of work processes on the shop floor was initiated. It was done under the auspices of a compromise with shop floor workers, who were told that the main purpose of this configuration was to support a more precise calculation of costs. The work was finalised but stopped, because of performance problems.

After these problems, the promoting coalition finalized their cooperation with the consultants, under a cloud of open conflict. The process of establishing cooperation with another consulting agency, claiming that they could solve the performance problem, led to a rather ambitious 'salvation' programme, involving heavy hardware and database investments. This programme was upset by a crisis at the ERP vendor, which destabilized the system, also internationally. Five years after the process began, the ERP system was finally abandoned. The enterprise then started discussing shifting to another ERP system. The financial support had been provided by the multinational owner, on the basis of the use of a particular MRP II System (Manufacturing Resource Planning System). It will probably lead to a third variant of BPR, but it was still under way when our study stopped.

Almost as a side theme, the direct competition between the BPR and ERP programme and the 'teams in production' programme started in the fifth year, after almost a year of parallel existence. The full reconciliation of the visions of, on the one hand, full control of the assembly process that was embedded in the ERP and BPR programme, and on the other, the enhanced autonomy and competency visions in the team programme, has yet still to be seen.

Consequences for Welfare. Although the process did not lead to physical changes, a number of more soft changes occurred.

The enterprise has developed a core group of managers and employees with enhanced competencies regarding project management and IT implementation. It has also had the indirect implication that a certain coalition is ready to develop new change projects in the future. Furthermore, it means that although one change project (the team project) over the last years has involved employees at the shop floor, as well as their shop stewards, it is not likely that the core group will involve the employees in future projects, as it is clearly not a part of the group's direct experience.

The project has revealed a potential for cost cutting. The establishment of the production teams coincided with the organization of the ERP-project. Key actors have therefore speculated that the administrative tasks seem to be carried out by a combination of a reduced number of administrative staff (since some of them were enrolled in the ERP-project) and production teams, taking over tasks that were previously done by administrative staff.

Finally, the process seems to have resulted in a strengthened Taylorization of the assembly work. A system for mapping of work processes and algorithms for planning work at the assembly lines by IT has been developed. It includes 1200 product numbers and involves mapping of assembly lines as resources, routes for product, and include time studies of operations at the shop floor. The new planning system will be integrated with route planning and probably be handled by production planners and not the production teams. All in all the shop floor workers will have a smaller decision latitude.

Case 2: A Danish Municipality: BPR as 'Managementification' of a Welfare Institution

In recent years, the focus in the Danish public sector has shifted from citizens to consumers, and individual service has taken centre stage. The changes that the public sector organizations were faced with, have been conceptualized through terms such as 'competition', 'outsourcing', 'exit by choice'. This 'marketification' of the public sector, reflects a new relationship between the public sector and the society at large (in particular the marketplace). It also involves a transformation involving new ways of organizing the administrative processes. Higher professionalism and standardization are required. In an effort to achieve better control, new instruments have been applied, such as outsourcing to private businesses, management by objectives, internal contracts and new local pay-systems. We label it as a 'managementification' of the public sector.

Burebjerg is a medium-sized Danish municipality (30,000–40,000 inhabitants), with 260 employees, organized in a 'usual' administration. Many more staff are employed in executing institutions such as schools, elder care, and road maintenance. In recent years, the budget of the municipality of Burebjerg has shown a minor deficit. This is mainly due to the decentralization of public services from the state and counties. Moreover, demographic developments in Burebjerg will increase expenses. It has been a clear political aim to avoid increases in the expenses of the municipal administration. The Burebjerg administration perceives itself –

particularly by the management – to be a modern, fast changing project-oriented organization. Management tries to develop internal change competencies by using external consultants, for instance by training employees to conduct the analysis and the implementation of organizational changes themselves. The cooperation between management and employees is good, and the level of unionization is high. Employees are usually well informed, when new projects are planned.

At the outset, the municipality's administration had an ambition of setting up a control service, involving an audit on correct and good language, and securing the citizens' easy access to well written information. The control service also aimed at rationalizing time spent on services in order to secure quality and increase services. It was created as a response to former budget reductions. In late 1995, the municipality laid off 20 employees, bringing staff reduction up to 60, over the course of the past 8 years.

Process. In early 1995, two staff members from the IT and finance department participated in a conference on BPR, and suggested that the BPR concept was used instead of the 'control service'. The overall purpose for the BPR project was then formulated:

> ...to conduct an analysis of the municipality services regarding both resources, content and verbal presentation... and furthermore ... it must be evaluated, whether the municipalities' service is produced in a rational and efficient way, e.g. with a minimal use of resources and with front office staff members who have adequate competency and responsibility (Terms of reference).

It was decided to hire a management consultant firm in order to conduct an education programme that could provide a selected group of staff with the necessary qualifications, regarding BPR and associated tools. Fifteen staff members were chosen from different parts of the municipality. The management consultants would also function as coaches, and they would monitor the overall quality during the BPR project. The decision of initiating a BPR project was solely a managerial decision, and in late 1995, the idea was already well acknowledged by the management. At the work council meetings, information about the project was provided, but there were no discussions on goals, content, strategy, selection of internal consultants, etc.

The following table shows the course of events:

Phase	Main Activity	The BPR Coalition	Neutral Actors	Competing Coalitions
Idea and planning	Project basis Training of in-house consultants	Management The Project Group Consultants	IT Department Department and group leaders Employees SU and SIO	
Mapping and develop-ment	Mapping work processes Developing new work processes	Management The Project group In-house Consultants IT department Department leaders A few employees	Other employees Works council Safety committee	
Impleme ntation phase	Create developmental contracts Introduce new work processes	Management Project group In-house Consultants IT department More co-workers	Other employees Works council Safety committee	IT department / IT-implementation

Figure 3.5 The political process of BPR in the municipality

The IT-implementation project and the BPR project were increasingly merging during the last part of the process. In the implementation phase, hasty and dysfunctional implementation of IT inhibited the full benefit. Missing and poorly co-ordinated training was partly the problem. Specifications to the IT-systems were haphazard and associated with a general lack of user involvement in design and choice of the new systems, as well as in missing support. During implementation of the new systems, the process caused production loss, and at the same time it increased the workload.

There were elements of working conditions present in the early programme declarations: job satisfaction and good work conditions were included in the terms of reference. These elements were, however, not expanded in the further course of the project. The programme developed through the initial training. The internal consultants were taught mapping and analysis, to develop new administrative procedures and finally employ the results in local development contracts. These process activities were supposed to provide the recipe for how to develop the political programme in order to accommodate substantial change in the organization.

Analyses of Strategies. In the beginning the coalition was based on a project group, the top management, and the external consultants. It was decided to place implementation in a group of in-house consultants It was a strategy aimed at disseminating the project within the organization, and an attempt was therefore made to recruit internal consultants from different departments. However, in practice most of the internal consultants came from the central administration; most were in their thirties and had an academic education. The argument for selecting them was that they were familiar with project work. The internal consultants were asked to come up with suggestions to be included in contracts, covering the participating departments.

Training of the internal consultants had three main goals: introduction to consultant work; introduction to the concept of BPR, and the establishment of a common frame of reference, including a common set of tools. The in-house consultants then interviewed employees, made detailed process mapping, time registration, calculation of potential time saving, etc. The focus was on potential re-engineering processes that were described in detailed process flows. The resulting changes were then described in 'developmental contracts'. These contracts were made for each participating department. The contracts were supposed to tie the department to the change process and make them part of the coalition. However, there was tension with employees who were sceptical of the BPR programme. During the process, the in-house consultants also isolated themselves more and more from the external consultants. This was partly the intention as a result of growing discontent with the external consultants.

Changes in Welfare. The BPR project ended up being intertwined with the increased use of IT in the municipality, and it was therefore the implementation of the combined strategies that changed the work.

In the Family Group at the Social Welfare Administration, the task of generating records on clients was moved from administrative staff to the social workers. The individual social worker had to write her record directly (by the use of the client module) at the PC immediately. As a consequence, the administrative staff would no longer generate the records on the bases of notes from the social workers. It was experienced as a deterioration of the work conditions, both for the social workers and for the administrative staff. Moreover, a weekly group meeting was abolished. It was supposed to be substituted by the use of the client module, implementation of a journal for clients, run directly on the PC during consultation. Also, a new database, made accessible for many different departments in the administration supported the idea of a higher degree of transparency in decision making, which apparently made the group meetings superfluous, from the in-house consultants' point of view. These changes were also viewed by the major part of the social workers, as a deterioration of the work conditions.

In the Technical Administration, a systematically prioritized database on maintenance needs for all buildings in the municipality was established in the building and maintenance department, and a standard scheme for building examination and coordination across categories of buildings was developed. Most employees saw these changes as improvements in working conditions.

Some positive evaluative statements were given and agreed upon by almost all employees in the Technical Administration. They considered IT as a possibility for supporting colleagues across different work functions, since the IT systems had helped to stan-dardize work processes. There has thus been an increase in IT competencies. The project had at least for some increased responsibility and from their point of view decreased bureaucracy.

The pattern for employee participation was on the one hand maintained, in the sense that the use of the formal works council continued. On the other hand, the change process actually strengthened a coalition of managers and employees, which is likely to be appointed for further change work in the future. In this sense, the BPR project has further undermined the possibility of gaining influence for those employees who are less resourceful.

Conclusion

BPR's entry into Denmark had three distinctive phases. In the first phase, the company projects were driven by multinational consulting agencies, and there was no public attention. In the second, books, articles and seminars were booming. And in the third phase, many company projects continued, again without much public attention.

The entry was facilitated through coalitions that were built around consulting firms with the professional associations as arenas for meetings between company representatives, consultants, observers, and others. Then at a later stage the first meetings developed into concrete cooperative partnerships between companies and consultants.

The course of events was influenced by the fact that the trade unions and the work environment institutions were almost completely absent. BPR poses a particular threat for officials and mid-level managers, but Union for Managers, the Union for Secretarial and Administrative staff, the Union for the financial sector or the Union for technicians remained passive and only commented on events. The only active Danish union was the Metal Workers Union (Metal 1994). Also work environment institutions such as the Labour Inspectorate, the Occupational Health Service, and and professional associations in the work environment field were silent.

The case studies of the two enterprises and the entire Danish process also show that the focus on cross-cutting business processes is the only stable element in the concept. Everything else is negotiated and changed over time. In other words, there is a limited stable content as a basis for hidden patterns. And the political process has taken place in such a way that the welfare dimensions are not noticeably articulated.

Welfare, perceived as participation, working conditions and competencies was not given systematic priority in the two cases. The explanation for this may partly be that no-one in the enterprise processes put it on the agenda, and partly that the BPR variants that are offered through books, seminars and consultants' concepts, also do not contain this dimension. The original dimensions in Champy and Hammer's book from 1993 towards the development of a new type of work had no success.

This study of the Danish reception of BPR re-articulates some classic dilemmas for the Scandinavian welfare state. Scandinavian working life has at least since the 2nd World War, found itself torn between two poles. On the one hand, foreign (primarily American) developing forces of an economic-rational orientation that have materialized in a succession of management concepts; and, on the other, a Scandinavian-based democracy and participation model, which constantly has had to reproduce, defend, and develop itself (Sandberg 1997, Clausen & Broberg 2001).

The management concepts have been imposed from the outside - en bloc - and they are missing crucial welfare dimensions, but it is unrealistic to hope for the concepts to get rejected, because the forces that unite behind the concepts, are too strong. However, they can and must be shaped in order to fit into the actual organizations, and it is in that process possible to integrate welfare elements in compromises between capital and work. It must happen at company level, but in that situation it can be difficult to mobilize forces that have the strength and the insight to affect the concepts in a welfare direction. The opportunities are probably better at the national and global level, where the political forces are better organized and more interested in transforming the concepts into tools for welfare.

Different strategies can be adopted in the attempt to make the concepts more welfare oriented:

- Alternative concepts can be adopted that draw on tools and ideas taken from those international business concepts that give the welfare perspective a high priority. Developmental Work, which we outlined in Chapter 2, is an example of this.
- The choice of concepts can be influenced, so that those concepts in their starting point give the development of human resources, working conditions, employee participation, and other welfare elements a high priority, are supported. Since the concepts are shaped in practice, this will, however, not by itself be enough to secure the welfare dimensions. Therefore it becomes relevant to:
- Interpret the opportunities and support strategies that give elements of welfare dimensions a higher priority, regardless of what concept we are dealing with.

The Scandinavian model has had to deal with huge changes, caused by the development of international capitalism and the related management systems that have emerged. These trends have been incorporated without fundamentally weakening the model. Through dialogue, critique and pressure these new forms of management have been successfully integrated into the Scandinavian tradition. However, uncertainty may still persist as to whether it is really possible to have a dialogue about, and a critique of the new streamlined management concepts that are being marketed with such a high degree of professionalism. But the concepts may, in all circumstances contribute to create more publicity on production and work, and thereby contribute to the further development of strategies for its development.

Chapter 4

Company Development Through the Employees

Introduction

Working life is undergoing immense changes. These changes are repeatedly analyzed and confirmed in any setting, where business development and working life are being discussed. The many management concepts of development have serious impact on these changes. On the one hand, we have the management concepts, as mentioned in the previous chapter; on the other, we have the concept of Developmental Work, developed by the Labour movement in collaboration with researchers in Denmark and the other Scandinavian countries. The idea behind the concepts is that the company in order to survive the increased competition in the future, must have the ability to develop. Also, it must be substantially more flexible to meet the alternating demands of the market and the use of new technology. Both approaches presume that the company is based on the competencies of the employees and their ability to independently plan the work in a flexible and suitable manner. This increased attention to a more goal-oriented development and utilization of the human resources in the work, is almost automatically linked to the necessity of securing a healthy and stimulating work environment to maintain, develop and protect 'the human resources' in the company. Developmental Work argues that the companies' interest and responsibility for the development, health and mental wellbeing of the employees can be linked to the employees' self-interest in having work that contains personal development and more responsibility. It is asserted that a connection, and sometimes even a merger, exists between, the reproduction and development of the employees as production factors, and, the employees' personal development that also includes minimizing the psychosocial strains and other health hazards in the work. 'The objectives of integrating preventive strategies into internal business processes are to promote total wellbeing and to develop skills, competence and awareness of responsibility' (Bullinger 2000).

A huge difference does indeed exist between the management-oriented strategies of human resources and the strategy of Developmental Work. While the first one represents a smooth philosophy of harmony, the latter is to a higher degree, aware of the existence of conflicts of interests and potential disagreements between management and employees. Granting the employees influence and control is in this case emphasized as a matter of crucial importance. This difference is in theory clear and fundamental, but not always so obvious in practice. A grey area from the 'toughest' management-controlled places at one end of the scale, to the more democratically oriented places at the other, sometimes exists in concrete projects.

In this chapter three different, yet coherent aspects of projects based on development of human resources are examined. The chapter is based on seven different company cases, where six of them are oriented towards Developmental Work, and thus, to varying degrees, emphasize the employees' influence. The exception is the BPR project from a social welfare administration already mentioned in the previous chapters. All cases can be characterized as ordinary workplaces that do not substantially differ from the average in technology, competence, and scale. It is the Developmental Work (and in one case BPR) in its practical reality, and we discuss the opportunities, problem and dilemmas it involves.

The first aspect to be examined regards the 'social cohesion' among the employees, their community, and solidarity. Do the strategies pose a risk that such communities undergo 'erosion', meaning that individualization will develop in the form of divisiveness and competition among the employees; thereby weakening the employees ability to protect their own interests? Or do they (also) include the opportunity to develop communities and maybe create a new connection between solidarity and individuality, based on autonomy and competence?

The second aspect concerns the achievement of influence and power sharing. In one of the seven cases, the Social welfare administration 'Blue', special emphasis has been given to an objective of co-determination. This case is in line with the strategy of Developmental Work and it is given a more thorough analysis, in order to address some of the issues related to co-determination. Can real co-determination be achieved, and at what level? Are there difficulties in undergoing the necessary learning processes? Is there any resistance to the changes? Does more influence mean greater job satisfaction and productivity?

The third aspect concerns risks in the workplace – the work environment. The question is, whether the human resource strategies by aiming at the development of the individual, also change the health risks, and whether such changes are met with suitable prevention. The focus is on potentially new psychosocial hazards, rather than towards the more traditional physical, chemical, and ergonomic hazards. Does the employees' awareness of risks in the work undergo change, and in continuation of this, do the strategies for risk prevention change?

The three sections of this chapter thus represent three different perspectives on resource projects; all except one are oriented towards the Developmental Work. The case on the Social welfare administration 'Blue' is redundant in all three sections, and it thus represents continuity in the chapter. But this aside, the sections are independent and they can be read independently of one another.

Development and Solidarity Among the Employees

Strategies for developing the human resources in the companies are both aimed at personal development of the single individual, and towards development of the relations between individuals. The intention is for the employees to perform in such a way that new goals are met, not only for the companies, but also for the employees themselves; especially in connection with the working life oriented approaches such as Developmental Work. This development inevitably affects the social relations of the employees – for each other, the management, and their trade unions.

It is expressed with particular sharpness in the Anglo-Saxon 'Human Resource Management' (HRM) literature. It is emphasized here that the management is the acting subject, and a strategy for how to directly attack the trade unions is often included (Gowler et al. 1993). The trade unions represent according to this version – the 'hawkish version' – a roadblock for the development of new forms of organization and new direct relations between employees and managers. This hawkish version of HRM has never really gained a foothold in Denmark. It is difficult to practice in a Danish context, with strong traditions of cooperation between trade unions and company management. It would be expected to create too much resistance, carry a high price, and most likely fail.

A softer strategy for development of the human resources has proven to be more relevant in a Danish context. This version of the strategy is based on the expectation that changes in the work – in addition to increasing productivity – will create good working conditions, and that recognition of the employees' valuable resources will bring about respect and security, and consequently a loyal relationship between managers and employees. In this soft version, concrete changes in the work and in the culture of the company become more relevant. It is a development away from the industrial assembly line and its uniquely collective worker culture. It is an opening that makes it possible for the individual worker to develop his or her specific competencies, and to take individual responsibility. The bureaucratic organization is broken down, and decentralization of tasks and decisions to single individuals or work groups is gaining entry. Also in the soft version, the social relations are issues of concern.

Richard Sennett (1998) has described a particular aspect of this development. In an American context, he draws a picture of a very flexible labour market, where the individual wage earner continuously works to develop, test and utilize his or her personal resources. It is, to some extent, driven by self-interest, but at the same time it is under pressure from the management and from competition with colleagues. While striving, he or she submits to a market logic that demands that the person constantly 'moves' – in employment, profession and geography. The person – and his family – loses their roots, and they are no longer familiar with long-term collective work communities and interest communities. The career becomes the only 'fixed point'. The individual becomes an isolated island in relation to colleagues, the company and trade unions.

Such a development looks extreme from a Danish context. The development of the human resources may potentially also lead to the creation of an attractive productive and social working life where the individual develops in a community with others. Hochschild (1997) demonstrates that the company may develop to meet an increasing number of the employees' needs, almost seducing the employees to a life devoted to the interest of the company. Such a development may have its positive sides in the form of community, development and identity. But it can also have its downsides, where the community is infested with competition and performance anxiety; where the employees' non-work oriented interests, for instance in a normal family life, are lost in a continuous effort to serve the company and the career. The development of the human resources involves a risk that identity and meaning for the employees in subtle ways turn back on the employees, and become social 'tools of oppression' (Casey 1995).

The development of the human resources may also create a so-called 'Company Corporatism' (Brulin 1989). Company Corporatism is characterized by being cooperation-oriented with independently organized trade unions at the local company but with no link to a central trade union movement. It has previously been seen in connection with totally different types of company culture – especially in small communities where large companies dominate the labour market for long periods of time, and the company has been highly dependent on the local work force, and at the same time, the local population dependent on the company for jobs.

Another related problem could be a heavy emphasis on development of the human resources of the core work force which may result in a strong and favorable position for the core workers, but poses at the same time the risk of loosing solidarity through isolation from common wage earner interests and more marginal groups of workers.

The Reaction from the Danish Labour Movement

From the outset, the Danish labour movement took a critical and negative position to the HRM strategy. The critique had two main points. The first one expressed fear that even though the development may lead to improvements of work and work environment, it may simultaneously increase individualization; it would then undercut the labour movement's position in the companies. The second one expressed the concern that the HRM strategy only represented a seductive and manipulating rhetoric, and that one should not expect any real improvements of the working conditions in a capitalistic economy.

But this attitude changed with the formulation of the strategy of the Developmental Work in the beginning of the '90s. The strategy placed the main emphasis on development of work and competence, unlike the previous focus on protection, salary and employment. This strategy was also a reaction to the new management strategies; it was an attempt to neutralize the threats and make use of the opportunities present in the companies' HRM strategies. Employers' need for the workers' resources became the cornerstone of a strategy that could include both increased productivity and a strengthening of the position of the workers and their organizations, thus resulting in better working conditions. The Danish Trade Union Congress' strategy stressed local company activities and intended the strategy to be implemented 'from the bottom up', as concrete cooperation projects between management and employees in the companies.

The formulation of the strategy in the beginning of the '90s was an attempt to revitalize the one hundred-years-old Danish model for cooperation and conflict solution between the labour market's parties. It was thus intended to be a part of the dialogue with the employers' associations. The employers' organizations have never explicitly recognized the Developmental Work concept, because they fear that it will be used, as a way to renegotiate the employers' right to set the terms for management. However, there are many indications that it was a difficult decision for the employers, because the labour movements' acceptance of the new principles of organization meant an opportunity to introduce new product concepts and organizational changes, with no significant resistance to the renunciation of existing 'restrictive' rules and collective agreements.

When the employers' organizations did not wish to cooperate, it became crucial for the Developmental Work to succeed at individual company level and to work with each company's strategies. Danish TUC, LO, made over a period of almost 10 years a huge effort to train shop stewards and members to introduce initiatives in individual companies.

The development of the human resources can thus have many meanings. It can represent fairly different strategies, and these strategies must sometimes work under very different circumstances. It contains not only opportunities, but also risks. It is therefore a wide-open question: what consequences these developmental processes will have for the social relations and communities in the companies?

Five different case studies show different tendencies, and they can highlight how change processes based on different strategies aim at developing the employees' resources, and consequently, how the social relations are affected. Three of the cases look at traditional blue-collar workplaces, each of which has very different work tasks. The latter two cases analyse two public service organizations that have identical work tasks.

Looking at a long term perspective all the projects must be seen as time-restricted elements in the companies' development of work and organization. All case companies are, in their starting point, traditional in their structure and culture, and they can in no way be called sophisticated. Although the employees' cultures differ, they are all embedded in conventional labour market relations and systems of collective agreement.

The Green Company

The workplace consists of 80 employees who maintain a churchyard. The employees include skilled gardeners and unskilled workers who perform manual routines and partly mechanized jobs. The workplace is under the Municipality of Copenhagen.

The development project started in 1996. At this time the workplace was traditionally managed by a number of foremen, who planned both the long-term and the daily tasks to be performed. Within this frame, the employees enjoyed great autonomy, but the work was quite monotonous and offered few challenges. A high degree of indifference towards the use of resources, such as work-time, materials and equipment was found. Also, the job performance only provided a low sense of meaning and quality to the workers.

The workers as a group had several features similar to a classic 'workers' collective' (Lysgaard 1967). They were united in defending traditional interests and in particular expressing resistance, when something happened that could be viewed as infringements on the part of the management. The foremen on the other hand, took charge through rules and orders. There was a high occurrence of absence, and a survey in 1996 revealed that the psychosocial work environment was very bad.

In 1996, the Municipality initiated activities with the purpose of reducing the incidence of sickness absence. The strategy was first and foremost to fight sickness absence through motivation and development of the work (development of the human resources), compared to more traditional control and sanctions. The employees' representatives in the Green Company heard of the initiative and that it was possible to get funding to carry out a concrete project. They presented it to their colleagues, who agreed to take part in a project on developing the work and reduction of the sickness absence. The churchyard's management also accepted the idea, but it was the initiative of the representatives of the employees that was the decisive factor.

From 1996 to 1998, a project was carried out that, to a great extent, happened on the terms of the employees. With funds from the Municipality, a consultant was employed who together with the workers' representatives and the local management, managed the process. Time and space for discussions on how the work could be organized, so that it could be both more satisfactory and more effective was granted. Slowly, an involvement in the workplace evolved, and a wish to take responsibility for the daily tasks emerged.

An important aspect of the process was the internal relationship of the employees. This relationship had, for a long time, been undergoing serious conflicts. A core of workers – later called 'the strong in-mates' – acted as spokesmen and were active in the regulation of the relations to the management on the one hand, and in the internal relations in the group of workers, on the other. Towards the management, they led a protective policy, a policy that also was very defensive and non-developmental. Internally, they were the ringleaders of a tough atmosphere that was part of a repressive regimenting culture that caused divisiveness between the professional groups and overall did not allow many individual trips or initiatives. This contributed to the bad psychosocial work environment and contributed to the involvement and the high absence.

In the beginning, many had a positive attitude toward the project. But after it had gone on for a while, the 'hard core' of workers was dissatisfied because of various disagreements with the management. The group was also sensing that it was loosing control, and it suggested that the project be stopped. In a decisive vote at a general assembly, the group was surprisingly outvoted: the 'silent' colleagues opposed the group and voted in favor of a continuation. This can be interpreted as the majority of workers' wish for changes in the work, but also as a rebellion against its dominating colleagues. It became a turning point for the course of events. The internal power balance 'tipped over', the hard core lost influence and gradually left the workplace.

The process was at times both dramatic and dynamic. The result was the emergence of a more responsible attitude toward the work and a better work climate. The sickness absence fell drastically. The development continued beyond the project period; slowly work organized groups were established and the planning tasks were delegated to the workers. New managers took over, which was a contributing factor in radically changing the cooperation between employees and managers, in comparison to the previous situation. The total outcome was thus a stronger position for the employees, as authoritative producers, better cooperation in general, and a securing of a workers' collective with local solidarity.

However, none of the employees saw the development they had partaken in, as a part of the trade unions' strategy of Developmental Work. The result was totally and completely the employees' own doing. Although there was public attention on the project, the trade unions also did not attempt to use the opportunity to include the project in its activities on Developmental Work.

The project and the process resulted in obvious improvements. Contributing factors were that the employees in the churchyard, themselves articulated their own wishes of how to develop the work. The fact that there was time and space for these activities, and also that the process was managed in an open and compromise-ready manner by the workers' own representatives and the process consultant, were also contributing factors. In the process, the employees developed their competencies and their collective ownership of the work. They also developed their community to become more 'spacious' for the individual person and probably more solidaristic. The process was, however, not seen as having broader relevance for wage earners and the trade unions.

The Building Materials Factory

It is a big old company that produces construction materials. The employees are mainly unskilled workers, who operate the machines. It is hard and monotonous work. The company was at the beginning of the project, managed in a completely traditional manner, and the cooperation between managers and employees was characterized by distrust. Often conflicts arose because of disagreements related to the daily tasks. 'We had to toe the line. As soon as they saw you sitting with a cup of coffee...what the heck, are you sitting there again?' [An employee on how it used to be]. And a foreman said similar things about the past: 'If you put anything up on the bulletin board, without the shop steward knowing it, there'd be trouble right away'. The workers had a strong community with inward solidarity, support for wage earner values and support for the common straightforward resistance to the managers.

In 1997, a consultant from a union-affiliated training institution, suggested that the company could participate in a large-scale developmental programme, initiated by the labour movement. It was based on a network of several companies, and it was funded with public money and strongly inspired by the strategy of the Developmental Work. The principal idea was that a shop steward and a manager would be trained together, with the purpose of taking responsibility for a developmental project in the company.

In the Building Materials Factory, the project idea was accepted by the management – and equally importantly: by the employees. The concrete content contained introduction of personal employee consultations with their managers. It must be called a relatively modest change, but a realistic goal considering the very stalemate forms of cooperation and the high level of distrust that characterized the company. After the two project leaders were trained, a number of training activities were set in motion for the employees, who chose to participate in the project.

Although the ambition of the project was limited, the process nevertheless had a noticeable symbolic meaning. The employee consultations were carried out over a period of time; but after this, some of the foremen were replaced, and the employees now refused to continue. Once again, the trust was broken. Nevertheless, the development after the project shows that it had (potential) significance, since it cleared the way for an acceptance of group organized work that was later introduced.

The process was, to a great extent determined by the fact that the two project leaders (the manager and a shop steward) developed a common understanding of 'the modern company'. The shop steward however, had to suppress his wishes and move forward at a slower speed than he wanted to. The other more old-fashioned shop stewards bothered him. They emphasized maintaining a strong resistance towards the managers. But he understood the necessity of giving the employees enough time to prepare the symbolic act of going to an employee consultation with the foreman.

The shop steward eventually developed an ownership-relationship to his company, where it gradually became the development of the company that was the primary starting point of his activities; before, it had been the observance of general collective agreements and group contracts. He put it this way: 'I am a trade unionist, and I think I do what's best for the employees in the company. Next after that, I do what is best for the labour movement. My point of view has caused me to get beaten up many times in various unions'.

The Sausage Factory

The company has approximately 70 employees of both sexes, of which most are women. All are unskilled workers. Before the change project was commenced, the company was traditional in every respect. The work was repetitive and routine and did not require much coordination. The few foremen managed the work in the usual authoritarian manner. The workers did not have any influence and responsibility for the daily production output.

Before the project's start, the chief executive became interested in new principles of management and work organization. At the same time, a larger corporation that gave group organization of the work a high priority bought the company. Also, the shop steward had in the same period attended conferences and courses on the Developmental Work, in the labour movement. The chief executive and the shop steward met and discussed principles of the Developmental Work, and decided to use one of the tools that the labour movement had developed, namely a method to conduct a survey of the employees' wishes for how to develop the work. When the survey was done, it showed that the employees were indeed interested in change.

In the introductory part of the project, all employees and managers were gathered for a two-day conference. On this occasion, ideas for new organizational and cooperative forms were evolved. The atmosphere was good, and a drama group performed, demonstrating potential opportunities and the difficulties involved in introducing new types of work organization. Ideas and suggestions were refined. The conference became a positive experience, marking the transition to a new era. The employees were therefore motivated, but also felt insecure when they were about to implement the new work methods. Many of them said afterwards that they had not really understood that the exiting, but also relatively abstract ideas that came up at the conference were supposed to be seriously put to use.

The chief executive immediately went ahead with the change process. Production groups were organized, being responsible for the daily operation, and many planning and management tasks were delegated to cross-sectional groups of employees. He also took the opportunity to initiate a number of tasks related to quality control and systematic production. After a few months, the employees' involvement had vanished. They did not have the overview of the daily work, they were stressed out, and they began to pick on each other. The productivity and the quality fell. After a year of 'chaos' as it was called, the board of directors fired the chief executive. The employees demanded re-election for the post of shop steward. A new shop steward was elected. The project was stopped and declared a failure. Although it started well, it never became the employees' project. They were happy to return to the old routines.

There are important reasons why the story ended with failure, despite the good intentions and the up-beat start. Partly, it was due to bad project management, where the employees did not get enough support and resources; partly, it was caused by the fact that the employees, from the outset had no experience with collective action and mode of thinking. While the workers were part of a wage earner culture and also were organized in the trade union, this culture was passive and opinionated. It was not a local wage earner culture that the workers had created in an active common learning process. The workers themselves explained that the majority of the employees were women, and that they belonged to a small and 'tight restrictive island culture under great social control'. Finally, it must be added that the workers were polarized between permanent workers and many temporary workers in seasonal positions. Thus no effective workers' collective existed to provide a starting point for the learning process that was set in motion. The shop steward stood alone among the employees with her initiative and involvement. And there was no direct support or assistance from the trade unions.

The Social Workers

The social workers' work is quite different from the forms of 'blue collar work' in the preceding cases. The individual social worker typically works exclusively with counseling, casework, and pedagogy related to a client. Rules and legislation govern the work on the one hand, and on the other, the purpose is to care for the client. The social workers are, to a great extent 'authoritative producers'; they are responsible for the task and they often act independently. But in practice, they can be exposed to inadequate resources, a huge work load, pressure on the part of the client and on the part of his or her own professional norms. And they are possibly also exposed to an unsatisfied need to develop their professional competence in certain areas.

Blue case: Development from the bottom up, but.... The social welfare administration 'Blue' did the project 'The Meaningful Work' (DMA) in the time period 1997 to 2000. Previously, from 1995 to 1996, the entire Copenhagen social welfare administration had worked with the psychosocial work environment, which in many places had become a hazard. A Government fund provided resources for the project, and the idea in The Meaningful Work was to continue the effort to improve the psychosocial work environment, without provision of additional manpower resources, by emphasising development of methods and tasks to achieve a more meaningful (and effective) work. An agreement was reached with a process consultant, and the project was organized with extensive inclusion of the employees.

The group of employees consisted of a number of different professional groups with different functions: social workers, social communicators trained by the City, psychologists, consultants, secretaries and others groups. The social workers composed the largest and most central group.

The employees did not beforehand make up an effective collective. The social workers appeared both work-wise, and culturally as individualists. And they emphasized the need for each individual to develop his or her, individual competencies. But in the project, the emphasis was primarily on creating a development community among employees, to serve to develop collective competencies and cooperation, in order to support the individual in his or her work. There was less focus on strengthening individual competencies, such as needed in relation to the client contact.

It was a mixed result. In three out of four departments, inter-disciplinary teams were formed. On the one hand, there was a tendency towards less hierarchy and more responsibility, openness and reciprocity among the employees, in particular internally in the individual team. On the other hand, not everyone participated actively in the decision process in the teams. And a tendency was seen where 'boundaries' between departments shifted to 'boundaries' between teams.

The process itself contained increased efficiency and conflicts. But overall, there were nevertheless reports of reduced mental strain and stress. At the same time, the experience of strains tended to change: beforehand, strains were primarily explained with lack of resources, whereas now, they tended to be explained in terms of social insecurity.

There was a tendency towards weakening of the traditional formal organization of employee influence. The safety committee, for instance, could not handle the psychosocial strains and only paid fairly sufficient attention to traditional physical work environment problems. But the psychosocial work environmental issues were treated in the new fora for co-determination, such as the department groups consisting of employee representatives from the work groups and management. And the solution of psychosocial work problems was rather perceived as administrative issues about efficient organization of the use of resources, than of conflicts of interest.

Red case (Burebjerg): Development from the top – a provocation that is rejected... . It is the same Municipality as mentioned in the previous chapter. It had over a number of years, steadily received more tasks, and the top management in the City's administration wished to give the City administration a so-called 'service check-up'. By consulting with a consultancy firm, it was decided to adopt the management concept Business Process Re-engineering (BPR). The introduction of more systematic IT in the work processes also became integrated in the project. The plan was to test the concept in several places, including in the social welfare administration which is the focus for this presentation. Formally the goal was to improve service for the users, to make the use of resources more effective, and to create job satisfaction.

The project was a top-down project. The employees were not included, and the consultants had poor understanding of the daily work tasks. The social workers' estimate was that the changes gave more administration, fewer and worse client contacts and less contact with colleagues. Although they could also see potential improvements, the main impression was that of more work and less meaningfulness. The project was seen as an attempt to rationalize work. But several saw it simultaneously as (another) silly management trick, and the social workers felt insulted.

The social workers compose a relatively active and committed group of employees. They were therefore also successful with making several professionally founded counter-demands (e.g. avoid using computers during client visits and the formation of teams). But the overall impression is that they exerted a quietly watchful resistance. The BPR project was carried out with only lukewarm support. The group of employees, including administrative co-workers, thus exerted defensive and passive resistance. The community was not internally weakened but maybe even strengthened a bit in the process. The process could have been an opportunity to develop common professional competencies more aggressively, but it did not happen. The trade unions were also not activated in the process.

Analyses

Three main points may form a basis for discussing the development of the social relations:

- Firstly: what social forces in the company could accommodate, or respectively hinder change? Did the various parties experience problems in the company? What are the identifiable wishes, resistances, and oppositions?
- Secondly: Was any potential for developmental community present in the company? This is a sort of programmatic concept that includes preconditions to negotiate and cooperate; a willingness and ability to look at the totality as well as partial interests; a willingness and ability to change one's own preconditions and positions. Part of the question is, whether any willingness is detectable within the management and does it have experience with cooperation? Among the employees, is there any coherent collective present? Is it very defensive, or does it have the ability to change? Does it have any experience with common action, and is it able to partake in negotiations and learning processes with other parts of the company? Does it have contacts to professional associations outside the company?
- Thirdly, what are the developmental processes that are used to develop common problem awareness and interest in change? Were the processes controlled from the top? Were they confrontational or were they consensus-oriented? Did the employees get enough time and resources to develop understanding and motivation? Did they reach relevant goals and suggestions for solutions? (Or did for instance 'fashion trends' or ideology characterize the suggestions?).

In The Green Company and The Building Materials Factory, the management had an interest in reducing sickness absence, fewer conflicts, and employing more flexible and motivated workers. The workers (in particular in the Building Materials Factory) could have an interest in reducing physical strain, and in more alternating and meaningful work. There could be motivation for change among the workers, in situations where the relationship to the management is conflict-oriented and defensive, and in particular in the first case, where a tough and tense tone is the norm in the internal social relations. In both cases, informal communities with highly defensive features had been formed among the workers. The communities operated as an internally protective solidaristic mechanism, but they also contained inner contradictions and discipline, especially in The Green Company and the Building Materials Factory. Despite their defensive appearance, these collectives demonstrated an ability to develop and gradually change their orientation.

In The Green Company, the workers' representatives dominated the process, assisted by an out-of-house consultant. At the same time, time and resources were given to concept development, discussion and projects among all employees. Internal showdown took place, and separations of the negative persons occurred among the workers. The development resulted in significant changes in the work organization, and it gave more coherence, independence and sense of meaningfulness in the work. It also drastically improved the tone and the internal social relations among the employees.

In The Building Materials Factory, the workers' shop steward was an important player, along with his management counterpart. Although the employee consultations were stopped because of disagreements, the consultations contributed to a shift in the workers' orientation and a readiness to later partake in group organization of the work.

In both of these workplaces, the workers safeguarded a productive and relative solidaristic local collective. The labour movement, however, seemed rather invisible. Although the labour movement had participated in taking the initiative to both projects, it gradually disappeared from the project participants' field of vision. No new professional awareness and wage earner culture, with a broader horizon than that of the company's, had emerged. Although the preconditions were favorable, the strategy of the Developmental Work did not become anchored locally.

In the third case, The Sausage Factory, the new owners and the chief executive were united in their wishes for new management principles, including group-organized work. Until then, the work was managed in a traditionally authoritarian manner, with much routine and no responsibility allocated to the shop floor. The workers expressed wishes for change, and their shop steward was inspired by the idea of the Developmental Work. Although the employees were part of a traditional wage-earner culture, and although they had common views on a number of issues, such as salary, work norms and management, it was a weak collective. There was a lack of experience, skills, and maybe also readiness to act collectively, and thereby develop learning processes and orientations together. In the process itself, the impression of bad project management is conveyed, because it delegated responsibility with poor preparation and no support to the employees. The result was a lack of overlight, internal conflict, stress and a loss of involvement and productivity. The project ended as a failure and became a 'negative learning process'. 'It is better to stay with the old ways.'

Although at the outset, there were forces in favor of a change of the organization, the project failed because of a lack of change competencies in management and among employees. Too abstract a management idea on the one hand and too abstract an idea of Developmental Work, on the other, may have stunted the project. No developmental community emerged. We cannot conclude that the solidarity among the workers was weakened, but the negative experience can in the worst scenario become a roadblock to a philosophy of a more effective solidaristic development.

The social worker case was different. In general, the social workers' work is more individualistic and linked to personal responsibility. A meaningful coherence exists, when time and the necessary resources for the clients are available.

In the first case, 'Blue', the employees and the management were both interested in a development, which on the one hand could develop and assist the employees, and on the other make the work more effective. The social workers' community was not well developed as a starting point. Their unity was to a great extent based on common education and common professional positions (solidarity with the clients), and it was to a lesser extent based on daily cooperation (meetings). The primary relations were to clients and other professional groups. The course of the project itself was organized with much co-determination and participation of the employees.

The result of the project was on the one hand, changes in the form of more maturity with the individual employees: responsibility, reciprocity, and openness, and also a sense of less mental strain. On the other hand, this positive tendency was broken by increased intensity in the work and tendencies for boundary setting among the new teams. There may also have been a tendency to emphasize the group formation in relation to the particular core tasks of the work, at the expense of overlooking the need for individual skill development.

As for solidarity and community, the conclusion is ambiguous. In the beginning, the community was indeed more founded in ideology than in practical daily cooperation. The individual's enhanced maturity and ability as a team player may have reinforced the potential for community and collective interest protection. This potential may, however, become blocked by group-based boundaries ('entrenchment') and a stronger identification with the organization. Also the division of work environmental issues in traditional physical and psychosocial issues, and the glide towards a more administrative, than interest-oriented perception of the work environment, can weaken the community and its ability to act.

In the second social worker case, Red, the management also wanted increased efficiency. But here the employees were quite skeptical of the plans to introduce BPR and IT. The process was managed from the top and the plans did not really take the actual conditions into account. This resulted, by and large, in a 'silently' waiting resistance on the part of the social workers. Neither important changes, nor improvements, were made in service and work conditions, and there were also no clear changes in the social relations, solidarity, or collective effectiveness of the social workers. It is fair to say that the project may have increased the demands and the strains, while it was going on, and that it has created increased skepticism towards other similar projects. It has also created a potential solidarity among workers towards the management.

Conclusion

The five cases show that in reality, 'development of the human resources' becomes a very broad and general term, representing a number of very different things. Thus, it is also difficult to formulate general links between the 'resource strategies' and their impact on social relations and communities in and across companies. What's new is that a break is underway with the old Tayloristic strategies, where companies are dominated by authoritarian bureaucratic structures, and where the workers exclusively view the company in a sharp dichotomy. But this new development is not clear and it is certainly not unambiguous.

Firstly, at the general level, we observe interests and motives that indicate change in management as well as in the workers. But there are other motives opposing the wishes for change: control requirements, carefulness and defense motives that can have a blocking effect. This is also due to the fact that there is no symmetry between the parties. The different interests do not automatically form a synthesis: there exists an imbalance of power, and some of the resistance is well founded. The divergences are also determined by power relations, the existence of which the management strategies have placed under a virtual taboo.

Secondly, the necessary experiences and qualifications may not be present to carry out successful changes. Not only the management's background, but also the ability or lack of ability of the existing workers' collective to participate in 'change communities' may be deciding factors. The traditional workers collective was often defensive, but not necessarily passive, and it might hold potential for more offensive initiatives. More individualized (i.e. divided) employees may on the other hand experience difficulties when it comes to developing collective effectiveness.

Thirdly, the change processes are not always clear. From the programmatic and optimistic point of view, we are dealing with learning processes; but it may be a fictional simplicity. Often the changes can involve regression, discipline and conflicts, if seen from other perspectives. A search process with room for a diverse set of experience processes, experimentation, and new understandings requires openness and shifts in established privileges and power bases. In this process, the management side has its productivity and control requirements; the employee side has its demands on protection. Both of these aspects can curb the possibilities of open learning processes. Often the workers' safety representatives play an active role, but it also looks like the labour movement in a broader context, has difficulties in asserting itself and in choosing a meaningful role in the change process.

When evaluating the interplay between development and solidarity in general, it is clear that in all cases the tendency has been to break with bureaucratic and Tayloristic work procedures; and the human resources have been put on the agenda as the long-term goal for development. The change processes have, at times, been dramatic. But the results are generally ambiguous; some are negative, others are positive: modest but noticeable and appreciated by management as well as by employees.

At the general level, we can also see that the development of the work has not caused the local solidarity that was present in the beginning to break down. This may be due to the kind of change processes that we just mentioned. It may also be due to the fact that the period we are looking at is too short (although the duration is 2–3 years). It may be part of a more extensive transformation of work and solidarity, locally as well as in society, where the results may not show up until some time in the future.

Finally, we may conclude that in none of the five work places we have described, has the trade union played any role in the development, except for the local shop stewards. This is particularly surprising in the three blue-collar workplaces, because the Developmental Work strategy was developed by the blue-collar trade unions, and in two of these, it was the labour movement that initiated the projects. In the three blue-collar workplaces, the preconditions of practicing the union strategy of the Developmental Work were as optimal as one could realistically expect, and the employees had relatively strong positions. Nevertheless, the change processes never succeeded in becoming milestones in the development of a new strategy for the labour movement.

In the long run, the labour movement's role may become undercut, if its strategy for renewal does not gain a foothold in the individual workplace. The labour movement's strength and legitimacy must be rooted in and be articulated through the individual workplace, so that the individual workplace may gain support as well reflect its own relation to the common policy and the common goals. Such a connection was more simple and easier to pinpoint in the traditional strategy of collective agreements on salary and working conditions. The renewal of this link between the labour movement and the individual workplace is crucial to the future of Developmental Work.

Employee Participation in Development of the Work

Employee co-determination and influence is a trend in working life. It is one of the labour movement's old demands, which has gained momentum with the strategy for Developmental Work. It is also an important element in the development of the human resources that the modern management theories are based on.

The labour movement's demand of employee co-determination has traditionally been aimed at the frame conditions of the work in the form of (among other things) salary and working hours, while the employer has had the unequivocal right to set the terms for the work ('manage and distribute the work'). These demands have led to collective agreements between unions and employers both at the national level and at the industrial sector level. The agreements were further developed with a system of shop stewards and works council at company level (Gustavsson, 1990).

Parallel with this development, the socio-technical tradition has pointed to the need for employees to control their own work. Mental demands of satisfaction in work would thereby be met, while simultaneously achieving a more highly motivated work force. Group organization was, in particular, seen as a means to this end. This tradition is continued in the idea of Developmental Work, where there is emphasis on the employees' influence on their own work, as well as the frame conditions for the work, which over time became integrated and part of the labour movement's strategy.

The management theories also build increasingly on employee inclusion. The human relation tradition has traditionally viewed employee inclusion, as an important way of motivating the workforce. With human resource management and the learning organization, employee participation as a tool for organizational development has gained broad recognition (Edling & Sandberg 1997). Also the tougher management concepts such as BPR speak of a certain type of employee co-determination.

In practice, the employee involvement has developed at three levels over the past 50 years in Denmark:

1. Through legislation, employee representatives have been guaranteed a seat on the boards of limited companies, and work environment legislation require election of safety representatives and safety committees.
2. Agreements between the main parties of the labour market have introduced a system of shop stewards and works councils.
3. Finally, increased autonomy, responsibility and competence in the work have gained entry – in a collective form by self-governing groups among other things. This type of influence has typically developed in a decentralized manner in the individual company, often with support and occasionally initiated by the labour movement, but with no central agreements and legislation to assist the development.

The first two levels concern representative co-determination, where elected representatives on behalf of the colleagues have the task of protecting everyone's interests, while the third level concerns direct co-determination for the individual employee. It has proven quite difficult to get the two representative levels to connect with the third level of increased autonomy for the individual person's own work. Group organized work has occupied a central position since the 1960s, in the attempt to develop autonomy in the daily work, however group-organized work does not necessarily provide influence at company level. Svensson (1983) has thus pointed to the fact that while the strategy of developing group-organized work does expand the influence on the work actually performed, it does not include co-determination over the development of work and organization. This conclusion has later been confirmed by a literature study of 56 surveys of companies with group-organized work (Hvenegaard & Jessen 2001).

The first experience with Developmental Work points to this problem, and also that it can be difficult for the employees to make use of the direct influence. In a study of 9 pilot projects with the Developmental Work in the governmental sector of Denmark (Hvenegaard et al., 1999), it was concluded that the management initiated the projects to a great extent, and that the actual employee co-determination in several cases was limited. The employees had difficulties articulating their own demands both to the development of their work and the whole organization.

The problem is confirmed by an extensive evaluation of the Danish fund for improvement of working life and increasing growth (Holt 2001, Arbejdsmarkedsstyrelsen 2001).[1] The shop stewards and the works council in the companies have, only to a limited extent, been included in the development projects. The evaluation furthermore points out that employees have been involved in the projects at a rather late time, but also that those projects which had a high level af employee involvement have been conducted with fewer conflicts. Most companies consider their development projects successful, but they also perceive that they have taken much longer and have been much more difficult to implement than they anticipated.

Although there are many reasons to increase employee co-determination and many projects with this goal can be considered successful, it is still quite difficult to

1 See Chapter 2 for an elaboration of this fund.

introduce and to make employee co-determination work in practice. We shall cast light on this problem by describing the development project in the social welfare administration Blue, already mentioned in the preceeding section.

In the analysis of the company case, a three-dimensional model for employee co-determination is utilized. The first dimension concerns the level of autonomy that can be operational, tactical, or strategic, depending on the duration of the decisions' long-term consequences for the company. The second dimension distributes the decisions in two main groups: 1) technical/task decisions related to the product, the production equipment and the production process and 2) administrative/planning decisions related to group processes and management in the group. These two dimensions are from Bailey and Adiga (1997), and depth of co-determination has been added as a third dimension, consisting of information, co-determination and autonomy.

The social welfare administration Blue is a public company with good preconditions for increased employee co-determination. The previous section focussed on social relations and communities. But in this section we will look more in-depth at the project in Blue while focusing on employee co-determination.

The development project in the Social Welfare Administration Blue

The social welfare administration Blue was a municipal company with about 120 employees, whose main task was to offer social services to the municipalities' residents in compliance with current legislation. The social welfare administration had completed the project 'The Meaningful Work' which is the topic for this section. This project had the goal of improving the psychosocial work environment through personal development, as well as through development of the working group and the whole organization. The main focus was on increased decentralization of competence and increased employee co-determination at all three levels. The project was to a large extent based on experience from a previous project on the psychosocial work environment that had caused a much improved cooperation between management and the employees concerning the development of the work organization and the content of the work. Both employees and management wanted to make use of this experience in the future development of the workplace.

The new project 'The Meaningful Work' was therefore established with a development organization based on a high degree of employee co-determination. The design of the project was based on a number of fundamental considerations regarding employee co-determination through dialogue-based courses of change. The approach was to develop the employee co-determination in the daily evolvement of the work, as well through participation in the overall tactical and strategic development of the work and the institution.

The organization of the employee co-determination was based on the following core philosophy:

- The individual employee had great direct influence on the content and performance of the daily work by enjoying great individual freedom (much competence in the task performance).

- In the teams, the employees had great direct co-determination on the planning and arrangement especially exerted through team meetings.
- At the department level, there was employee co-determination on the department's strategy, development, and operation through the representation of a coordinator from each team in the department committee. This group consisted of the department manager, a coordinator from each team, and maybe one or two core staff members.
- For the whole organization, employee and middle management, co-determination was exerted through participation of the department manager and a representative from each department in a coordination group. This also included the chief executive of the administration, the deputy chief and an employee representative (shop steward) from the works council.

This co-determination system recruited employee representatives (and managers) via the operational organization. This was a form of organization that had a structure similar to that of the statutory health and safety organization, composed of employees from departments in the organization, but with no formal consideration to trade union affiliations. While being a co-determination system, it was also a system that via its 'flat' structure (few leaders) and great employee co-determination, was an organizational necessity to secure the operational aspects of the organization. Communication and cooperation between different teams and also between team and management must be secured. In order to include the formal cooperative system, the vice president of the works council (a shop steward) was included in the Coordination Group.

Employee Co-determination in Teams and Departments

An example from the Employment Department can serve to illustrate how the employee co-determination in the teams and the departments was exerted. In connection with establishing the team structure, an employee co-determination system was established in the department. It consisted of a Department Committee and a Forum for Discussion of professional issues. Both fora consisted of representatives from the various teams of the department in addition to the department manager and a staff member. The representation rotated every six months – with the shifts between the teams spaced out over a three months period, in order to avoid a total replacement of representatives every six months. These fora met two hours at least, every second week.

The reasons for selection of this structure:

- The teams were the organizational units that the department was organized around. In the teams, the employees could gain direct influence on the daily work tasks and work organization. This co-determination was exerted at the team meetings.
- The employees could – via representatives – achieve co-determination on the entire department's development through the two fora: the Department committee and the Forum for discussion of professional issues.

- In a department with only one leader, there is a need for a communication system to give the department cohesion. The active participation of the employees in the various meetings and committees was the main tool for the communication.
- The development of several different fora for dialogue could make use of the many different competencies in the organization to benefit the organizational and professional quality and learning.
- By rotating the coordinator role in these fora, all employees would, over time, be able to get a better overview of the entire department, and it would train the employees to participate in the dialogue on tactical and strategic issues that are traditional management tasks.

The main task of the Forum for Discussion of professional issues was to secure stability, development, and dynamics in the social-professional work. It was a very important forum, because it dealt with decision-making in many concrete the social cases. The aim of the Forum was to secure professional development, practice coordination and work procedures. The Department Committee was the overall organizational forum and cooperative body, where it was possible via representatives to gain co-determination on the tactical and strategic decisions.

These were the expected function of the organizational structure. Now we will turn to the practical experience with this structure.

Co-determination as a Possibility or Reality in the Social Welfare Administration Blue. In the entire period, the Department Committee as well as the Forum for Discussion of professional issues was continuously in operation and worked on a diverse range of issues, cf. the box below.

The Department Committee	The Forum for Discussion of professional issues
• Strategy and development in the department • The relation to the rest of the organization • Work organizational issues • Technological and construction related issues • Administrative issues • Personnel issues • Training issues • Professional Issues (primarily as overflow from the Professional Forum) • Work environmental issues • Issues related with collective agreements	• Long term professional development • New social legislation • Professional issues • Common guidelines for descisions on social cases • Administrative procedures for social cases • Professional cooperation between the teams • External cooperative partners • Education

Figure 4.1 The tasks of the two fora for co-determination

The employees were generally satisfied with the function of the Department Committee and the Forum for Discussion, although at times it was unclear what tasks, form and practical outcome these fora were supposed to have. After a more explicit description of goals and tasks it became clear for the employees. Some dissatisfaction existed though, because the department manager, according to some employees pointed out too often that he as the manager, had the ultimate word. It caused the employees to doubt whether the dialogue in the Department Committee had any real value.

Problems for the Employee Co-determination. Good formal opportunities for employee co-determination were created in the social welfare administration. It turned out to be difficult, however, for the organization to transform the opportunities into reality. It was difficult for the managers to hand over influence, and it was difficult for the employees to make use of the possibilities for co-determination. A number of issues regarding work load, group dynamics and the very introduction of co-determination opportunities contributed to hinder the implementation.

In many cases, it was difficult for the mid-level managers to enter into a real dialogue with the employees concerning the perspectives of the co-determination system and also about the necessary descisions. Instead they tried to delay the process, narrow the perspectives, or omit putting important issues up for discussion. The mid-level managers were themselves in doubt about what to use the fora for, and they were not sure whether the fora were there to stay, or whether they would soon disappear again.

The employees had never before participated in the tactical and strategic decision-making. These tasks had previously been reserved for the management – at best with a certain inclusion of the shop stewards. Many employees had difficulties seeing the tasks of the Department Committee as a real work task. In the beginning, the meetings were seen as a heavy unnecessary duty and they were given a low priority: no preparation, no follow-up, passive attendance, or absence. It was clear that the employees were far from making use of the objective opportunities for co-determination, offered by the existence of the fora.

There was, overall, a passive resistance from some of the employees as well as from some of the managers. This resistance was in line with the traditional bureaucratic culture, where changes were received with a shrug and ignorance – in the hope that they might disappear again so that the *status quo* could continue. This attitude was somewhat changed after the chief executive for the Social welfare administration was replaced. This chief executive represented the new ideas of the organization, and made it clear for everyone that this was something that was going to continue – also after the first trial period had expired.

When the teams were established, it was implicitly presupposed that the tasks that the coordinators had, in both the teams and in the two fora, should be performed within the total time that the teams had available. In practice, the tasks became an extra workload for the employee who was elected to be coordinator, since they were added to the traditional tasks. A later calculation showed that up to six hours a week was spent on coordination tasks. In addition to the restricted time for the teams, the extra workload for the coordinator thus contributed to prevent the co-determination fora from working optimally.

In practice, there was much insecurity as to where the boundaries for co-determination were, although the commission at the overall level was quite clear. Different mid-level managers had very different practices. In the beginning, there were no clear task descriptions and the employees' role was not sufficiently discussed and defined. The establishment of the two co-determination fora was thus caught by the classic dilemmas of employee inclusion in change processes. On the one hand, the framework, the content etc. cannot be arranged beforehand, because the employees themselves need to be involved in defining them, and on the other hand, the employees ask for framework and guidelines, in order for them to have a sufficiently well-defined arena to act in. However, the co-determination bodies eventually came to work better in the course of the years that the project ran.

The training that was initiated to strengthen the employee selected coordinators, turned out to be insufficient, although it too was improved on the way. One of the difficulties was that the coordinators worked for a limited period of time and the replacements were at different times from team to team. It was therefore difficult to establish a continuous development of qualifications for this task. In addition, some employees were very committed to the new opportunities, while others were not. It was primarily young people who saw the opportunities, while the older people more often remained passive or focused on the disadvantages.

The group dynamics also played a significant role. In one of the departments in the Social Welfare Administration, there were three teams with almost the same objective conditions: work tasks, work load, manning, size etc. But despite the common conditions, they all worked very differently in relation to the Department Committee. One team worked professionally as well as socially optimal. It constantly brought suggestions in and took active part in the debates that were raised in the Department Committee. The other two teams had problems with the social dynamics of their groups, and the energy was restrained by this situation. There were no resources for active participation in the co-determination bodies. One team was significantly more absent from the meetings than the others. This team had many fights over the social-professional work content, but few personnel replacements. The other passive team was more present, but had trouble contributing with anything. The team had social conflicts and a considerable number of personnel replacements.

Social conflicts in the teams and between the employees are a constraining factor for the development of an extended co-determination system. But these conflicts can have a variety of causes: they may be due to conditions in the work itself (management, organization, work pressure etc.), and they may be due to conditions that are 'brought in' with the participants (personal problems, conflicts etc.). The exact causes can, however, not be determined in this case.

The Scope and Depth of the Co-determination. During the project and the decentralization process, a significant part of the competence was successfully transferred to the individual teams. A distribution in accordance with the three dimensions for employee co-determination, shows that the teams had high autonomy regarding the operational issues, and low autonomy regarding the tactical level, and a high influence in almost all issues regarding the strategic level, but only in the form of co-determination. It was primarily a number of issues at the tactical-administrative level regarding bonuses, evaluation of individual work effort, and initiation of disciplinary actions that the individual teams did not want to influence –

or such as were taken care of by shop stewards (e.g. bonuses). However, bonuses can be influenced, but not due to systems established by the project. The influence was organized through the traditional system in Denmark for co-determination via collective agreements and the shop steward system.

A number of transversal general conditions at the strategic level, pertaining to the entire social welfare administration also existed. For natural reasons, the individual teams had no direct influence on them.

	Case and client oriented tasks	Administrative tasks
Operational level		
Autonomy	• Arrange individual methods • Determine the order to perform tasks • Contact internal support • Determine daily production goals • Contact external support • Correct deviations in 'product', method or process	• Plan coffee and lunch-breaks • Assign production tasks to the members • Contact collaborators and clients
Co-determination		• Arrange overtime
Tactical level		
Autonomy	• Arrange weekly or monthly production goals	• Plan holidays • Choose group coordinator
Co-determination	• Plan preventive measures (legislative update, method innovation) • Evaluate or select new equipment/methods • Determine success criterias	• Plan training and education • Choose new team members
Primarily management decisions		• Determine the individual bonuses of group members (co-determination via shop steward) • Evaluate the individual work effort • Initiate disciplinary actions
Strategic level		
Co-determination	• Determine the need for equipment/method innovation • Determine long-term production goals – quantitatively • Determine long-term production goals – qualitatively	• Define the training needs for the group and for individuals • Determine the size of the group. • Determine the group's work tasks

Figure 4.2 Distribution of decision power on type, and task, and depth of decision

Despite the many barriers in the beginning of the project, the employee co-determination had been successfully integrated into the organization. Through the team organization, the employees had achieved good opportunities for exerting co-determination, and after the initial skepticism had passed, they had become more motivated and qualified to exert this co-determination. In addition, a representative employee co-determination had taken place, organized through the Department Group, the Forum for Discussion of Preofessional issues and in the Coordination Committee. These fora were also arenas of co-determination at the tactical and strategic level of transversal issues that went beyond the individual teams. It was also clearly defined that it was the management that made the final decisions at the strategic level regarding the development of the work and the organization. But through the various representative fora, the employees had an opportunity to influence these decisions.

Employee Co-determination Attached to the Operative Organization. Via the bodies of employee co-determination, a close link between the operative and the developmental tasks was created in the social welfare administration. At the team meetings, attention was on the team's situation, and the team members had the competence to make decisions. If the issues went beyond the team, the coordinator passed the issue on to the Department Committee and from there to the Coordination Committee. In these two bodies of co-determination, a responsible manager for the relevant area of the organization always attended, so that the necessary decisions could be made.

The advantage of hooking the cooperative system up to the operational organization was more direct co-determination on the direct working conditions. The various departments had gained a more independent power position in the institution and more room to make its own decisions, but still within the general goals and framework determined by the management. It was ensured that the management competence available in the respective bodies merged with the various issues on the agenda. This secured direct leverage. The representatives would represent a team or a department, rather than professional groups, as it often happens in the traditional trade union organization.

It can, therefore, be a problem for such an organization that the interests that are linked to the various professional groups can more easily be put on the back burner. No-one has the role of representing the professional groups in the various bodies. Often the representatives from the dominant professional groups have seats in the decisive bodies and exercise the greatest influence. This will give the smaller and more peripheral groups (e.g. cleaning personnel or secretaries) a harder time in being heard (Mathiesen et al. 1999).

It is a dilemma that if area representatives and professional representatives are to be there simultaneously, the bodies will become too big. This has both economic and operational consequences. A large body with many people will not be able to develop the same dynamic, depth and precision in the discussions as a smaller one. In order to somewhat compensate for these problems, a representative from the works council participated in the Coordination Committee; but only to a limited extent, because there were many different professional interests, and the representative thus worked more as a senior shop steward does, who is protecting the interests of several different groups.

Many other issues that normally would be dealt with in the works council or in the Safety committee were solved in the new system. In the Department Committees, the manager's and employees' opposing views, such as a department's discussion of the conflicts between social workers and the secretaries, would often be dealt with as a social-professional issue, related to the work tasks. If the same problem had wound up in the Cooperation Committee, it would have had a long range of professional policy/organizational demarcation lines, and then the case would have had a completely different character. Likewise, there were many issues, such as cooperative difficulties and actions towards employees with frequent sickness absence that were solved in the departments.

Management and employee representatives wished to make the employee co-determination system in the social welfare administration into the official cooperative system in order to substitute the works council which was established in accordance with the collective agreements. But the trade unions were reluctant because it would involve many representatives, who would not have the same protection against dismissal that the shop stewards had achieved through the collective agreements. When writing this the two systems still exist side by side, and one of the weaknesses is that the employees in the new system do not enjoy the same protection against dismissal, as do the shop stewards in the official system.

Conclusion

This case shows that it is possible to develop direct as well as representative employee co-determination on both the operative conditions and the tactical and strategic conditions in the company. But it did not take place by itself. It was a long process in which the formal framework for autonomy and co-determination for the employees had to be put into effect through developmental processes, where both employees and management had to learn to use the new opportunities.

This kind of learning process involves a number of barriers and difficulties. There will often be limitations in the mid-level managers' and employees' skills and willingness, or it may be a lack of clarity in the competence and the role of the employees in the co-determination fora. Work pressure and conflicts in the team or in the department may also hinder the process.

The case is an example from a public company with good preconditions for introducing employee co-determination. Experiments with employee co-determination at the workplace had taken place already before the actual changes, and the group of employees was relatively well educated. It was an organization that was totally dependent on the knowledge and commitment of the employees. It will often be a different situation in private companies. They often have hourly-paid employees and the company may feel that they are less dependent on their knowledge and commitment. The motivation for introduction of employee co-determination may therefore be relatively minor. There is often considerably less room for influence on the daily work, and it will be more difficult for the mid-level managers to delegate the influence and for the employees to make use of the new opportunities for co-determination.

New Working Life Strategies and the Perception of Risk

The increased importance of developing the human resources also affects the work environment, and it is, to an increasing degree being used as an element in the company's strategy. This means that one also can find many examples in work environment goals that are part of projects to develop the human resources. They may be:

- integration of the work environmental activities in the management systems;
- prevention of hazards integrated in production innovation;
- involvement of the employees in planning and performing the work;
- focus on the common goals for competence development.

This does not mean that the work environment problems so to speak are automatically resolved through the management's prioritizing of the human resources. On the contrary, the new production concepts are, by many, viewed as a horror picture of a new work culture that will spread to all aspects of life and break down social cohesion, thereby corroding the personal identity and the psychosocial reproduction (Sennett 1998). There is a positive opportunity which may evolve from increased involvement of the employees. But the risk is that the work swallows everything, and it is often pointed out that the development carries along an increased pressure on the work force, resulting in stress and burnout. Increased employee participation may also lead to individualization with respect to individualism and divisiveness (as previously discussed in this chapter) and to temporary employment conditions where the employees have no real influence on the workplace.

This duality in the development of working life poses a series of questions. First and foremost, how does the development in working life affect the existing work environment, and does it create any new ocupational hazards? The integration of the work environment into the developmental strategies also raised the question of whether any changes are happening in the main-stream perception of the work environment and in the associated preventive strategy.

So far only a few studies have focused on these connections (Csonka 2000; Hasle & Møller 2001; Jessen & Hvenegaard 2001); these studies point to the fact that both the positive and the negative developmental opportunities are present. However, what we need are more concrete suggestions for what the conditions are, that determine the balance between the positive and the negative side, and also for how the positive side can be encouraged at the expense of the negative.

The philosophy behind Developmental Work is that the work environment must be integrated in development of both work and company, and that health and well-being should no longer merely be defined as the absence of hazardous effects, but as a good working environment, including development of competencies, commitment, and ability to take responsibility. A good working environment that safeguards against wear and tear and disease, is no longer just a right that the employees must fight for, but a precondition for the workforce to perform optimally. The question is then, whether it is really possible to secure the work environment in this way in projects that aim at development of the human resources? In three company cases, we shall further examine this question. But before we do so, it is necessary to discuss the transformation of the work environment concept.

A New Paradigm for the Work Environment

Projects aimed at development of human resources are often rooted in different (primarily management) concepts and they take very different concrete forms. Despite the differences, there are a number of common elements that constitute goals and visions for the intended change in almost all the change projects (Naurbjerg 1999, Csonka 2000). The most frequent elements are:

- A more hierarchical leadership
- The establishment of a group based work organization
- The employees are given more responsibility for execution of the work
- More variation in the tasks, for the individual as well as for the group
- Continuous competence development
- More flexible employment conditions
- Establishment of increased direct influence in the work, as a supplement to the traditional representative influence co-determination.

All these elements must be assumed to have influence on the work environment in terms of both hazards and prevention strategies. This development of the work has affected the work environmental discourse in society, and two competing paradigms have emerged: the ‘hazards paradigm’ and the ‘development paradigm’.

The first paradigm is rooted in the traditional work environment perspective, and it is developing towards an understanding that the classic physical/chemical work environment problem to a great extent are under control, and that it is necessary to concentrate on the psychosocial hazards. The psychosocial work environment is, however defined by the professionals in the work environment field in the traditional manner. It works just like the physical/chemical work environment that takes its starting point in scientifically documented causal relations between hazards and effects in the form of ill health (Arbejdstilsynet 2000). Thus the paradigm aims at development of preventive strategies for reduction and control of the health hazardous. The work environment professionals are, therefore, still basing their work on the hazards paradigm.

The developmental paradigm offers, however, some new insights into the connection between work and its negative consequences. While the starting point is increased influence on one’s own work and opportunities for personal development, prevention has been redefined from protection against damaging hazards to a development of the individual and the organization that prevents problems *per se*. Development must be based on the individual’s ability to promote one’s own health through appropriate behavior and in promoting his or her mental wellbeing through personal development and increased involvement in the organization the individual works in.

In the analysis of the two paradigms, it is necessary to define the working environment broadly, and on this basis look at changes in the connection between work and work environment from three different perspectives:

- Changes in the most serious hazards in the work.
- Changes in the employees' perception of the risks at work, and which risks should be given priority in a preventive strategy.
- Changes in the preventive work environmental activities.

The focus is thus on the work environmental activities, defined as systems, priorities, and competence associated with the prevention of occupational hazards in the company. The hypothesis is that the development projects offer a new work environmental discourse, and that it has great impact on the work environmental actvities and thus on the underlying risk perception.

The Three Case Studies

The development in the work environmental activities and thus also the two paradigms are analyzed on the basis of three cases. They show that the new production concepts will have considerable impact on the work environment. This is not only because of new psychosocial hazards in the work, but maybe even more so because a change has evolved in the actors perception of risks in the work, and also because new structures have been established to protect the local work environment inside the company.

The three companies have completed developmental projects that all give priority to a better working environment and are based on extensive participation of the employees. The projects have been studied over a period of two and a half years from the beginning to the end, with special focus on the work environment and the local work environment activities.

The Explicit Goals of the Projects. The three case studies all had explicit goals that mentioned a combination of better work conditions and increased productivity. This shows in the following quotations from the projects' objectives:

The Social Welfare Administration Blue. The objectives are 'to create integration between organization, management, and cooperative development, and also work environmental improvements, since these often happen independently of each other…', and 'that focus is moved from work hazards to development in the work'.

The Sausage Factory. The goal is: 'that the company creates a better workplace through employment security and a good physical and mental work environment' and… 'a yearly growth of 15% and an increased revenue of 5% of the net income is created through cultural and structural efforts'.

The Fresh Food Terminal. The goal is 'to improve the work environment by making the individual jobs broader and by giving them more content, by introducing group organization of the work, and to give the individual more influence on their own job. Employee development, job development and more autonomy are the means to improve effectiveness and customer service and to secure continued growth'.

The projects thus made an attempt to integrate the work environment with the organizational development. A better work environment appears on the one hand as a means to creating growth and increasing productivity, through a more joyful work and involvement in the job. On the other hand, a better work environment appears as a goal in itself; where the projects are supposed to create work with more content, more security, personal development and increased employee influence. The productivity objectives can be expressed in percentages, whereas the work environmental objectives are less exact, and the results (that come later) are harder to document. The belief in the connection between the good work environment and productivity was not so much founded in the actors' concrete experiences, as in ideologically founded 'common sense'.

The Methods of the Projects

The projects took quite different routes, but overall, the strategies and the choice of methods to create the development in the projects were relatively identical. All the projects included concrete changes in the organization that do not differ much from other developmental projects. The three companies were primarily trying to achieve a more flexible organization with shorter internal and external communication flows, and to make the employees more accountable for the decisions and scheduling tasks that previously were performed exclusively by the mid-level managers.

The methods that were employed in the projects can be summarized in the following figure:

	The Social Welfare Administration	The Sausage Factory	The Fresh Food Terminal
More tasks for the individual	• Participation in developmental groups • More tasks for the individual	• Participation in committees • Rotating coordinator role	• Everyone is educated to be able to perform all job functions
Competence development	• Education of coordinators • Individual supervision • Team development	• Training courses in production and teamwork	• Training courses in production and teamwork
Greater responsibility for the execution of the work	• More decisions are delegated to the social workers • Full autonomy on social cases	• Responsibility for quality assurance is delegated to quality committees • Task distribution executed by the groups	• Task distribution executed by the groups
Group organization	• Teams responsible for task distribution and professional development	• Permanent production groups • Coordinator responsible for task distribution	• Work groups with rotation between the tasks among employees
Less hierarchical management structure	• Professional supervisors disappear	• Decisions are delegated to production groups	• No
Technological development	• Increased IT usage	• No	• No
New roads to co-determination	• New departmental committees and a coordination committee	• Establishment of a great many task-oriented committees	• Project management group
More flexible employment relations	• No, but lots of overwork	• No shifts and seasonal work are maintained	• No, but large personnel turnover
Flexible market relations	• Focus on better citizen service	• No	• No

Figure 4.3 Comparison of methods in the three case companies

The projects aimed, primarily, at functional flexibility by improving the capability of the employees to exucute more different work functions. In all the projects, a goal-oriented competence development was included that aimed at both concrete 'production competencies' and at soft competencies, such as the ability to handle responsibility and teamwork.

The organizations became more flexible by introducing group organization of the work. At the same time, the number of supervisors and mid-level managers was reduced (in two projects) with the intention to integrate the immediate management tasks in the work; thereby, increasing management flexibility. As a consequence the employees gained more influence on the direct work, including planning, execution, and communication. This involved an increased responsibility for fulfillment of the predicted production targets. It was particularly relevant for the two production companies, since the social workers already had this responsibility before the project. Technologically, there were no big changes. The IT usage was gradually increased, yet it was only in the social welfare administration that it happened to such an extent that it had an impact on the work.

Through the projects, the companies sought primarily to achieve greater internal flexibility. The development of a potential (numerically flexible) workforce was not a significant goal. All the companies were already exploiting the opportunities for a relatively flexible employment of manpower (seasonal work, short-term employment, etc.). On the contrary, it was an underlying goal to be able to hold on to the manpower. For instance at the Sausage Factory, training courses were offered for summer temps during the winter season.

None of the courses brought about a total reorganization of the companies, and far from all goals were achieved. Social Welfare Administration, Blue, that merely perceived of the project as one of a long series, afterwards maintained the structural changes, but continued with renewals of the organization. One of the central insights was that changes take time, and that this project was only the first step in a new direction.

The Sausage Factory stopped the project and closed down the autonomous groups, when productivity fell instead of rising as anticipated. The corporation moved the fresh food terminal to another geographic locality, and the new work organization was not transferred to that locality.

The Employees' Assessment of the Work Environment

In questionnaires[2] as well as qualitative interviews, the employees were asked about their experience with the physical, the ergonomic, the organizational, and the psychosocial work environment.

In the Social Welfare Administration, *Blue*, an effort was made to improve the ergonomic and the indoor air quality in the individual offices. The employees thought that the conditions had improved, but generally the employees viewed the physical and ergonomic strains as minor, when we compare them to the entire SARA population (see Chapter 2). There were only a few changes in the work

---

2 The questionnaire methodology is described in chapter 2.

environment that were seen as important [3] for the study period of two years. The increased use of IT was stated as the most important reason as to why there seemed to be higher demands with respect to carefulness in the work. The introduction of IT required, among other things, that the documents that the individual social worker should create become more public. The increased influence through the new Department Committee structure contributed to a sense of an improved information level. At the same time, however, the employees stated that the influence through the elected representatives fell considerably. The possibility of receiving social support from the closest manager was seen as reduced, and there was an increase in the number of conflicts in the work. The employees explained this as due to the removal of the professional supervisors group, which meant that the employees were expected to make more decisions on their own. The highest strain from the work stems (as estimated on the basis of the questionnaires and confirmed in interviews) from a high work pressure and emotional strain in connection with the caregiving work for the social clients. The employees in the Family Department (that works with children's conditions) and the Employment Department (that works with people in socially strained situations) viewed it as particularly difficult to reach a balance between the formal framework (time, funds, physical possibilities) on the one hand, and the problems they are supposed to help resolve (abuse, hardship, incest, violence a.o.), on the other. Many describe this problem as the fundamental cause of psychosocial strain, and they do not think that it has undergone any change.

As expected, the Sausage Factory's employees described the ergonomic strain as a big problem. The work in the production was typically repetitious work. Other hazards such as noise and coldness (the work is performed under low temperatures) were to a greater extent, perceived as a necessary and acceptable part of the work. The new group work and in particular the demand to participate in the many extra task committees, were seen as an increase in the mental demands of the work. At the same time, the employees felt that the support from the closest manager had diminished significantly. The new work organization meant that the demands on carefulness in the work seemed to increase. The greatest change in the work environment, however, was the increase in conflicts, gossip, and badmouthing among the employees. It was explained as partly due to an unsuitable bonus agreement that contributed to creating competition and mistrust between the production groups and partly due to the difficulty for the employees in meeting the new demands of cooperation regarding production-oriented tasks.

The Fresh Food Terminal's employees thought that the new job rotation was an improvement of the ergonomic conditions; there had been good cohesion between the new tasks and the training offers, and also the speed of the changes had been acceptable. The social support from the closest manager was, however, also here viewed, as significantly worse, despite the fact that the mid-level management group was not reduced and that the managers were closely involved in the development project. The conflict level rose significantly here. It was explained as due to the

---

3 A change was estimated as important if the change between the first and the second questionnaire was higher than five percentage points on the respective scale (Limborg 2001b).

group structure and an antagonism between, on the one hand, the employees who viewed the company as 'their workplace', and on the other, those who were in short-term positions and merely saw the job as temporary work. The employees found that the physical work environment was all right. The main problems in the work were a bad social atmosphere, colleagues who had no respect for agreements and good practice, and mistrust caused by the removal of time-honored privileges for individual employees, when the group structure was introduced.

To summarize, the lessons learned from these projects are that the physical work environment conditions were not significantly affected by the organizational changes in the projects. They were neither improved, nor did they deteriorate. The attention given to the physical problems was also not increased – rather to the contrary.

The work environmental problems that the employees have highlighted are connected to two problems, where one stems from the work task and the other from the cooperative relations. The first problem is linked to the demands in the daily work. In the production companies, there are greater demands to quality and effectiveness. Among social workers, an intense work pressure is also mentioned. The second problem concerns the new demands for teamwork from the group organization. In all three companies, this was viewed as the most significant change – along with the first line management's reduced ability to lend the necessary social support for these changes. The result is described in surprisingly similar terms: as social conflicts, badmouthing, and internal power struggles between different groups.

Changes in the Work Environment Activities

The projects took up organizational resources from the companies. The various groups that provided the framework for the employee participation, in all the projects, were manned with 'fiery souls' – employees who wanted to achieve personal development and meaningful work by taking an active part in the project. Since the work environment was also involved in the projects, the project structure challenged the formalized activities in the safety organization. In several cases, the elected representatives also became involved in the projects, but eventually exchanged the role of negotiators (as representatives for the employees) to the role of project makers.

In the Social Welfare Administration, the new influence structure became based on department committees that included the department manager, team coordinators, and sometimes selected employees. The department committees were again represented in a central coordination committee. In the course of the project, this structure was made permanent, with one change, however, that the employees should now be elected and not just be included at their own initiative. In the last phase of the project, there were initiatives to formally merge this new structure with the works council and safety committees, but, as mentioned above, it was met with resistance from the unions. In the project period, the safety committee lived a quiet life in the social welfare administration. The mandatory meetings were held but mostly had an informative character. The resources were spent on the new structure, and the work environmental issues were transformed to discussions of competence development, teamwork, and cooperation between teams and departments.

The Sausage Factory's safety committee also barely existed while the project was running. A few concrete work environmental improvements were made during the project. An active safety representative, who was later appointed safety manager by the management, initiated them in a cooperation with the occupational health service. A number of different committees were established and the production groups were to provide representatives for these committees. They were, respectively, concerned with machine maintenance, personal hygiene, first aid and safety, clothing, improvements, cleaning, orderliness, and carefulness. None of these were directly responsible for the work environment, but, nevertheless, they dealt more or less with various aspects of the work environment. Due to resistance from the employees, this complicated committee system never fully became operational. The employees thought that too much production time was lost by participating in the numerous committees. Conflicts and increased levels of mistrust in the employee group also put a damper on the development of the committees. The attempts to create a dialogue regarding these problems, in the existing or new meeting arenas, therefore failed.

The Fresh Food Terminal had a long tradition of well-operating and active work environmental activities. A former safety representative had been a 'fiery soul' in this work that for a number of years, had resulted in good welfare conditions and a good physical and ergonomic work environment. It was achieved by obtaining technical aids and by making suitable technological choices. Before workplace assessment became legally mandatory, the safety committee had already performed a systematic registration and prioritization of the work environment. These activities continued in the course of the project. The newly elected safety representative, who was also active in the project's steering committee, emphasized the psychosocial work environment, and he sought to integrate it with the systematic work environment activities. The work environment activities therefore developed in two ways. One was related to the daily operation. The maintenance department, to a larger extent, took care of maintenance of the technology and the aids, and the department used the opportunity to introduce additional work environmental improvements by them selves. The safety department, however, still handled any new problems that might arise. The development tasks constituted another way, to which category the psychosocial problems were assigned. Thus it became part of the project to handle conflicts and to support a development of the teamwork in the groups. Improving the social relations between employees through courses and direct social support to the groups, including a psychologist from the occupational health service, was greatly emphasized.

Despite great differences between the projects, a coincidental shift in the perception of what constitutes the most significant strains in the work was present in the three companies. The importance of physical and ergonomic hazards was reduced, either because they really were controlled through technical improvements, or because it was perceived that everything that could possibly be done about it, had been done. For instance, neither the employees at the Sausage Factory, nor the employees at the Fresh Food Terminal, considered it a big problem that the work was performed in very cold production facilities, as long as suitable work clothes were handed out. Likewise, a number of the problems that previously were prominent in the discussion about the work environment, such as heavy lifting, chemical substances, indoor air quality, and office ergonomics, had been resolved to what seemed a satisfactory extent. It means that the technical prevention was viewed as a natural part of the production apparatus and that it was included in the procedures for maintenance and technical development that apply to the production apparatus. At the Fresh Food Terminal, a large part of the responsibility for the physical work environment was thus placed with the manager who was responsible for maintenance.

The problems that the employees now focus on as extremely important – in the questionnaire as well as in the interviews – are the deteriorated social relations among employees and a lack of social and professional support from the closest management. These are problems related to the changes in the organization of the work that the development projects have introduced. At all three companies, there is a perception of an increasing number of conflicts among the employees. Still, the conflicts have not led to a perception of a lower possibility for support from colleagues that is anything close to the perception of missing social support from closest management. Some of the explanation is to be found in the development of a feeling of belonging to the newly formed groups, where one finds support within the production group or the professional group, at the same time as conflicts arise between 'competing' groups.

New Strains or a New Perception of Risk?

The new problems concern relations between the employees, and between the employees and the management. If they are observed through the traditional hazard paradigm, the changes can be seen as the hazard and the conflicts as the negative consequence. This understanding leads to the perception that the problems must be prevented by protecting the employees against the changes. Such an approach can either lead to a rejection of changes, or it can lead to demands for more resources for development of the employees' teamwork abilities; for instance, through increased course activities or consultancy support for the groups. The next step could be to make demands on the framework conditions, such as resources (time and labour) and professional and social support to conduct the new tasks and to meet the new social demands.

The last possibility relates to the developmentally based paradigms of the work environment which are stated by the most active project makers and 'fiery souls' – but only to some extent. The development paradigm totally contradicts the hazards logic, and articulates a perception of risk that is not based on an understanding of new hazards, but instead emphasizes positive developmental opportunities, as a means to resolving the negative work environmental conditions (if the the work environment is named at all).

The employees and the management are increasingly expressing a developmentally oriented perception of risk, where experiences of personal and collective experience of problems play a completely dominant role. The employees, in all three case studies, concurrently state that the new demands in the work are difficult to meet. This is partly the case for the new professional demands associated with conducting new operations. But it concerns, particularly, the new and higher demands for more responsibility for the work and the commitment for teamwork and cooperation with groups and individuals across the company. At the Sausage Factory, the employees, for instance talk about how their traditional 'slaughterman-jargon' suddenly seemed inappropriate, when they were giving colleagues directions or criticised their work.

In the developmental paradigm, there is a lack of generalized knowledge on how these types of problems are to be handled. So it becomes increasingly the informal culture and values of the company that determines what is 'just and fair'.

The action perception is, to a great extent, brought in from the development projects themselves and it is based on a philosophy that progression through increased competence and assistance from consultants – or from the management – can reduce the problems. The attempts to develop traditional preventive strategies were thus only partly successful. In all three companies, training on teamwork was conducted, although of variable extent and quality. The mixed experiences from these courses made it clear that social competence cannot be learned by offering a 'Directions For Use' guide. Courses on teamwork that were conducted and detached from the daily work turned out to have very little utility value. In addition to this, the social workers also pointed to the necessity of increasing time and manpower resources, besides increasing professional support, as central strategies for prevention.

The element of conflict is affected by increased employee influence in the work. Conflicts arise between competing production groups, between permanent and temporary employees, and between professional groups who have different attitudes toward the work. Conflicts are no longer connected to a general conflict between employer and workers; rather, the situation is that several informal conflicts are going on, in all directions in the organization.

A shift takes place from formality (knowledge, rules and formalized negotiations) to informality, when the situation is more vague and unresolved. An old stabilized state of equilibrium is displaced, and it is not clear beforehand, when and where a new stable equilibrium is to be found.

Conclusion

As a point of departure for the discussion of the three case studies, it is important to emphasize that the strains that have turned up in the companies must be viewed as strains that stem from two sources: one is the change process itself, which can be experienced as strenuous. Another is the permanent reorganization of work.

It is, however, difficult to make a general distinction between the two, because most companies currently must undergo change activities, and will do so for the foreseeable future. It can therefore be difficult to identify a final work organization that is allowed to remain stable for a long period of time.

The three cases all point to the fact that changes of organization and management structures, with extended inclusion and development of the employees' resources, in many ways change the work environment. The following conclusions are significant:

- The employees' participation in developmental projects may lead to a higher priority of giving psychosocial problems.

- A significant increase in psychosocial problems related to cooperation is perceived in the work, such as conflicts, cooperative difficulties and lacking support from the management. The problems arise from the new work organization with autonomous groups, where the employees are given more responsibility and they gain influence on the execution of the work. This breaks down the social patterns associated with the former work organization.
- The reason why the social conflicts and lacking social support are perceived as strenuous seems to be a combination of two factors. Firstly, there is an individual sense of dissatisfaction; and secondly, these problems appear to be causing the malfunction of the new cooperative relations that were supposed to create the anticipated individual development and increased effectiveness of the work.
- With regards to the perception of increased social dissatisfaction, there are only few suggestions on formal work environmental hazards that can remedy this problem. However, all three change projects considered need for training and supervision in teamwork and conflict handling. The conclusions from the three cases point to the fact that the effect of such activities is limited, if they appear merely as a course activity detached from the work. Personal supervision and direct support in the work, for instance, to develop the way a work group operates, seem to be essential preconditions for making the changes work. The perception of actions that can prevent the psychosocial strains bears on individual solutioins, because of missing skills in handling social conflicts.
- In several cases, a polarization of the employees' perception of the strains is observed. In some cases the division is between older and younger employees, in other cases, between different production groups or professional groups, or the split may be between the permanently and the temporarily employed workers. It looks like the traditional dichotomy between management and employees is breaking down and giving way to a polarization between subgroups of employees, where the individual also plays a bigger role.
- The perception of strains seems to be rooted in the concrete conditions for the individual to solve his, or her, work task. This seems to contribute to a change in the traditional perception of the work environment as something associated with the physical and ergonomic conditions. More emphasis is placed on the execution of the work and on its organizational and social framework, both in an individual and collective context.
- Prevention (primarily technical) of traditional physical and ergonomic hazards are, increasingly often, considered an integrated operational task and is thus given a lower priority in the awareness of the work environment.
- In relation to the work environment activities, the new forms of organization of work opens up for the establishment of a number of new meeting arenas that naturally put work environment on the agenda. These arenas are often connected to a project organization, or to the execution of the work, and they are not typically formalized representative bodies. They are often based on 'fiery souls' and temporary committees, and they have only limited

competence beyond the limited scope of the task. In the social welfare administration, however, the new meeting arenas have been formalized.

The three cases indicate that the development paradigm is challenging the hazards paradigm, when assessing work environmental problems in the 'developmental company'. A significant problem is that the development paradigm only has a poorly developed concept of risk. It is true, however, that in connection with the psychosocial strains, a fairly extensive body of scientific knowledge has been developed. But it is still seldom transformed to a company-oriented local resource of knowledge, compared to the traditional physical and ergonomic work environmental problems. The legal basis for regulation of the problems which related to the new psychosocial problems is similarly poorly developed, and it is today far from providing a foundation on which to establish norms for the work in this respect.

This problem is reinforced by the fact that this type of developmental projects is often surrounded by a 'win–win ideology', where it may not be legitimate to point out the problems for the employees related to the development. This makes it harder to discuss prevention of the negative consequences of the development. It becomes difficult to take on the problems, until they have escalated to large proportions. If at the same time, the formal organization of the work environmental activities is weakened, it can be difficult to safeguard the work environment during such developmental projects. The responsibility for the day-to-day protection of the work environment becomes opaque, and it can lead to over-emphasis on individual accountability.

The cases, however, also indicate that awareness of these problems can secure discussions and subsequent initiatives to find the necessary solutions. This possibility is confirmed from other studies, where an effort has been made to develop the work, with explicit inclusion of the work environmental activities in the developmental projects (Mathiesen & Hvenegaard 2001).

Final Comments

The three aspects of the work that have been examined in this chapter – community, co-determination, and the work environment strains – are closely connected. The human resource strategies often (but not always) introduce more influence over the work and certain developmental opportunities for the individual – along with a changed demand structure and new forms of cooperation. This makes it possible for another relationship to the work and to the management to evolve. But the changed demands and cooperative forms can simultaneously cause new strains and risks. Altogether, new assessment of the relationship between advantages and strains for the employee, and, indeed, a new self-knowledge in relation to the work, seem urgent. Does it create individualism, increased competition and divisiveness among the employees? Or are such changes accompanied by abilities and readiness to be united, to find common understanding and work for the common good? The answer to this is ambiguous. Although there may be strong incentives, interests, and material circumstances that favor certain developmental features rather than others, no automatic and inevitable consequences are to be identified. The development always contains a subjective element with the concerned persons, in the form of orientations, power and resources that can lead to a variety of actions, organization and policies.

In our cases, we have observed composite and ambiguous developments. We have seen how the employees in the social welfare administration Blue were relatively successful in gaining influence. The extensive participation of the employees at all levels, and also the decisions' connexions and attachments to the operative organization were important features. But also the employees' previous experience with participation must been seen as a positive contribution. The result was less hierarchy and more responsibility, openness, and reciprocity among the employees. On the other hand, it must also be noted that the learning processes caused difficulties. Not everyone took an active part; resistance and conflicts arose in the course of events. There was also a tendency for new entrenchment to emerge between the groups and between departments, where previously entrenchment had existed between employees and management.

Such developmental features must be related to changes in the strain pattern and in the perception of risks in the work. To sum up on the Blue social welfare administration, The Sausage Factory, and the Fresh Food Terminal it may be said that the employees experienced increased demands and higher strain in relation to the task (quality and effectiveness), but even more so in relation to the social relations. Demands for decision making, responsibility, and cooperation took centre stage. There was less support from the mid-level managers and more conflicts between the employees. The physical work environment was – generally speaking – neither better, nor worse off, than before. But it now received less attention. The psychosocial conditions came more into focus. In general, the employees now felt more satisfied with their work.

These features are part of a broader tendency to view the work environment as a link in a developmental paradigm, where strains are dwarfed by the advantages of (personal) development associated with the content of the work. The more traditional hazards paradigm, where the worker is an object (or victim) of hazardous strains, is consequently on the retreat. Thus, in the cases we also saw a tendency towards a separation of the protection of the employees' interest in traditional work environmental issues on the one hand, and psychosocial issues, on the other. Such a division – it is often said – may carry the danger that crucial protection of interest is played down and that the developmental interests become individualized.

Are there any changes in the employees' communities and in the way they represent and defend their interests? In the five companies that focused on this issue (The Green Company, the Building Materials Factory, the Sausage Factory, the social welfare administrations – Blue and Red), we could not establish that the communities were being eroded. In one company, the solidarity had clearly improved, and in another it had most likely improved. In both of these places, there were, at the same time, improvements in the organization of the work in the form of more cohesion, autonomy, and thus meaningfulness for the individual. And in both places, a maturity evolved to some extent among the employees, in the form of responsibility, involvement, and openness, both regarding the tasks, and regarding the cooperation with colleagues and management. The cases demonstrate that more involvement in the work does not necessarily lead to more individualism in the form of competition, divisiveness, and loss of solidarity. It is possible to unite more individuality with solidarity in the work. But there is certainly no guarantee. The most important factor in our cases seems to be the process conditions that a project yields. The chances of a positive development in the quality of the work, as well as the influence and the solidarity of the employees are strengthened by including all employee groups, by granting time and resources for them to articulate and discuss experience and wishes, by granting influence to all parties, and by preserving transparency in the decision process, as well as in the result.

Such experience is important for the employee-side to expand and to further specify. The labour movement could play a productive role here, to support the employees, as well as to collect and communicate their experience. *But it is striking, how invisible the trade unions have been, as players in the concrete cases that we have studied.* The Danish TUC has been active in formulating the vision of Developmental Work; but in our cases, this interest has not been transformed to a concrete and purposeful practice.

Chapter 5

A Good Work – Quality and Values in the Job

Introduction

Good work is an ambiguous concept. It can mean that the frame conditions for the work are good, so that the work environment is right and it is possible to perform the work under satisfactory conditions. It can also mean that the content in the work is good, so that the work is done properly in order for the product to be of good quality. In this chapter, we examine what the content dimension of the work means to the employees, and how the employees relate to the development of values and goals for the quality of the work.

In a survey from 1993 of a cross-section of Danish skilled and unskilled wage earners, 83% voiced the opinion that if they could freely choose their work, it would be of major importance to choose a job where 'I feel I have done a good job'. The survey also revealed a growing interest in immaterial issues in the work – i.e. issues that are not about salary, in particular among younger members (Madsen 1997). At the same time, data from the SARA project's own questionnaire survey pointed to the fact that it is important for the wage earners and their job satisfaction to feel that they have a meaningful job (see Chapter 2). More recent research indicates that influence and meaningfulness in the work can contribute to reducing stress and burnout; even a monotonous and tedious work can be perceived as a good work, if it feels meaningful and involves good social relations (Karasek & Theorell 1990, Isaksen 2000).

There is not necessarily a connection between satisfaction and quality in the work. Many wage earners find other aspects of the work, such as the salary, work conditions, social life, etc more important to them, than the quality of what they do. They may feel that they have a good job, although the products may not necessarily be of high quality. And on the other hand, many high quality products, such as Persian rugs for example, are produced in miserable working conditions. There are, however, many indications that it is important, both to the work satisfaction of the employees and to the quality of the products, that the employees have a subjective involvement in the work.

If, however, the quality of the work depends on the employees' own contributions to the development and improvement of the product, a coherence will necessarily have to be created between the subjective perception of the quality of the work and the standards for quality set by the surroundings. Developmental Work places special focus on the worker's own perception of the content and the quality of his, or her, work and on the opportunities to develop a better product. In order for the employees to be able to take responsibility for management tasks, development, and quality of their work, they must also have the possibility of getting involved in the content of the work and in the quality of the product.

The question now, is how the employees' perception of quality in the work is linked to the standards of quality, set by the management. And also how they link to the external requirements to the product and the company, set by the market, by authorities and by players in the context that the companies are part of.

- How are standards of quality built? What dilemmas and contradictions do the standards cause in the relationship between employees, the management, and the surrounding society?
- How are such standards changed, as elements of change processes? What does the employees' subjective perception of quality in the work mean, and how do the employees gain influence on the standards for the execution and quality of the work?
- What is the impact of efforts to develop the quality of the work for the employees? Do new opportunities for meaningfulness in the work arise, or do the employees feel the requirements to quality, as an additional work pressure? Are new relations between employees, management, and society created around development of standards for the quality of the work?

This chapter discusses lessons learned from three areas – quality management, environment, and care. These areas have been analyzed in the SARA project in order to find out whether these three areas contain opportunities to develop 'a good work' and what the conditions are that affect it. The analyses in the chapter take their starting point in qualitative studies of a number of private and public companies. These are workplaces where the work is either performed on the basis of the Developmental Work concept, or where initiatives have been taken toward employee involvement in either quality development, care-giving, or environmental considerations.

Values in the Work – the Work's Content and the Product's Utility

The work's content and meaning to the employees, has not been a frequent topic in research on working life. Often, the question on whether the work is meaningful to the workers is not even raised; it is never asked what the employees might perceive as the work's value and goals. The same is true for quality and environmental management systems that are based on the premise that set goals are transformable into unambiguous instructions and regulations for the employees.

In some schools of management and organizational development, it becomes a management task to motivate and engage the employees, among other things by making the work meaningful to them. Unlike these schools, traditional research in occupational health and safety and working life research have often taken for granted that work in itself is meaningless or that the meaning of the work is irrelevant, since the workers have no influence on it anyway. The work environmental research and effort has thus focused exclusively on the framework of the work itself: salary, working time, speed, work hazards, rules for influence, etc. This framework is of course also important to the employees' life conditions. But one must also be aware of the dilemmas and contradictions that arise for the employees, between, on the one hand the goals and values they attribute to the work, and on the other, the demands to accountability and involvement that the management imposes on them.

Most often, the employees take considerable pride in their work and their professional competence. This pride is, however, often contested by demands of the work that make it impossible for the employees to live up to their own standards for a well-performed work. This individual dilemma is often connected to major conflicts and contradictions between on the one hand, the users and society's standards and ethical norms and on the other, the economic considerations of the companies. The employees are thus expected to make considerations over the content of the work even though the framework does not allow room for it. The employees handling of these dilemmas may result in various survival strategies. But how they handle them also holds the possibility of power shifts; because issues become politicised that, so far, have been repressed as a-political. The quality issue thus reaches much further than to the individual company.

Employees' Role in the Development of Quality

The quality of the work that is created by the employee plays a role for many employees' job satisfaction. It plays a role at to the value that is attributed to the work and the 'professional pride' that goes into it. In 'craft professions', creating quality in the work is directly connected to one's own professional knowledge, skill and experience; however more routine work contains the knowledge of and training in what constitutes good work. An integral part of professionalism is to know what a well-performed work is, and on this basis, standards of quality and practicality anchored quality awareness are developed. Inversely, industrialism and the division of the work processes has most certainly also developed a more instrumental relationship with the employees to the work and to the meaning of the work for the quality of the completed product.

Many employees will probably feel dissatisfaction when delivering 'bad work'. It involves the risk of a bad psychosocial work environment, if the employees take on or are given responsibility for the bad quality. This problem can be reinforced, if the employees feel that they have no influence on conditions with which they are dissatisfied. Employees choose in some situations, to refuse to take responsibility for bad quality in cases where calling for the management's attention to the problem has been futile. For instance, the slaughterhouse workers in a company have, in interviews, claimed that they do not personally buy the products that they produce, because they do not think the quality is acceptable.

On the other side, the awareness of producing a good product or of 'delivering' a good service can make a work meaningful. Some employees in the food industry have said that it is professionally more challenging and satisfactory to produce organic food, because the raw materials are treated more delicately in accordance with traditional crafts methods, using the natural qualities of the raw materials. Likewise, the employees in a hospital kitchen have said in interviews that preparing good food for other people makes the work meaningful.

However, the employees have rarely any influence on the instructions, procedures, etc., that are being used. At the same time, sudden shifts in directions are imposed, because the management observes that the market's demands have changed. The management's perception of the necessary and obtainable quality will thus, to a higher degree than the employees' perception of quality, be influenced by the competition in the marketplace and the economic framework (Ullmark et al. 1986). There are examples of how the companies' management refuses to take responsibility for the quality of a company's product by referring to the market's demands and other external conditions (Wilkinson & Willmott (eds.) 1995). In interviews with women working in the Danish food industry, Annette Bilfeldt refers to the women's statements regarding their frustrations over reduced quality: 'Before, one could pack what one wanted to buy, you can't do that now'. At the same time, it leads to fearing the consequences of the company' competitive power – including fearing for one's own employment in the long run (Bilfeldt 2000, p. 210). Annette Bilfeldt refers also to the fact that unskilled women in the food industry build 'know-how in quality and the factors that influence the quality'. Consequently, they feel frustrated if they have to compromise and send bad products off – for instance when a foreman feels pressured to send the products off quickly in order to not fall behind on processing the orders. In some cases, the pressure becomes twofold: the work must be performed fast, and goods must be sent off that would normally be scrapped (Bilfeldt 2000, p. 209).

Quality Control as the Answer to Quality Problems

Some companies' and institutions' responses to quality problems have been to introduce quality control with formulation of quality policies, quality objectives, control procedures, process descriptions, specifications, and instructions.

In connection with the introduction of quality control, the employees often undertake courses on quality awareness – as a reflection of the management's view that the employees' attitude to quality is insufficient or that the quality of their work is problematic. This issue is ideologically founded, since the quality of products and services in most cases primarily depends on the management's decisions with respect to the framework of the work: choice of technology, acceptable cost level, etc. The ideology that affects many quality control projects is at the same time ambiguous. On the one hand, employees are viewed as a hindrance to achieve the right quality, and the employees are expected to follow the management's recommendations on procedures and specifications. On the other hand, it is also expected that the employees are creative and that they are ready to call attention to quality problems and their possible causes (Wilkinson & Willmott (eds.) 1995).

Setting the quality of the company's products and services is rarely an area of quality control, where the employees are included. This seems to be the case, not only in areas where the employees as workers with accumulated work experience may have knowledge of how good quality is achieved, but also in areas where they, in their role as citizens or consumers themselves, can have experiences linked to the product or to the service (food, caring for patients, etc.). Therefore quality control often becomes a question of involving the employees in the company's or in the institution's development, on terms defined by the management.

In quality projects, terms such as 'employee involvement' and 'empowerment' are often used, but the framework of the objectives that have been set by the management will often restrict it. However, this also means that the management depends on the 'support' of the employees to achieve a satisfactory production. The more divided the work is in a company or in an organization; the more reduced the management's possibility of getting an overview of the causes of bad quality. This means that employee loyalty in some cases is obtained by making the salary depend on the number of mistakes, or by increasing the supervision of the employees by collecting data on the individual employee's work by using information technology. (Wilkinson & Willmott (eds.) 1995).

The employees' inclusion in the practical organization of the quality work seems to hinge on the company's tradition for employee inclusion in other types of organization.

The more established the tradition of inclusion, the more the employees seem to be included in for instance writing instructions for their work (Hentze 1992). Company consultants in quality control have been criticized for having a simplified understanding of the work in the companies that is to be quality assured and for not respecting the employees' insight in the daily work (Hentze 1992) and (Wilkinson & Willmott (eds.) 1995). In some companies, it is the consultants (or the management) who write the instructions that guide the employees in their work. In other companies, the employees ask to write the instructions – in order to make sure that the instructions describe the actual daily reality (Hentze 1992). It may however, cause problems in companies where the employees are not used to formulating anything in writing. Therefore in some companies, the consultants have written the instructions – after a dialogue with the employees.

The company's development up until now, besides the future prospects for the company, can determine whether conflicts will arise between management and employees in connection with quality projects. In a British electronic plant, the employees thus felt pressured to accept the management's initiative in connection with a quality project, because they feared that their plant could become the next in line in the corporation to be closed down. The employees were to report repeated errors to their supervisors and they had the opportunity to partake in error-preventing activities. The employees experienced it as a more challenging way to work. But simultaneously, the work was perceived as more physically strenuous, because it was intensified, and it became more mentally strenuous due to increased responsibility, fear, and insecurity, as a result of the practice of reporting errors (Wilkinson & Willmott (eds.) 1995).

Quality Control and Work Conditions

Quality control may have both positive and negative consequences for the work conditions. In several studies, it has been referred to as positive that daily nuisances for the employees, such as unsuitable workflow are removed. Clarity on the part of the management regarding its expectations to the quality of the work can remove insecurity among employees, but causes new or increased insecurity when people are laid off because of 'too many errors'. The increased usage of information technology gives the management more opportunities to get an overview of information on the behaviour of the individual without using direct physical supervision (Hentze 1992) and (Wilkinson & Willmott (eds.) 1995).

Some quality projects may cause some intermediary management levels of organization to be removed between management and employees by 'abolishing' mid-level managers or by reducing their number. This means increased demands on the employees' control of their own work. However, it is far from certain that the employees gain more influence on the framework of their work. Viewed from this perspective, quality control can be characterized as increased responsibility of the employees for their own exploitation: Increased attention is required in the daily work – but it is not accompanied by any increase in real influence on their own work (Wilkinson & Willmott (eds.) 1995).

In the SARA Project, the relationship between quality and work has been given a particularly thorough examination in two case studies: an industrial enterprise that produces food and two hospital kitchens.

Quality in the Sausage Factory

The Sausage Factory that was described in detail in Chapter 4 was well known for its quality products. It had, up until now, had a conventional hierarchical work organization. When the SARA Project was introduced to the factory, a redesign of the work organization was initiated. The core of this redesign was the establishment of autonomous groups with very extended responsibilities. The project was not a success. It was stopped after about a year as a result of low productivity and high dissatisfaction among the employees. A disagreement between employees and management regarding the product's quality was what finally wrecked the project.

The packing department did not want to pack a series of badly produced sausages. Because of work and order pressure, the chief executive decided that they, contrary to the usual procedure, should be sold to the customers instead of being returned to the meat processor. That did it for a group of employees. The employees were summoned to a post-work meeting and a small group of editors was formed with the purpose of writing down the critique and passing it in to the chief executive. In the paper, the entire project was criticized. The intensified animosity among colleagues, due to the competition between the groups was called to attention. A new 'sausage master' was requested, the group structure was requested to be ceased and equal pay reintroduced. The critique led to the firing of the chief executive. The group organization was maintained, but the many committees were terminated and the groups would no longer have a number of functions, beyond the production.

A range of factors caused this project, which among other things involved increased employee responsibility for the quality, to gradually be met with resistance from many employees. The causes were among others:

- There was no connection between the responsibility that was imposed on the employees and the competency they were given to make the necessary decisions.
- The critique of too low a productivity was experienced as unjust, because a number of new work tasks were imposed on the employees.

- The tradition of equal pay for the employees was discarded because a bonus system for salary was introduced.
- The bonus salary system was perceived as unjust, because it only rewarded on the basis of the production volume and not on the basis of the many other functions that were imposed on the groups.
- The social relations in the employee group deteriorated because of pressure from the changed organization and differences in salary.
- The employees did not think that they were being sufficiently informed by the management and the shop steward, and they felt that they had no opportunity to state their opinion.

The project thus contained an attempt to give the employees increased responsibility for the product quality. But the problem was that responsibility and competency were not connected. The employees did not get enough training and time to control the quality, and their decisions were revoked. The other causes for the employees' critique show that a project that gives the employees more responsibility for quality can run into problems if the project puts existing norms under pressure (here equal pay), and the employees do not feel they have the opportunity to influence the project. The project also shows that the ability of employees and management to make use of 'collective spaces for dialogue' takes time to develop. There were weekly coordination meetings and employee meetings, but they were only used to pass on information and resolve practical problems.

Team Organization and Food Quality in Hospital Kitchens

The SARA Project has made a research study of two large-scale kitchens in connection with the introduction of team-organization of the work. The kitchens produce food for hospital patients and for the personnel in the hospitals. Quality has not been in direct focus in the project, but in the interviews with the employees, reflection on quality has been present. The employees have had considerations on when to assume responsibility for quality and when to deny it. In the interviews, visions for the quality have been formulated.

The two kitchens that the SARA project has followed are part of a combined kitchen organization for all five kitchens in the county. A small top management with a food director and a deputy director is heading the kitchen organization and underneath it are the five kitchens. A food manager, titled 'executive food manager', leads the five smaller kitchens. The largest kitchen is led by a group of three area food managers. The kitchen organization reports to the county's director of health and to the Health Department in the county. The political leadership in the form of the county council and its Health Department set the economic terms for the kitchen organization.

Three meals are prepared every day: a breakfast, a lunch and a dinner. The food must be prepared, placed in portions on trays (which may be characterized as assembly line work) and the dishes must be washed.

Preparing the food takes place as three different productions:

- 'the smorgasbord', where the breakfast and the smorgasbord for dinner is prepared;
- 'the hot meal', where the hot dinner meal is prepared;
- 'the diet meal', where special care is given to diabetics, heart patients etc.

In addition, the dish washing forms an independent department.

Besides preparing the food per se, there are work tasks such as planning the menu and shopping and scheduling the personnel, that is all done by the management.

The service assistant project was started as a response to a requirement from the county to save money on the operation of the kitchens. Back in 1994, the county council suggested outsourcing the food production with the result that the employees in the largest kitchen went on strike. The two trade unions (respectively for skilled employees and foremen and for unskilled employees) worked together to form an alternative to the outsourcing. Their proposal had the principles of Developmental Work as its starting point and the trade unions argued that the work could be developed at the same time, and money would be saved. The project was based on the premise that 11% would gradually be reduced from the annual budget. The county accepted the proposal. The core of the change project was the formation of a kind of team structure in the kitchens, where the daily planning was to be led by a skilled employee. A team coordinator in the form of a person in the kitchen's daily management would have the overall responsibility for the team's production. The unskilled employees should commit themselves to taking a service assistant education with courses in hospital porter work and cleaning work, supplemented with a module on kitchen hygiene, food preparation, etc. This would involve a pay raise. A three-week team-building course was part of the education. Courses in team building were also given to the skilled employees and to the managers.

Several of the employees claimed that making good food for other people was what gave meaning to the work. Several employees expressed dissatisfaction either with the raw materials or with the finished food. Some employees had chosen to repress their previous sense of responsibility for the quality, because they had witnessed a mid-level manager ignoring their calling for attention to e.g. the bad quality of the raw materials that were delivered. The employees had chosen to mentally deny responsibility for the bad quality, since the manager had not followed up on the critique.

Others said that it was frustrating when some of the temporarily employed young people sent a bad product out to the patients in the wards. Many of the young employees were doing weekend and vacation work or they only intended to work in the kitchen for a short period of time to make money for later studies. These young people often did not have the same understanding for how to arrange the food so that it looked neat on the plate and on the tray.

In the team-building course that the employees were exposed to, it was emphasized that the employees now had to take responsibility for their work. This was by some employees, perceived as a provocation: 'Who the hell do they think they are? They say we have to work in teams and take responsibility for our work. We are already working in teams and we feel enormously responsible for our work'. The course that was bought ready-made from a consulting firm was thus badly suited to the company's conditions.

The nurses and the assistant nurses in the wards did not always remember to tell the patients about the existing opportunities of having specially prepared meals delivered, and this was another frustration for the employees. The interviews with the employees show that some employees have visions of how the work could be better performed, by having a more direct dialogue with the patients. Thus a few employees expressed a wish of establishing a dialogue with the patients on the food quality: by changing the organization of the work in such a way that the employees in the kitchen could partake in serving the food in the wards and thus have a more direct contact with the patients. They would like to be able to follow the product all the way to the user. Today the only feedback is a postcard or a letter to the editor from previous patients – usually with praise. A food committee has been established at the individual hospital, but only managing employees and dieticians are represented.

In the smaller hospital kitchen, the employees expressed that they were frustrated with the lack of opportunities for dialogue between management and employees in the planning phase of the team organisation, because of a very tight time table for the work of producing three daily meals. Daily kitchen meetings were held, but some employees felt stressed if the meetings slightly exceeded the time it was supposed to end. Often, employees were absent due to sickness, and this meant that the individual often had to perform extra job functions. In such situations, the employees could not concentrate on the morning meetings, but were instead thinking of the extra work ahead. The team organization meant that the individual team was given time for a monthly meeting in the work time. The experience was not altogether positive. In some cases, the meetings were cancelled – as was previously the case with the department meetings in the large kitchen. The employees in one of the teams were frustrated that the team coordinator was unable to get support from the management for the wishes of, e.g. repair of equipment, that were brought up at the meetings. Frequent stops were thus contributing to a stressed work situation because of the tight time schedule that a hospital is subject to with three daily deliveries. The frustration deepened because the team perceived that their team coordinator made them responsible for the many problems with the equipment.

Some of the previous experiences with team organization shows that it can be difficult to change a work organization with a very detailed task division – in particular when increased productivity is required at the same time because of downsizing. In some teams, the team organization was thus initiated with the team scheduling, when the daily cleaning and the more thorough weekly or monthly cleaning was to take place. The reactions from the employees varied. Some chose not to take on more tasks than they could handle, while others took on more responsibility and typically they were the ones to take on heavy-duty cleaning tasks. Also in this case, there were some employees who felt that there was a lack of support from the management. They did not feel that the management had any understanding that the cuts caused increased work pressure.

Perspectives for an Employee Oriented Perception of Quality in the Work

The experiences from the two development projects show that employees can feel very responsible for the quality. If there are problems regarding not being able to deliver a satisfactory quality, some employees react by distancing themselves from the problem and denying responsibility. This may, for instance, happen if it is perceived that the management does not follow up on the cause of the quality problems that the employees have called to attention. In other cases, internalization may take place where the employees feel a daily frustration with the bad quality.

The projects also show that the use of ready-made concepts for team organization, which are often very ideological, can be very offensive to the employees. For instance, when they lecture the employees on the importance of taking responsibility for quality in the work. The employees may think that they have bent over backwards already to take this responsibility, and sometimes despite the efforts of the management.

The experiences also show that there may, in a group of employees, be very radical and well-developed visions for development of quality in the present work. This shows a potential for quality development that goes far beyond the visions that management and employee representatives might have in a project, based on the introduction of team organization according to the principles of Developmental Work.

It seems to be a general problem for the employees to have enough time, space and personal relations for a dialogue among themselves and with the management – both regarding the daily production and the ideas that are present among the employees to change the organization of the work.

Environmental Sustainability and Working Life Development

In the course of the last decade, environmental issues have been put on the agenda in modern companies. Environmental management becomes integrated in the companies' management system, environmental declarations and organic products are gaining a foothold. Environmental relations are in general included in product innovation and planning. These changes in the companies have been called an organic modernization (Hajer 1995 p. 261), where there is an effort to adjust the environmental demands to the economic conditions and subject them to demands on profitableness. They may be viewed as a reaction to demands from society towards a more sustainable production system. Sustainability is, however, from the outset a much broader concept that also encompasses a social and an organic perspective on the societal development as a whole. It therefore goes much further than the initiatives to organic modernization that can be observed at company level.

Traditional working life research and trade union philosophy has tended to view environmental efforts in companies as a parameter of competition that primarily is initiated by the management as a reaction to authority demands and customer demands. The employees and the trade union reaction is aimed at safe-guarding the work environment, skills, and influence in connection with such initiatives, so that the employees are not further strained in their working life. But this perspective seems somewhat one-dimensional. Possible potentials for the employees' working life that are latent in any production change (no matter how small it may seem) are really overlooked in this perspective. 'A second look' is needed to explore such environmentally improving production changes that may primarily be initiated on the basis of competitive considerations, but which also hold broader societal perspectives.

In recent years, a new school of thought has developed in Denmark in regard to working life and in the labour movement; new efforts in new areas and initiatives towards a trade involvement in a sustainable development are being developed. (Some examples among several: General Workers Union about organic farming, Food Workers Union about a sustainable working life and Danish Trade Union Congress about green industrial policy). Danish TUC has, in its presentations on Developmental Work raised the environmental issue as an important element. The two dimensions of TUC's three-dimensional vision on the developmental work indeed pertain to the products' societal relevance and sustainable character and also to the companies' environmental sustainability and social responsibility (see Chapter 2 and Børsting & Bruvik-Hansen 1999). A series of issues pertaining to the employees' role in the developmental process are raised now that the environmental issue has been brought into focus. This is done both on the part of the large organizations and in particular very concretely at the individual companies in the form of diverse environmental conversion projects. It is therefore relevant to examine how these environmental production changes unfold in an employee and working life perspective. Theoretically, it means that environment and working life, as research fields, to a greater extent, need to become conceptually united, and the concept of sustainability is well suited for this purpose. A 'humanization' of traditional environmental philosophy is needed, because it is often dominated by an expert oriented natural science approach that is often just implemented as a pure top-down controlled management dictate at the individual company.

Several concrete studies of the employees' participation and involvement in environmental issues exist. They show that the employees are into environmental issues and that they are interested in participating in environmental work at the companies (Jørgensen et al. 1992 with a questionnaire survey and case studies in Lorenzen et al. 1997 and Christensen et al. 1997 and 1998). The organic issues are, however, mainly not represented as research topics in social science research on working life. And inversely, there is very little focus on the role of the employees in the development of environmental improvements and organic production in environmental research. The employees most often view this link as a pure work resource and venue of work related knowledge in relation to the company's environmental activities, rather than as an independent and active player in the societal development of sustainability (Miljøstyrelsen 1999).

We shall take a closer look at the problem in this chapter, and we shall try to answer two central questions: How do the employees participate in environmental changes at work – is it only a changed work load or does it create involvement and development in the work? What does it mean to the employees to contribute to environmental improvements in the work and in the products – does it bring along a new professional pride and increased attention to environmental conditions or is the environmental understanding that the work requires miles away from the understanding of environmental problems and sustainability that one develops as a citizen?

Developmental Work and Sustainability

Sustainability and risk are concepts that place the work and the use of the human resources in a societal context. The sustainability requirement links the work and the product with its societal consequences and thus it links the working life with the social life. Employees are also citizens with political influence in the local community. Employees act as consumers and employees compose a necessary resource for the company. The employees thus form a composite political player that links the company with the surrounding society. Through the work and the work relations, the employees' involvement in environmental conditions can take place, for instance as exertion of influence on the customers; or as a development of new ideas for environmental improvements. The work place can be viewed as a political arena where reflection and reactions to the works' organic consequences can be developed in the sub-political public of work colleagues, customers, suppliers, management and others. Despite the adherence to a predominantly hierarchical company structure – and also by introduction of environmental changes – the management will, in practice, have to pass a minimum of control over the practical outcome on to the actual executors with the risk of losing control and possible unpredictability to follow. It therefore constitutes some latitude for the employees to exert power that can be used in a company perspective, as well as in a societal perspective.

This has relevance for the individual executor of production – the employee – not only in his capacity as a competent professional executor, but also as an ordinary person, consumer, and (local) citizen. Spotting the places where the environmental issue in the company are not just about increased sales opportunities to benefit the company's position in the increasingly tighter competition thus becomes interesting. The issue goes beyond this narrow criteria and lives as an all-present collective societal problem that pertains to all of us as employees, management, consumers, and as ordinary people in general. Environmental changes in the company may thus be viewed, as a potential opportunity to view the product and the way it is produced – the work process – in a more coherent way. The goal is to overcome the split between being an executor of the product and being an every day person, a discrepancy that for instance shows in the frustrations that can emerge with being employed in an environmentally polluting company.

Furthermore, this is a potential source of new social orientations and professional identity that could counter the extensive individualization that the labour movement is struggling with today. The essential point in one of the most commonly quoted survey's in Denmark on values and attitudes to work (Jørgensen 1992) was precisely that an increased interest for immaterial issues was present in the wage earner group, while the traditional collectivist labour movement issues did not engage the members to the same extent (Madsen, 1997). Considering the tendencies towards a decreasing involvement among the members, it thus seems obvious that the labour movement must begin to take these issues far more seriously. It constitutes a potential for a new social orientation and community feeling that is based on a common responsibility and interest for the environmental problems' societal consequences. It takes aim at a more extensive kind of solidarity that transcends the traditional focus on pay and that simultaneously could constitute a collective link and a feeling of community among the members. In doing so, it could compose an alternative to the individualized service orientation in the relationship to the labour movement that is increasingly affecting many members. By making room for a common environmental orientation, a basis could be formed for new social identifications. Furthermore, involvement in environmental politics could strengthen the employees' orientation towards and struggle to develop professional and skill competencies that could contribute to a professional pride in the work.

Experiences with the Employees' Participation in Environmental Politics at Work

In the three companies that we have studied, introduction of environmental management, environmental certificates, and organic restructuring of the production have been put on the agenda. We have studied how the employees have taken part in the restructuring and what it has meant for them. The three companies are:

- A mid-sized printing house that has introduced a certified environmental management system and environmental declaration of their products.
- A small producer of bread and mill. The company has been an organic pioneer with close relations to organic and bio-dynamical grain growers and an organic involved clientele.
- A super market chain with associated traditional local bakeries, where a part of the chain has been turned into organic bakeries, while another part is about to undergo a similar change. Three bakeries are actually participating, besides one that is planning to shift to organic production.

The Organic Modern Company

The subject of our study is a mid-sized printing house, operating in a very competitive situation. The shift to certified environmental management and environmental declaration was part of a number of efforts, where the company wanted to be on the leading edge of the surrounding demands to quality, the natural environment, and the work environment. The shift did not bring about big changes in the work. Rather, the company was certified for its handling of the environment conditions. The biggest change was that the environmental and work environmental problems of a physical-chemical nature were registered, prioritized and integrated into the management system and that an employee was given the task of heading the environmental and quality control. The shift had particular importance for the use of chemicals, i.e. for print colours, solvent agents, cleaning agents and others chemicals, among other things for the photographic processes. The work environmental problems of physical nature, such as hard floors, heavy lifts and environmental problems in connection with energy, paper usage and such, were also included. The psycho/organizational work environmental problems were on the contrary forced out, as something that was irrelevant in connection with environmental management. Shifts, stress, no time for the employees to exchange what they have learned, opportunities for a changed work organization, and the tight order management were issues that never were dealt with as real problems. Individual employees were heavily involved in environmental issues and put a great effort into the safety committee and in contacts with colleagues, but most viewed the environmental management primarily as a management concept that posed new demands on the work's procedures and registration of products and materials. An environmental officer played a major role for the projects and the BST was pulled in [BST=Bedriftssundhedstjenesten, a national institution with extensive local presence, assisting the companies in their improvement of work environmental and some time also their impact on the external environment].

But the room for developing the organic awareness turned out to be narrow. Time pressure, the difficulty of allotting time for the employees to perform environmental work, and work-shifts, made it difficult to hold general assemblies and the lunch break was in fact, abolished. These were conditions that according to the environmental coordinator, made it difficult for the employees themselves to take over a bigger part of the environmental work.

Several interesting opportunities for developing the environmental work in the company however also turned up:

- The printers' long struggle for a better work environment was a good basis for acquiring knowledge on the external environment that has now become associated with the work environment in the mind of the employees.
- The printers were aware of and wished to avoid risks associated with chemical substances – but they were in a dilemma, because of the extra time and effort it takes to use less abrasive agents.
- An environmental coordinator was given an important role as communicator between the societal knowledge of environmental consequences and the workers' actual experiences concerning the execution of the work. This was a communication that took place at many levels in the course of the change process: For instance, as a staff meeting, a questionnaire to the employees, short courses, every day dialogues and small experiments.
- A dialogue and an influence process took place 'from below', where the most environmentally aware employees convinced the others to also give up the abrasive chemicals. Some of the arguments were that it caused unequal work conditions, when some workers spend more time than others on the work, and because it contributed to improve the printers' work conditions in general that the abrasive agents were phased out.
- The printers took an active part in the experimental innovation of new chemicals and new processes, since they tested new products from the suppliers for their practical usability in the work.
- There were opportunities for increased communication with suppliers and (through the environmental coordinator) for increased communication with BST and other consultants regarding environmental conditions, for instance regarding choice of colour, paper usage, printed image, and the need for communication.
- When there was room for visions and dialogue, the organic considerations were right at hand. The group interviews thus fostered exchange of experiences and ideas as to how the 'good environmentally safe printed matter' should look and be produced. For example, the paper must be used to

the maximum, print colours must be natural, the printed part cannot touch the edge, the print colours must have their life cycle evaluated.

But a fundamental ambivalence was at the basis of it all and made it hard for the printers to whole-heartedly support an organic dimension. One of the printers put it this way: 'When printers go down to get a coupon for the lottery, they will pick 50, because it means more work for them. You have to do your part to get jobs for the profession'. The resource consumption for, among other things, unnecessary advertising and printed matter, you cannot change as an employee – and it is your livelihood. But it was evident that an awareness of this paradox was acutely present.

The Organic Pioneering Company

Alongside traditional companies that become established on market conditions, there are company types that are based on alternative objectives. Cooperatives, inventor companies, organic agriculture, and organic pioneering companies on other frontiers are examples of this. It is interesting to study how the employees have participated in the development of such an organic pioneering company in the production of bread. The company built on a bio-dynamic philosophy on preserving the life-giving forces in the ground and on a spiritual community of people and nature, as formulated by Rudolf Steiner, among others. The company was part of a network that often included personal relations to bio-dynamical and organic growers, and to stores and institutions that buy the products. Thus, it constituted a link between grower and consumer that involves storage, mill, and bakery. In recent years, the company had received more attention and it stood out as an important source of inspiration and as an innovator by, among other things, developing recipes with original types of grain, with organic ingredients, and with baking methods where artificial additives were not used. This had caused increased 'industrialization' of the production with an increased number of employees that had required reorganization toward an increase of quality control and environmental management.

It turned out that although the company was built on a foundation of respect for the work and the craft with relatively good work conditions, the employees were not included in decisions and considerations on developing the production. It was the initiator and general manager alone who would interpret the ideological principles and who would prescribe methods and ingredients in the organic products. The employees were expected to be involved in the quality of the work, but not in the concept behind it: 'You can be engaged in the work, without being engaged in the idea itself' according to the manager. This meant that on the one hand, the company could recruit ordinary workers from the local area, without requiring them to form an opinion on the ideology behind the product, as long as they did a good job. On the other hand, it meant that the manager did not expect that the employees contributed with their own understanding and interpretation of what is organic sound – and yet, they had to maintain the attitude toward the environment and quality that the manager had built his company around. So we found a top-down controlled approach, a rather patriarchal type of management in this organic pioneer. Some work environmental problems, such as work speed, were solved as part of the overall ideology of respect for the work and for the environment. But others were overlooked or given a low priority. According to the 'workplace assessment', this was, among other things, the case with physical problems with flour dust, slippery floors, bad lightning, temperature conditions, bad space conditions, and mental strain due to stress and poor planning.

The employees expressed satisfaction with the workplace and took pride in the quality of the products. The social community was particularly praised, and so was the quality of the product. The employees viewed themselves as co-producers – along with the entire workers' collective – of very special products, and they perceived that they had an interest in protecting this standard of quality. Although they viewed the company's ideology as slightly too fanatic, they did respect the product, and they did not think the price it cost was too high, because they knew how much care and effort that had been put into it.

The company was totally dependent on the employees investing their sense of responsibility, their involvement, and their professionalism in the work. From carefulness in placing the correct declarations on the products in order to maintain credibility, to mastering the technique of baking so that the quality of the bread could be evaluated, the company was dependent on the employees. It was not enough to use a stop-clock when baking. The manager thus made the criticism that the bakers were more oriented towards baking times than towards the product itself. Much of what the bakers were educated in, had no use here, whilst alternatively several were not even educated bakers, but had been trained in the company. Furthermore, the company was quite dependent on the employees' own cooperation and flexibility in order to make the many links in the daily workflow work together, meet the changing orders and not the least bring new ideas and recipes into the production.

The company was placed in a rural area, dominated by traditional agriculture, and the employees were usually not familiar with the company's values when they started. Therefore, they often met them with scepticism, but they eventually became respectful of the results and they began to make the organic philosophy their own. Some had also developed a critical awareness of the environmentally problematic aspects of their spouse's agricultural production at home. But there was nothing in the work organization that directly aimed at developing the employees' organic understanding and participation in the development of products and processes.

Organic Conversion in a Grocery Chain

The third case company is the bakeries of a major grocery chain. A top management decision was made that all the 72 bakeries of the chain were to make the change to exclusively organic production of bread as well as of cakes by a particular date – at the same price as before. There were many reasons for the conversion to organic production:

- The company has an ideological front position since it both operates as a consumer organization and as a store. The company is therefore based on political goals of combining credibility, health, quality and environment awareness, with the business management. It was, however, getting increasingly difficult to secure deliveries of pure raw materials to the bakeries in the form of GMO free corn, grain without straw shortening, salmonella free eggs and the like. A transition to organic raw materials would potentially solve this problem.

- The bakeries have undertaken an independent development as a decentralized crafts oriented production with central management of agreements with suppliers, economic and baking technological consulting and demands for recipes and assortment in the stores. In the beginning of the '90s, a conversion of the bakeries had taken place. They became subject to a common concept of crafts-oriented bread production, based on common recipe development and natural ingredients. It was decided that there was a need for a new concept in order to make the individual bakeries more dynamic.
- The management had succeeded in negotiating agreements with suppliers that could secure deliveries of approved organic raw materials at prices that were only slightly higher than standard raw materials. The products would, therefore, not be significantly more expensive, since the prices of the raw materials only constitute a small part of the product's cost price.
- By simultaneously converting a whole chain, a market advantage of greater sales, as well as economic large-scale operation advantages could be obtained, since it did not necessitate two separate production lines in the bakeries.

Since a main element in the strategy was the surprise momentum in having the conversion take place all at once all over the country, only a few employees were involved in the plans from the outset, more than a year before the conversion. While the common employees were only informed 3 months prior to the conversion, only the master bakers and the first assistants in the stores received a 1–3 day course to learn the new methods and principles that they had to pass on to others when back in the bakery.

The strategy succeeded in the first round, and a large number of articles and interviews with happy and proud employees and booming sales testified to this fact. Later, there were many problems. Some of the most significant problems were dry bread, margarine that caused problems, assortment that was imposed on the bakeries, difficulties in getting the bakery's own recipes approved, difficulties in finding suitable decorations, local specialities that had to go out of production which caused dissatisfaction among the customers, and bread that was too expensive compared to the locality's usual prices, etc. In addition, bread and cakes that were previously made from ready-made mixings now had to be made completely with basic raw materials. For the good baker, it could produce a much better taste – but it could also go terribly wrong, if the baker did not know his craft. The biggest problem was, according to the employees, the decoration of the cakes. The colours disappeared and the fruits of the season and various sugary things could not be used for decoration, because it had to be strictly organic. Special problems arose in the strawberry season, when the suppliers of organic strawberries fell behind. A number of bakeries in the chain left the organic concept and a number of customers left too. On the other side, new customers arrived, who explicitly preferred the organic bakery and therefore also became new customers in the supermarket. All in all, the situation had stabilized after two years with increased sales and success in certain areas, mostly in the big cities and with falling sales and in some cases conversion to partly non-organic production in the rural areas.

To the employees, it meant turbulent work conditions for a year after the conversion:

- A lack in participation, commitment and ownership of the conversion – but acceptance of the conversion, partly because it was the management's strategy and partly because the employees would like to help the environment.
- New demands in the work, new work environmental problems in particular with regard to registration and control and that it was now harder to be allowed to make the bakery's own assortment on the basis of local conditions.
- New professional challenges which were welcomed by some, while others left the workplace.
- Experiments and development of new solutions to problems and tackling of problems.
- The joy of working with pure raw materials, to create the product from the bottom up, to develop one's craft and professional skill with the bakers: 'The good thing is that you don't have to deal with all that magic powder, which you don't really know what is. Now there's just salt and sugar and yeast…'.
- The joy of being able to tell the customers exactly what the ingredients were, to feel the product was safe with respect to risks, and to be sure that the organic control was all right with the sales people.
- The perception of ecology was, for many people, restricted to the aspects that they themselves meet. It is about the content of the product, but it is not seen in relation to cultivation of the grain and the ground water, or it is about the pure raw materials, while the major environmental problems are left out.
- A few individuals put things in a wider perspective and questioned the environmental profile of the company that was perceived as stained and contradictory, when the sugar was brought over here all the way from Brazil, and when some of the bakeries could opt out of the organic concept.
- A dialogue on environment with the customers, with the family, with people in the street: 'So, you have gone organic at your place. I wonder if we can trust it…'.

In the conversion process, the management had obviously not gone out of its way to get the employees involved in the ideas behind it. But the employees have had a positive reaction, and they have made a strong effort to make the conversion a success and to explore new ways to create a good assortment of bread and cakes. Furthermore, they have taken an active part in the local debate on ecology. Scepticism comes from the surroundings and regards, in particular, whether one can trust that the products are completely organic, and the employees had to be well prepared to also tackle this scepticism. Professional identification was about the good craftsmanship and the clear message to the customers: 'Our cocoa has a stronger taste of cocoa, cinnamon has a stronger taste of cinnamon, the baked goods now have a more pure taste' and 'it makes you feel mighty proud when it looks attractive'.

Discussion of the Lessons Learned from the Companies

In all three cases with environmentally oriented conversions, we found resistance to the changes that were imposed as a result of the conversions. It was especially grounded in irritation with the increased registration and with control over work processes and raw materials. There were work tasks beyond what people saw as their normal work, and which contained an element of outside control of the work. In the bakeries, the ecology rules required a meticulous registration of what goes in and out of the bakeries. With respect to the printing house, the critique was centred around the quality control and environmental management's extensive control of the whole process. This resulted in a notation procedure of huge proportions, and furthermore, it was a threat because it gave rise to disloyal informing between the employees. In the beginning, the employees were, in general, annoyed with the troublesome work procedures and task expansions, but seemed surprisingly fast at getting used to them. The consideration for the guarantee of the product's organic quality seemed to balance the increased workload. The following statement from a sales person in the chain's organic converted bakery points to this: 'I think that it is also, at the same time, what benefits us that we can stand by the things we have'. However, it is an issue whether this acceptance from the employee side was the result of a real change of attitude related to the importance of spreading the organic production. Or whether it should rather be viewed as a result of the management's success with the attempts to 'discipline' their employees to accept the conversion, as a common project that primarily is aimed at increasing market shares. With respect to the practice and control that took place in all three companies, it was the second that got the most appeal. The training courses and information meetings that have been held in the grocery chain were, for instance, primarily concerned with the management's intention of emphasizing the modern and rational – the pragmatic – aspects of such a conversion. In doing so, it was also stressed that there was no intention to make visionary and idealistic changes of society behind it.

A perception of ecology as a way to use one's craft, once again, right across the company, was present at the same time among the bakers in the grocery chain. The crafts-related qualities were central to the baked goods, rather than the time it took to bake it. It was also viewed as a professional challenge to have to make everything from the bottom, rather than use factory-made mixtures.

Room for Experiments and Development of Environmental Improvements

As previously mentioned, experiments were made by the cleaners at the printing house to clean the printing presses by using soap instead of organic solvents. The employees made use of their professional expertise and experience in testing the cleaning ability of the products, and they currently reported the results to the supplier. The supplier could then change the composition of the products in accordance with the printers' directions. This took place alongside the company's otherwise top-down environmental politics that is characterized by an absence of formal employee influence. At closer examination, it turned out, however, to contain practical and concrete employees influence by way of the professional everyday insight. Something similar could be observed in the organic converted bakery, where they had big problems producing organic confectionery that were as colourfully brilliant as that conventionally made. Not only did it cause problems in relation to the customers' expectations of confectionery's appearance, but also in relation to the bakers' own perceptions of professionally acceptable products. The bakers tried to solve this problem by experimenting with alternatives and by using a good deal of professional fantasy. A substantial problem was the extensive use of food colour. It turned out to be difficult to get organic food colour when it was not in season. After some creative thinking and practical testing, an employee found out that organic beet juice could be used as an alternative in the winter season to decorate the cakes. Even without a formalized inclusion of the employees, it turned out that there was a certain room for the professional development of the employees in an environmental direction that both contributed to develop their own work and that served the company's interests.

Discipline to Assure Organic Quality

A source of dissatisfaction in the grocery chain's converted bakeries was the management's prohibition of bringing non-organic products into the bakery, as well as into the store. The rule was applied very strictly, since non-compliance would be a cause for dismissal. Also in this case, the employees were accommodating and accepting. They interpreted the prohibition as an attempt to avoid sending out confusing signals to the customers. Overt use of non-organic products by employees could be a source of customer distrust, as to whether the production was really exclusively organic. The understanding and goodwill of the employees in complying with this control provision is thus remarkable. They considered it to be in place for their own good, because it contributed to strengthening the customers' trust, which they considered a factor of crucial importance. A baker's assistant made the following statement regarding the requirements: 'I didn't think it annoying, because it also gives me a clear conscience to know that it is just not allowed and that I can get fired if I do it. It makes me think ahead and decide not to bring Kærgården [non-organic butter] in here. I'll have to leave it in the lunch room'.

Sustainability in the Concrete Professional Practice

Work involves dealing with Nature. This is true even for the office work that deals with electricity, paper, PCs and other machinery. The work place in question contains specific relations to Nature, and the individual job or profession involves certain ways to handle Nature. The changes of the companies' environmental politics will thus also have specific and different consequences for the work's content and the environmental perception associated with it. There are great variations in the immediate consequences that the changes will have for the work. It depends, among other things, on whether the changes are related to the finished product's organic character, which is the case in the food industry. Or whether the environmental improvements rather pertain to the substances and the chemicals that are used in the manufacturing process and therefore have a more direct impact on the employees' health. These implications have different significance for the employees, dependent upon what product and type of production we are talking about. In the case of the bakeries, the narrow consumer orientation in the grocery chain's bakeries and, indeed, also in the bio-dynamic bread bakery, focuses on the product and the product's purity in the eyes of the consumer. This implies that the consumer's trust in 'keeping your promise' is of pivotal importance, while the way it is produced seems less interesting. With respect to the printing house, the work process is far more important. The environmental improvements pertain to a great extent to chemicals that are dangerous, not only in relation to the external surroundings – the outside environment – but they also contain a significant health risk for the executor of the concrete work process.

Sustainable Professionalism

We have been unable to find any great differences within the trades represented in the study with regards to opportunities for developing a sustainable professionalism. In the printing trade, a clear connection between environmentally safe production and acceptable work conditions was present in the mind of the printers. A very clear perception of 'what is good for the environment is also good for us to work with' was made explicit here. In their professional wishes of a good product, they asked for simplicity and less use of colour. They criticized the use of glazed paper in for instance, periodicals; and this can be interpreted as a sign of resource awareness. The conversion to using vegetable colours and cleaning agents was an obvious example of the union of considerations for the external environment on the one hand and considerations for the work environment on the other. This union was taken for granted in the view that 'what is healthy for us in the manufacturing process is also good for the environment in a broader sense'. When a well-functioning environmental coordinator was employed, her work area did in fact contain conditions pertaining not only to the external environment but also to the work environment. These two areas were to a great extent viewed as two sides of the same coin. This linking of the outside environment with the physical work conditions is in sharp contrast to the baking profession. Here the organic production appears, as the ultimate goal; that the work conditions to a greater extent will have to merely adjust to and be subject to. This is also the case in the bakers' view. Here, the external environment and the work environment will therefore tend to be in opposition to each other, since the organic end result is the determining factor. But at the same time, the environment is to both the printers and the bakers a source of innovation and professional development that is meaningful to the individual.

Development of the Human Resources – Visions Opening in the Work

It is remarkable that despite the many restrictions and resistance towards changes, there are nevertheless elements of freedom to the needed experimental development, in which the employees' subjectivity and their professional skill capacity can be expressed. It has furthermore been remarkable that the employees – despite temporary irritation in the beginning – overall had exhibited positive support for the environmentally safe production conversions that they from the outset did not have any say on. Although one could have expected a widespread resistance to change, closer studies showed that this was far from the case. In many ways, an involvement was found in the environmental conditions that exceeded the management-dictated conversions and that pointed towards a sense of responsibility and reflectivity in relation to the work's content and the demands for professional competency.

With reference to the analyses above, we thus see clear tendencies to develop the employees' social and professional orientation in the work, in the direction of a well-developed perception of sustainability and sustainability awareness. The environmental perception is shaped in the interplay of, and across the employees' many different spheres of life, and it is associated with ambivalence and contradictory perceptions and feelings. If the employees were granted a more active place in the company's environmental work, an extended and practice-based awareness in the employees, with respect to their perception of the environment and sustainability, could be opened up. The employees would be able to affect the companies' production practice and agenda, thereby influencing society in general. However, our cases also clearly demonstrate that many barriers exist that could hinder such a development, because of a conventional hierarchical management practice that rarely dares to make room for such a subjective development of the companies sustainability perspectives 'from the bottom'. One can say there is a need to counter the management's apparent fear of – or resistance to – changes and to create the needed free spaces for professional experiments with an environmentally professional practice. This is the only way that environmental conversions can have a real delivery potential in a broader societal perspective and contribute to overcome the company's limited here-and-now-oriented rationality.

A clear picture of employee involvement thus emerges in the companies' environmental politics. Employee involvement is an important part of a strategy to develop working life, as it has been suggested in the Developmental Work strategy. The employees participate and are engaged in the work even though bad conditions are imposed on them. Also, they soon acquire a sense of satisfaction and pride in the results that is not observed in many other change processes where insecurity related to the consequences and increased pressure on the social relations yield dissatisfaction and stress.

The fact that the changes pertain to a 'common good' – a more sustainable society – we see as a potential for a community feeling, and social integration factor and an orientation among employees that goes beyond the individual company. At the same time, this potential new orientation can foster a more wide-ranging and societally relevant perspective than that of the conventional trade and salary focus that so far has been a cornerstone of the labour movement.

Quality in Elder Care

To give care to users of social and health services is often viewed as something that gives identity to the employees in their work. To be a doctor or a nurse is thus often spoken of in terms of a 'calling' and the work in this sector is supposedly often chosen because the employees want to 'work with people'. On the other hand, it is also an area that has given rise to discussions of 'burn-out' in particular in recent years. The employees feel that it is hard to meet their own standards with externally imposed demands and limited resources.

In recent years, the social and the health sector have been increasingly subject to downsizing and efficiency drives, while at the same time, there has been increased attention on the quality of the services. This has led to the introduction of different types of quality control systems and organizational development projects. What does it do to the employees to be exposed to the double pressure of trying to meet the standards of good nursing and having to do so with fewer resources? Can organizational forms be developed that give the employees the opportunity to develop quality in the care-giving work? How would quality in the care-giving work be perceived from an employee perspective?

The consideration to residents and patients can have a very strong effect, because there is an immediate contact and identification with the people. To counter this, the employees may develop an instrumental attitude to the work, as a strategy of avoiding the strains of trying to meet the surrounding's demands and expectations without having the necessary resources to do so. There are also instances, however, of the attitude towards other people having changed in the social and health sector. It has in some places changed from a view of the elderly, the sick and others, as being difficult, helpless and ignorant to a view of them as people with resources, who should be more included in the arrangement of their own nursing and treatment.

In the following, we shall discuss quality in the care-giving work, while taking our point of departure in theoretical analyses of the care-giving work and experiences from case studies at four nursing homes in the SARA project.

Central Characteristics in Care-Giving Work for the Elderly

In the following, some of the central features of working with care for the elderly that have been identified by researchers in the field are presented.

The Practical Care-Giving Work. Care for the elderly contains:

- Physical nursing, i.e. attending to practical basic functions such as personal hygiene, serving food, help with eating, dressing, help with visits to the bathroom, dispensing medicine etc.
- Care that goes beyond the physical nursing, such as going for a walk, adjusting the hearing aid, watering the flowers, making sure the reading lamp is turned on in the evening, escort to therapy, hair dresser, pedicure etc.
- Emotional care for example conversations, holding hands, talking with relatives etc.

Working with the relatives consists of collecting information about the residents and their needs and lending support to the relatives (e.g. to the spouse of a resident with dementia). It also involves arranging that relatives escort the resident to a doctor who is a specialist or to a dentist, or to go shopping for shoes, clothes etc.

Care-Giving – a Work that Involves Head, Hand and Heart. The Norwegian sociologist and care-giving researcher Kari Wærness emphasizes that care-giving work requires emotional insight into the needs of the person, who is being cared for. Therefore, the caregiver must be able to handle 'the relationship between head, hand, and heart in the care-giving work' (Wærness 1996, 1999). According to Kari Wærness, the care-giving work as wage-labour thus contains a practical side as well as an emotional side (Wærness 1982, 1990). These two dimensions of the work cannot – or rather should not – be separated. The Swedish social researcher Martha Szebehely (1995, 1999) points out that an instrumental attitude toward the work is fundamentally irreconcilable with good care-giving, and this is at the root of some of the central dilemmas that characterize the work with caring for the elderly.

Involvement and Withdrawal. In the conduct of caring for the elderly, the caregiver is continuously confronted with quality requirements. The fact that other people's quality of life is connected to the quality of the caring that is given, brings content to the work. The receiver of the care (or the relatives), the colleagues and the caregiver him or herself all have views of what good care-giving is, and they all make demands on the care-giving work.

But the care-giving work is full of contradictions because it contains both involvement and non-involvement at the same time. A caregiver must both get involved with the individual person's needs and must also honour the workplace's requirement to execute the present work tasks – regardless of how few employees are there to carry out the work. Therefore, the caregiver will have to choose and withdraw from parts of the care-giving work. This constitutes a central dilemma in the care-giving work: that the involvement in the work can become a strain.

Elder Care as Wage Labour. When conducting care for the elderly in the formal economy through salaried care work, it is the nursing home's routines and goals for the work that the caregiver's work is based on. The professional care-giving at the nursing home is therefore qualitatively different from the care-giving that is performed as an unpaid activity in the family, where it is the family ties that are at the roots of the care-giving attention.

Professional care-giving work contains similarities to the care-giving work that is carried out in the family. The receiver of the care should for instance have clean clothes, food, medicine, fresh air and emotional care. But a professional caregiver goes home, when the workday is done. The employee is not contacted outside the working hours, newly arisen problems are resolved by the colleagues, and he or she can change to another job or be dismissed.

Because senior care is wage-labour, there is room for detachment – compared to the care that is conducted in the family sphere. The work is conducted in return for a salary (not because the caregiver is the son/daughter/daughter-in-law/spouse) and the employee returns to his, or her, own situation, when the workday is over.

The Meaning of the Relations. Professional care is conducted in a relationship, where one party (the receiver) is dependent on the other party's work (the caregiver). This relationship contains not only reciprocity, since the receiver has an interest in the care and the caregiver has an interest in the work; it also contains conflicts of interest and different goals (Schmid 1999).

The relationship between the caregiver and the person who receives the care is determining for the quality of the work (Szehebely 1996). Although the care-giving work may not in the beginning contain deeply engaging relations between the elderly and the employee, they may over time evolve in this direction. The work is performed within personal relation ties between caregiver and care receiver. It matters to the receiver who gives the care, and it matters to the employee who the person is that receives the care (Szebehely 1995). Good relations between caregiver and resident are important in conducting the care-giving work. To personally know the receiver of the care and the person's care situation is totally central to the work (Wærness 1985).

In order to make use of the contextual knowledge and evaluate the care receivers' changing needs for care, it is necessary that the caregiver becomes as qualified as possible to make decisions and make priorities. It is also essential that he or she has the necessary time to become knowledgeable about the receiver of the care, in a dialogue with the person.

The Organizational Framework for Care-Giving

However, it is not enough to know what to do, one must also have room for making it happen. The conditions for the care-giving work are therefore, among other things, also an issue of the work's organization. The two American social researchers Abel & Nelson (1990, the citation here is from Szebehely 1995) point to the fact that a bureaucratic organization is not suited to the work's attention to the individual. A potential contradiction is therefore present between, on the one hand, the routine making, the specialization, and the standardization of the work, where the decision-making is detached from the execution. And on the other, the caregiver's interest in acquiring knowledge about the individual resident and also the caregiver's interest in having the space to make use of this knowledge.

Rossmari Eliasson-Lappalainen and Marta Szebehely (1998) point out that the institutionalized senior care contains a risk of curbing the elderly people's autonomy more than there weakened state justifies. Senior care contains a risk for an unequal power-relationship between caregiver and care receiver, between institution and individual. The sub/superior dimension of the care relation depends on how the professional care is organized and also on what room for influence the elderly has access to (Szebehely 1995).

The sociologist Grete Korremann (1987) demonstrates in a study of domestic aids, how it is possible to counter the potential power imbalance. She shows in her study how the domestic aids, which are exposed to rationalization efforts of their work, protest that they cannot give the same care as previously. In their protests, they argue not only on the basis of considerations to their own work environment, but also on the basis of the needs of the elderly. In doing so, the domestic aids link their own demands to the work to the caregivers' interest in providing good care.

Identification and Distance

Senior care is characterized by being connected to stagnation or regression, as opposed, to for instance, childcare that is connected to development and progress. The receivers of senior care are in the last phase of life, and it can be emotionally demanding for the caregivers to be continuously confronted with the condition in the work (Szebehely 1995). It can trigger an – unconscious – psychological mechanism that makes it attractive to give the practical nursing a higher priority in comparison to the boundless and invisible emotional work (Nicky 1992). Such 'escape manoeuvres' from what is difficult to be confronted with and which there is no time to do thoroughly can be reinforced by limited resources, so that the emotional work is given second priority.

The Employees' Perceptions of Ideal Care

Although professional care gives the employees more room for distance than that which is present in the informal care-giving work in the family sphere, the employees express involvement in the residents and intentions to give good-quality care (Bilfeldt & Hofmeister 2001). Care-giving work as wage labour holds specific identification aspects, because the work is associated with insight in and responsibility for other persons' well being. If the work is going badly, it is not 'just' like in a store, where the customer is treated badly or in the industry, where a damaged product passes the sorting. A bad workday happens at the expense of another person, who is personally dependent on the result.

Two Developmental Tendencies

Kari Wærness (1992) discerns two different cultures in the public care that do not go well together: the housewife culture and the medical bureaucratic culture. While the housewife culture to a great extent, can be called invisible, oppressed and ridiculed, the medical culture has been the dominant one. The high priority given to the medical culture has meant that the users' influence on the content of the help has been downsized in exchange for more professional and bureaucratic standards for what is good work. This has contributed to creating a distance between decision-makers and employees.

Quality and Wellbeing at Four Nursing Homes

The SARA project has evaluated a change experiment at four nursing homes, where work has been done on issues of management, cooperation, wellbeing and worker absenteeism. The reason for the experiment was that frustrations due to high absenteeism and a failed effort to getting it reduced, had accumulated. For this reason, the City of Copenhagen, among others, wanted to initiate change projects that would hold new perspectives to explain the causes of the problem of high absenteeism. The idea behind the change projects was to focus on wellbeing in the working life with the goal of reducing the absence. The basic purpose was to support the organizations that participated in their development of learning processes, in order to be able to tackle conflicts and negotiations, thereby improving the opportunities for managing the development in the organization. It was about reducing negative stress factors in the psychosocial work environment, to bolster the staff's resources and to encourage their well being and health.

The content of the projects varied widely from one nursing home to the next. At one nursing home, quality control in the form of a specific model was introduced. At another nursing home, they also worked with quality control, but did so through discussions among employees regarding daily work routines. At two of the nursing homes, they worked with development of a common professional profile. All four projects aimed at creating a collective framework for increased employee influence on the care-giving work. Through the projects, an attempt was made to heighten the quality of the care and to reduce the feelings of stress and inadequacy for the individual.

The nursing homes participated as trial institutions, with the goal of examining what the job factors are that have significant influence on personnel well being. This well being status was to be used to initiate changes related to personnel and work organization, so that the employees would gain increased access to competence, responsibility, and personal development. In the actual implementation of the project, the four nursing homes had worked with various themes in the interdisciplinary project groups. In addition, the nursing homes had chosen a variety of different tools, methods, and strategies. The different choices were, among other things, due to the nursing homes' different preconditions, for instance in relation to work organization, management forms, and employee involvement.

Nursing Home one: The Quality Control Project 'Resident Evaluation'. One of the two nursing homes that worked with quality control was conventionally hierarchically organized, with much authority given to the department managers and with an extra management level in the form of mid-level managers, placed right under the department managers (first assistants). The top management was concerned with changing the work organization by gradually delegating responsibility. This effort ran into problems in practice, when the management found it hard to delegate and the employees found it hard to take responsibility, because they were used to having the management make the decisions.

This nursing home had problems with well being and cooperative problems, and it had frequent replacement of junior staff as well as at the management level. There was no tradition for discussing the work conditions in a collective setting. The safety committee and the working committee had only been established just prior to the start of the project 'Absence and Presence'.

At this nursing home, it was decided on the basis of the management's wish, to work with the RAI residents' mapping system. The starting point was that the residents' needs had to be mapped, so that the residents could receive the care and nursing, including potential rehabilitation and treatment that he or she needed. RAI is a tool to evaluate residents (Resident Assessment Instrument). The residents met this tool for the first time at an interview with new residents, where a form was filled in with detailed information on the individual resident. On this basis, a yearly evaluation was performed. The department nurse filled in the RAI form (it also involves input from the following professions: physical therapist, physician, and nursing staff). The resident's contact person became involved together with a representative from day, evening, and night shifts, besides the resident's relatives.

By use of this resident classification, the functional level and need for care was mapped, and on the basis of work-time studies, the extent of the needed work-time to the execution of the care, was estimated. This evaluation of the resident's profile and the development of this over time would then form the basis for quality control and development of care plans in the nursing home.

Despite the project group's serious and detailed work, it was not possible in practice to get the RAI system established in this nursing home. There was neither the necessary time, sufficient qualifications in the management and employee group, enough resources for training in the RAI system, nor enough stability in the personnel group because of many dismissals, available for the implementation. No opportunity was available to build and pass on experience and knowledge on how to perform the RAI evaluation, and to transform the results into practice.

There was no real employee debate or reflection, on what RAI would mean in the daily work. Neither was there much interest from the employees on the topic – despite the fact that among the employees, there was great individual interest in providing good care.

The principal and the vice-principal had hoped that the RAI system together with a training system for people with hemiplegia (the so-called Bobath system) could be used as a lever to establish higher quality in the physical nursing. The management had eyed the introduction of norms of quality as a possible shortcut to a productive cooperation on providing good care. But the employees did not associate the RAI system with something that, in practice, would lead to better care or work conditions. They saw it instead, as yet another demand that was made on them, without providing the necessary time. The employees were more occupied with the many cooperative conflicts and the problems that followed the many dismissals, preventing an attentive care, where the individual resident could be cared for.

Nursing Home two: The Quality Control Project 'Daily Work Routines'. The second nursing home was a modern organization, where they had already worked with organizational changes towards increased employee influence and highly decentralized decision-making. At this nursing home, the starting point was a mapping of the work routines. This institution had traditionally focused on discussions of the work conditions. It had developed a well-functioning shop steward system with a working committee and a safety committee, where employee interests versus management interests had become a topic of debate as well as conflict.

In the project 'Absence and Presence' the work organization became a theme in the project 'Daily Work Routines'. The discussion was extended to cover the whole organization – all departments, day-, evening- and nightshifts were all involved in the discussion on work routines and co-operation. 'What are we doing and what can we do differently?', the project group asked the other colleagues in the project that was nicknamed 'Project Time Robbers'.

The management's interest in the project was to save time, in addition to establishing a dialogue and exchange experience across the institution. The employees defined, to a great extent, the task distribution themselves. The project was followed closely and debated broadly among the employees, and it formed the basis for implementing changed forms of cooperation and work routines.

The project was a great success. A very broad group of employees worked across the daily group divisions with 'purging' inappropriate work routines and procedures. New work routines were established on the basis of the knowledge the employees had and on the basis of the new understandings of the cooperation that were gained by discussing the daily routines and workflow, in a collective reflection process. To the management and to the employees, it was beneficial to partake in defining the work, on the basis of an employee-oriented insight in the work.

But to the residents, such efficiency approach can be both positive and negative. It is positive, if the work then allows more time to be utilized for care and nursing – it is negative, if the room for dialogue between residents and employees that must form the basis of the work's organization, becomes restricted.

Discussion: Ambiguities in Quality Control in the two Nursing Homes

Eliasson-Lappalainen (1998) points to the fact that quality control contains a risk that the work becomes overly organized through top-down-control and division of the work, where standardization weighs heavier than does the needs of the individual people. The danger is, as she writes, 'to adjust people to the institution rather than the reverse'. The responsibility is then moved to the individual employee and becomes an issue of how to meet the institution's standardized description of the work.

The organization's formal goal was flexibility in meeting the needs of the individual resident. Nevertheless, it was stated as a rule by the employees themselves that the evening duty should make sure that all residents were in bed at a certain time of night, so that there was time to clean up before the night duty came on. Such a rule had a very strong position in the daily life, and one of the reasons was that the employees themselves have been part of formulating the rule.

The RAI system also contains a danger that the residents' own wishes will be in a weak position in the professional evaluation that is prepared in the RAI form. Quality control contains a positive dimension: that the receiver of the care becomes informed of what care he or she can expect and what care he or she is entitled to, and the employee is likewise clearly informed of the tasks that must be executed. The negative dimension is, however, that there may be a risk of reduced influence for the resident as well as the employee, in particular if the importance of the dialogue between resident/relatives and employee is played down, as a basis for the daily arrangement of the work.

Quality control may ultimately – unintentionally – become a standard that can be used as a defence against demands from residents, relatives and senior organizations, concerning better care. It could be argued that the care described in the norms of quality has already been delivered. Eliasson-Lappalainens and Szebehely studies of senior care in Sweden (1998) show that 'the softer aspects of the care' take second stage to nursing, because the emotional and situation-related aspects are hard to describe in a detailed work plan.

The project 'Daily Work Routines' contained an ambiguity. On the one hand, the important preconditions for good care: employee influence, employee involvement and an effective cooperation, were present. On the other hand, this quality control contained the risk of a detachment from the residents.

'Daily Work Routines' contained an element of Taylorization of the care-giving work, since the work was divided into even more clearly defined partial operations than before. The care-giving work was quality assured by the employee, so that it became clear who should execute what tasks, and also how much time should be spent on each individual task.

A detailed top-down management of the work with division of the work functions gave the caregiver at the end of the chain, limited room for executing the care in a dialogue with the resident. The work was thus performed on the basis of detailed job descriptions, where everyone was expected to behave the same way and be treated as equals. By specializing and standardizing the work, a treatment approach was developed that increased the staff's power over the resident. When the work was planned, either in the group or higher up in the hierarchy, with detailed work approaches, goal statements and precautions, the resident's individual interests and wishes were in a weak position against the institution.

Nursing Home three and four: A Common Prioritization Between Physical Nursing and Social Care

In nursing homes three and four, the focus was placed on the care-giving concept. It was decided to explore the dilemma between the practical and the emotional side of the care-giving work. The employees thus had to become able to handle this dilemma, inside the employee group, as well as in relation to the residents and the relatives.

Nursing Home three was characterized by having a rigid and hierarchical structure with no inter-disciplinary dialogue between the departments before the project started. Here, the issue was that the employees should learn to prioritize between physical nursing and social care. Taking the individual employees' skills to a higher level should reinforce professionalism, so that the person became able to make priorities between visible and invisible care, with respect to the residents' needs. A department manager described this dilemma in the following way:

'I have employees who finished their education as assistant nurses 20 years ago, and they have a completely different set of values regarding what work they are supposed to deliver. They value what is visible, because that is what the employee is judged by. You must preferably move around physically all the time and not sit down, because sitting down equals doing nothing.'

At this nursing home, which at this moment perceived itself as an inter-disciplinary project-workplace, a greater understanding and respect for one another's work had been gained through the project work, and the social care had thereby gained acceptance. The project had initiated a dialogue between different professional groups and departments. An organizational culture had been developed where the employees had gained more influence and where they accepted responsibility for a common workplace. The work groups had made the importance of discussing the different sets of values visible, and the employees had learned to use them to help each other.

A person from the management group said: 'We have learned much about cooperation, how we can help each other, and how important it is that we are honest about the things we do not master.'

Nursing Home four was characterized by having a hierarchical structure with a tradition for good cooperation. This nursing home entered the project because well being problems had arisen such as dissatisfaction and loss of work enjoyment. The problem was recognized to be a perceived conflict between the management and the employees on the content of the care. Many from the employee group thought that the management group neglected the care principle, and that the management group only wanted nursing. The management group thought it was encouraging care giving. It was thus a communication problem where people were talking past each other. The project group was asked to work with making care-giving more acceptable and measurable. They divided it respectively into Care by the Family, that contained the areas that the nursing home expects the relatives to take care of, Personal Care that contained the areas that the resident him or herself is able do, and Care by the Staff. Care by the Staff was again divided into three types of care:

- Planned Care-Giving
- Spontaneous Care-Giving
- Knowledge-Based Care-Giving

The 'Planned Care-Giving' covers everything that is arranged beforehand, for instance shopping trips, bus trips, events in the departments, etc. These are the activities that can be cancelled in case of high personnel absenteeism. When they are nevertheless carried out, it may happen at the expense of the physical nursing. In such situations, the caregiver may have to choose to ignore parts of the care-giving work.

The 'Spontaneous Care' is, for instance, the ability or opportunities to talk with a resident when he or she needs it. Or, when the weather is good, to go for a walk with the residents who want to. In practice, this is difficult because of the resource situation, which is the reason why the employees often cannot perform spontaneous care functions.

The 'Knowledge-Based Care-Giving' is executed on the basis of the personnel's knowledge about the individual resident's habits, such as for example that the resident does not want ice in his juice. The execution of Knowledge-Based Care-Giving presupposes knowledge of the residents' life history and background. It is often acquired with help from the family. In Knowledge-Based Care-Giving, it is emphasized that the practical work is done with an emotional and knowledge-based understanding of the care-receiver's needs.

At this nursing home, project 'Absence and Presence' had meant that care-giving work had become defined, which eradicated the previous conflicting perceptions and communication misses that were present in this area. This had set a new process in motion, where care-giving was put into words, since the things that were involved in the care-giving were now written down, and in this way an attempt was made to try to make this work visible. A department manager expressed it in the following way:

> I think it is important to put words on the care, because it is not measurable. When you then pull it [the description] out one month later, you can see that some things have happened that you have forgotten in a busy day. It is also a tool that makes it possible to give each other advice on what is being done, precisely because we cannot make production measurements. Putting words on the actions, however, requires that it is structured so that time is assigned to do it.

On the basis of the inter-disciplinary project work in the project 'Absence and Presence', these two nursing homes decided to give care-giving a very high priority, even though it might happen at the expense of the physical nursing.

> If a resident needs to hold hands, this may receive higher priority than for instance changing a slightly stained dress. We very much hope that the relatives will understand. We are well aware that care-giving is an invisible element, but it is so much easier to see the stained dress and complain about it (vice principal).

By awarding care a higher priority at the expense of the physical nursing, the intention was to collectivise the choices and the withdrawals that the employees had previously handled alone. The priority of these sets of values could cause many conflicts inside the personnel group as well as in relation to the relatives. An assistant nurse stated the dilemma in the following way:

> Years ago, they had to be scoured and scrubbed every day. But I now have a less rigid view on it and would rather sit and talk with them or go for a walk. I look more at those things today. But that's where we are when we are faced with the relatives, if they come and demand certain things.

In the relationship with the relatives, choice and withdrawal can cause conflicts in making priorities between the visible nursing and the less visible care. The relative can interpret grubby clothes as an indicator of a general lack of nursing and care. But the missing change of the dress can also mean that the caregiver gave high priority to Spontaneous Care for the respective resident or for another resident.

By making a booklet, an initiative for action on consensus processes between players with different interest positions (the residents, the relatives, and the employees) came about. The caregiver was continuously faced with demands on quality. It was therefore of great importance that the institution had a common professional profile that could identify the dilemmas that existed in the daily work, to reduce the stress load. With a common emphasis on the background for why care was given a high priority, the intention was to resist individualization, where the person's own standards of quality and lacking possibility of meeting them, lead to stress. With a clearly defined basis for handling demands to the work, they hoped to facilitate strengthening the relationship between employee and resident/relative.

By differentiating the care concept and distinguishing between Planned, Knowledge, and Spontaneous Care, the intention was to give the employees a common basis on which to arrange their work. An attempt was also made, to extend the employees' room to enable them to work in a flexible and spontaneous manner. While choosing the explicit theme of giving care more importance in relation to nursing, the goal was to make it clear that care of high quality could not just be governed by routines and job descriptions.

Focusing on the contradictions of a theme, does not imply that they are resolved – choosing not to give the residents a bath for an extended period of time in order to provide emotional care, is a contradictory choice. But by creating a common basis for arranging the work, an important step was taken in the direction of collectivizing the responsibility for acceptance of and withdrawal from work tasks.

In these two nursing homes, the project had developed a framework for negotiation and cooperation, where professional knowledge could be exchanged and it was possible to lend support to one another. This reduced prior conflicts that were caused by diverging perceptions and miscommunications in this area.

A Broader Perspective – Better Working Life and Better Care

The project has not only made some of the opportunities, dilemmas and learning processes visible that the work with senior care in a nursing home contains today, it has also shown what preconditions it takes if a project is to both improve the caregivers' working life and the care-receivers' daily life. In the following, we shall suggest some strategic efforts that have the potential to further this goal and thereby be instrumental in securing a general improvement of the work with senior care.

The Necessary Dialogue on Interests in the Care-Giving Work

The involvement of the employees in the work does not necessarily imply that the residents and the caregivers have the same interests. It is important to establish the areas where there is common interest, as well as the areas, where there are conflicts between residents', relatives', and employees' interests.

Focusing on common interests and different interests may create the basis for discussions and testing of different ways to arrange the work, so that the employees' demands on resources and work conditions can currently take place in a dialogue with the elderly, their organizations, and the relatives.

It has importance for the quality of the working life and for the quality of elder care that the organization of the work sets goals for and provides room to develop care that meets the individual person's needs. In order for the work to continue to be meaningful, the residents' needs must have a central place in the organization of the work.

Quality Development Through Differentiation of the Care Concept

Routines and job descriptions cannot be the only tools to organize the work. But since the emotional work is invisible and immeasurable, a risk exists in practice that it will be the physical work that is defined as the real work, when there is a time pressure. Differentiation of the care concept (Planned Care, Spontaneous Care, and Knowledge-Based Care) may be an important step on the way to demonstrate the importance of having access to exercising Spontaneous Care. It may also show the importance of establishing the necessary knowledge on a continuous basis for execution of the Knowledge-Based Care.

With this differentiation, the project managed to emphasize the importance of giving priority to the Spontaneous Care and ensure that its basis in the here-and-now judgement of the individual's needs, is evident. By doing so, the employee is granted support in giving priority to execute the emotional and context determined care – if necessary at the expense of practical nursing. The dilemma between practical and emotional care does not thereby disappear, but the responsibility becomes a collective issue.

Improvement of the Employees' Wellbeing in the Work

The interdisciplinary project cooperation in the project 'Absence and Presence' has helped to ensure that the employees have developed in the direction of taking on increased responsibility and adjustment to changes through learning processes, where testing new forms of cooperation and delegation of the responsibility have been central. The employees claim that the move towards sharing the responsibility has increased the job satisfaction.

But coinciding with this positive message the employees are, in general, experiencing increased feelings of powerlessness and stress in the daily work, because the work pressure has gone up. This means that it has become much more difficult to do what you want to get done. For instance, personnel as well as residents complain that the residents almost never leave the nursing home. There has also been an increase in verbal complaints from relatives, which feels very frustrating for the staff members, who think they do everything they possibly can.

This dilemma has not lessened in recent years and cannot be 'resolved' with a single development project. Some react with burnout and absence and others will therefore have to work harder. In case of sickness, the employees for instance take over other employees' residents, which make withdrawal from the usual nursing functions a necessity. This causes increased stress load:

> We rotate when somebody is ill, we have to because the residents must at least get up and eat. We can skip a bath. That is not a life necessity. I have periods where I feel O.K about it and others where I feel badly. If you work for a long period of time while the place is understaffed, you get tired and feel that you're not doing your job very well. If residents are sitting there with long nails, unshaved, and other ordinary things you'd do, I feel badly about that [nurse assistant].

Learning and Collective Exchange of Experience

The project did not only provide room for a collective exchange of experience and reflection, it also provided access to formal learning, in connection with the handling and execution of the emotionally demanding elements of the elder care work.

But knowledge alone is not enough. It is important that the organization provides room for employee influence on the work's arrangement. The work's organization is pivotal to the care-giving work. There exists a potential contradiction between, on the one hand, setting up routines, specialization, and standardization of the work, where making the decision is separated from the execution. And, on the other, the caregiver's interest in acquiring knowledge about the individual resident and having the possibility of letting this knowledge form the basis of the work's arrangement.

In the four cases, the most significant changes have been the inter-disciplinary project work. In addition to bringing about some concrete changes, the inter-disciplinary project work has meant that the management group has become more unified and more dialogue-oriented. The establishment of transverse project groups with management participation has meant that the employees have developed more contacts across the departments and thereby created a common workplace identity, plus they have developed a belief that you can change things for the better, if you make an effort. It has also created the breeding ground for an understanding of the importance of taking action on an on-going basis, in preserving the well being.

The knowledge that is gained through the projects has resulted in reflection and new insights on the reality that exists in the daily work with elder care. By providing room for action in relation to an open collective dialogue on the forms of cooperation, the projects have contributed to permit that the participants not only have worked with existing experiences, but also have produced new ones. The opportunities for new forms for cooperation have thus been made visible.

Quality and Values in the Development of the Work

The change projects that have been dealt with in this chapter have all been very different, but what they have had in common is that they have aimed at developing the employees' involvement and responsibility in the work. In all the projects, the employees have actively participated in the change projects and they have been highly motivated to contribute to develop quality, environmental considerations and better care. Even under difficult conditions and troublesome work procedures, the employees have tried to meet the standards for quality, environment and good care that they found were meaningful.

Most of the analyzed change projects have been management initiated. In some cases, employee representatives have taken part in planning the change process, as a reaction to problems at the workplace, in the form of threats of cutbacks or high sickness absence. The response to management-initiated projects has differed from workplace to workplace and from employee to employee at the same workplace. Resistance against the change projects build up, if the projects increase the control of the employees, if the work pressure rises significantly, or if the project creates conflicts among the employees.

Conversely, management initiated projects may also become accepted, if they offer an opportunity for the employees to develop the meaning they see in the work – for instance that organic baking methods make it possible to develop the professional baker identity. Or they may become accepted, if they offer an opportunity to build support for issues that the employees have already brought to the management's attention, such as substitution of chemicals in the printing houses, in order to protect the outer environment. Bringing them to attention is also seen to improve work environmental problems that have been in focus prior to the environmental problems.

Internalization, Detachment, and Politicizing as Employee Strategies

The demands of the work, and the possibilities of meeting these demands are central to the employees' well being and to their opportunity for developing meaning in the work. The employees' opportunities to develop a collective understanding of the demands to the work and to develop a personal identity in the work, is a central issue. The more the work is split up physically, organizationally and time-wise (for instance by being executed in shifts), the less the employees' chances of creating a collective room for dialogue between employees regarding quality, care-giving or environmental considerations. The opportunities for development of a collective understanding are central in the daily work, as well as in connection with change projects.

What happens if the employees cannot meet the goals that have been set for the work or if there is a conflict between the employees' perceptions regarding the work's objectives and the demands that are made? On the basis of the case studies, three employee strategies can be identified: internalization, detachment and politicizing. These strategies should not be seen as strategies the employees can freely choose between, but rather as strategies shaped by the work place's traditions and the way that new demands and efforts are introduced. Likewise, there may be differences from workplace to workplace within the same area, or from employee to employee in the same workplace.

Internalization means that the employees internalize the demands and the responsibility, and personally take on the responsibility of meeting the demands – whether it is their own demands or demands that come from the outside. This internalization may result in a greater mental work strain. In particular with respect to nursing and care, it can be difficult to draw the line for what is good enough. Furthermore, if direct or indirect sanctions for not meeting the norms or instructions are in place, the mental work strain is reinforced. This is, for example, the case, if it is possible to receive a bonus when certain demands are met – and it is perceived as difficult to meet the demands with the work speed that is the norm. Or if the employees feel that the relatives of residents in a nursing home do not accept the employees' giving priority to the non-visible care (such as time to go for a walk with the residents) as opposed to the visible care (such as changing a stained dress). The management initiated environmental projects show that the employees, to a great extent, accept the management's strategic considerations (such that for example the employees are not allowed to show up with non-organic goods in a supermarket that bakes organic bread). Or that they find it acceptable if an existing problem (such as high work speed in a printing house) is not put on the agenda, although a change project contributes to increase the problem.

Detachment means that the employees do not accept responsibility for demands that are perceived as enforced from the outside, or for demands that they cannot meet within the framework of the work and the norms for work effort that they find reasonable. Mentally, the employee does not accept responsibility for bad product quality or bad nursing, because it is ascribed to bad or unreasonable conditions. This strategy can be very ambiguous, if one is confronted with the consequences of the bad conditions, because quite a lot of energy is spent on keeping an awareness of the consequences at bay. Repression may also occur, if employees have for instance pointed out quality problems, but do not feel that they themselves can influence the quality of the purchased raw materials and the management does not attempt to solve the problem, despite the call attention to the problem.

Politicizing involves that the issue of the relationship between demands and resources is made an object of negotiations and discussions between management and employees or representatives for the employed. The intention is to create the needed conditions in the form of, for instance, working time, post-graduation courses, and influence on the arrangement and implementation. Depending on the norms at the workplace, or in the branch as a whole, politicizing can lead to demands to reward 'the extra effort' in the form of personal recognition or a different status in the workplace or wage compensation. Depending on the perspective of the politicizing, it may appear as an instrumental attitude to new efforts; or to a new area, by focusing heavily on for instance, wage compensation. Politicizing may also occur, if a change project, after a while, is seen to carry negative consequences (such as when the employees in a food producing company opposed a change project, because they saw that it created divisions among the employees). A certain occurrence may be the straw that breaks the camel's back (as when the employees in the quality committee sense that their competence is undercut by the production manager, when they cannot accept packing a lot of goods with a poorer quality).

As a strategy, internalization and politicizing both call attention to the individual employees' involvement. Individual 'fiery souls' may take on a role that makes the new area an opportunity for individual personal development and they may take on a new role in the company as coordinator, foreman etc. The qualitative demands to the work can thus create meaning in the work that may contain collective as well as individual elements. The opportunity for the employees to develop a collective understanding of their own and other people's expectations to the work, and thereby, develop a collective identity in the work, takes centre stage in the development of meaning in the work.

Quality Through Professionalism and Dialogue

Two management strategies seem to oppose one another in most of this type of change project. An instrumental approach where the norms that apply daily are presented as orders – and not as professionally and ethically justifiable norms that are put under debate in the workplace. Another approach opposes this. Here the employees become enabled through professional skills and dialogue to be involved in defining norms and conditions for making them reality.

The instrumental approach risks running into a rigid form of consensus – with many inherent frustrations, cf. the discussion of internalization, repression, and politicizing. It is important to maintain that there can be ambiguities in balancing the considerations to values such as quality, care, and environment on the one hand, and the consideration to the work conditions more broadly on the other. It is, at the same time, important to maintain that the subjective relations – with internal as well as external players – are important for the employees' participation in the setting of standards for the work.

A potential risk exists that the employees – despite their influence – will feel frustrated, because it is difficult to find the right balance between responsibility, competency, resources, and social support. This frustration and the ambivalence in being involved cannot always be solved at the individual's workplace. The nursing homes' bad economic conditions are the result of a societal downsizing of an area that the individual nursing home cannot resolve on its own. When workers in the graphic industry question the necessity of glazed paper, the individual printing house cannot necessarily solve this problem. The printing house will have to reduce its production or find other production areas. These discussions call for other fora than the individual workplace. And here lies an important task for the labour movement in the future. But it is not a task that the labour movement can handle alone. It is important to establish a dialogue and cooperation with social movements, environmental organizations, users etc. to develop more comprehensively oriented strategies that take quality, care and the environment into consideration, as well as the work conditions.

Chapter 6

Perspectives for the Development of a Working Life Policy

Work is political. This understanding is central to the first five chapters of this book. The development of work not only involves a number of decisive political and social consequences; it is also to a great extent a result of complex political processes. The development of work is not just a predetermined consequence of the global economic and technological development, as often claimed. The economy and the market set a framework for the development of work, but the concrete formation of work is primarily the result of a political process, where many players inside and outside the company have intervened in the development. In Chapters 3, 4, and 5, we have studied this political process at company level. In this concluding chapter, we will discuss the politics of work beyond the boundaries of the company, and we will point out dilemmas and opportunities for an active work policy, carried forward by organizations, institutions, national states, and the international community.

Work policy is here defined as the – official and unofficial – policy pertaining to the future of work, as carried out by public authorities and institutions, by labour unions and business organizations and by the companies (management and employees) themselves. The work policy includes:

- Policies in the companies, pertaining to work and its development.
- Labour market policy, except for income policy and social security.
- The educational policies, relating to qualification and competence development in working life.
- The commercial policies, aiming towards organizational and competency development.
- The technological policies, focusing on working life.

A Hundred Years of Struggle Between Formalization and Humanization

The dominant trend in the 20th Century's development of work and production has been characterized by formalization represented by Taylorism, Fordism, and bureaucracy. An attempt has been made to transform the individual in to a living machine in a company that has effectiveness and resource optimization as its goal.

This development had a major break-through in the beginning of the 20th Century. Since then it has evolved and formed many variants. In the 1990s, the formalization has been carried forward by new management concepts, such as, for example Lean Production and BPR. Even though these new concepts reject previous principles for organization of the work, they are nevertheless fundamentally rooted in Tayloristic philosophy with their praise of the extensively registered and in detail controlled organizations.

Concurrent with the introduction of new technology, the formalization has resulted in an enormous increase in effectiveness and productivity. But it has also had its limitations. The advancing formalization has suppressed the productive potentials that are linked to involvement, loyalty, affinity, understanding, insight, and creativity. The formalization has de-humanized the work, with a number of negative effects on the work force's ability to renew itself. People in formalized jobs are now exposed to a huge risk that their health will deteriorate and also a risk that their qualifications will become obsolete, because their jobs stop them from learning anything new.

All through the century, a counter-movement has therefore been present, where attempts have been made to develop forms of production and organization, where humans and their needs, to a greater extent, could be in focus. This is true for a number of different schools such as the Human Factor approach in the 1920s; the Human Relation approach in the 1930s; the Human Resource and the Socio-Technical approaches in the 1960s; the Cultural Theories in the 1980s; and The Learning Organisation in the 1990s. The Scandinavian Developmental Work is also part of the counter-movement.

In the last decade of the 20th Century, the humanization frontier seems to be making headway. A huge amount of literature has been written on the importance of developing human resources with respect to empowerment, development of competence, commitment, and regarding the involvement of the employees. The main argument is that formalization leads to a lack of flexibility. The unpredictability of the markets and the character of technology necessitates flexibility and thus a humanization of the work.

In particular in a European context, many initiatives have been taken to develop a partnership to humanize the work place – a partnership between state, work, and capital. The European Commission has, in association with EU's employment policy, in a number of documents expressed the strategic importance of such a partnership in Europe's competition with USA and South East Asia (Wobbe 1992, European Commission 1997 and 2001).

There are limits, however, as to what international institutions can do for implementation of an active work policy. The EU's role in this area is limited to general political formulations, and the spread of information, affecting attitudes etc. The work policy must necessarily be locally and nationally anchored, because the institutions through which it can function are local and national. But the work policy may gain international support by the spread of ideas and experiences.

Employee Participation as the Common Good?

At the root of the partnership to humanize work, we find a perception that if the process is properly organized, the management and employees as well as society at large, can benefit from developing the human resources. The company may gain flexibility and the employees may gain a better work environment and greater job security. Society may achieve more growth and lower social costs:

- Humanization of work makes economic sense for the companies.
- Humanization of work gives the employees a better working life.
- Humanization of work reduces exclusion, increases the work force and reduces society's costs of public assistance.
- Humanization of work supports fundamental values in modern society: the free play of the individual with responsibility towards other people, influence and democratization, also in the realm of work, master of one's own life.

These ideas are broadly accepted, but in practice they often turn out to be difficult to implement. The opportunity to implement the ideas differs widely from trade to trade and despite the many good intentions, the flexible organization that emphasizes the development of the human resources, is far from extended to all parts of economic life (EPOC 1997).

Difficulties in Involving the Employees

Employee involvement and employee development does not just happen. The case studies in the previous chapters show how difficult it can be to implement the employee-based development of work. Indeed, there are several good reasons why success (despite the favorable conditions in Denmark) is so far relatively limited.

- The ownership may be a decisive hindrance for employee involvement, because the owners may think that they lose control of their property if they let go of control over production and work, even when this control runs contrary to humanistic principles for development of the work. In private companies, globalization with international ownership has been a crucial hindrance when important decisions for development of the work are made far away from the employees. An example from the case studies is the descision of the owners to relocate the Fresh Food Terminal to a different part of the country in the middle of the development project. In this context, it has crucial importance with respect to how long-term the owner's planning is. While there are clear indications that a long-term profit can be maintained or strengthened with a high degree of employee involvement, this is far from always the case when short-term more immediate profits are the goal. In public enterprises there is also a strong owner interest, where politicians set clear limits to the development of the employee influence.
- Many new ideas and concepts are still marketed and spread that are formalistic in nature. They do contain aspects on humanization of work, as shown in Chapter 3, but in the practical transformation from concept to concrete work, these opportunities are rarely explored. And they are often tempting for the management because they promise a fast pay off even though more systematic measurements of the outcome are much less convincing.
- Although there is goodwill, the implementation of employee inclusion is neither easy for the employees nor for the managers, as shown in Chapter 4. The difficulties for managers, as well as employees, can be that they have

> been trained to do something else. Change creates insecurity. The employees may feel that new work environmental strains arise. The community is threatened. For the management, it is also a problem that it must let go of control which may seem additionally threatening.

Fundamental changes must take place in the relations between management and employees in order to be successful in creating a high degree of employee involvement. The employee is not just a purchased commodity which the employer can access in the period paid for. The employee becomes a subject who is equally concerned about what is produced and how it is produced. The results from the SARA project show that the meaning of work, the quality, and the utility of the production involved, seem to have much more impact on health and welfare than previously assumed (cf. Chapter 2). It therefore becomes more natural for the employees to get involved in the development of production and service output, both in terms of quality and environmental development.

The interest in the work's result also implies that the employees, to a greater extent, carry the societal interest and consideration into the company, as described in Chapter 5. Our studies in these areas indicate that employee involvement makes fundamentally new relations possible among employees, employers and society, where industrial relations in the companies are related to societal environmental conditions, usefulness and social responsibility. Completely new relations between work and other societal domains have thus been created. Agendas that were previously outside the sphere of working life are introduced in working life, and the wage earners' acting in working life interacts with broader political issues in society, as intended in the strategy of the Developmental Work.

This development is not for free. The employee involvement may also lead to increased pressure on those same employees. The employees are made responsible for effectiveness and quality of their work, in conditions with little time and few resources. It is the employee who is responsible for making the right decision and who personally has to carry the consequences of the decision. This may be experienced as a heavy burden. High levels of control makes it possible to handle more strains, and if the employees feel that they can master the situation, it compensates for some of the pressure that the company, as well as the employee, is exposed to. However many people are rarely in this positive situation. To some employees, the increased responsibility is only experienced as a pressure with no significant positive opportunities involved. To those people, the result is increased mental and physical attrition, succeeded by the risk of exclusion from the labour market.

Goal-oriented and qualified work that runs parallel with employee involvement, competence development and environmental improvement can greatly prevent these problems; nevertheless, the problems can explode when an effort is put into organizational development without a conscious awareness of the problem in its entirety.

The positive interplay between development of the human resources, improved work environment, reduced exclusion, and greater productivity does not come by itself. It requires an active work policy based on an understanding of the dilemmas and opportunities involved in this interplay.

An Active Work Policy

The company is the central arena for the work policy's development. The way the company develops its work policy is most often rooted in the past and influenced by the culture, the traditions and well-established personal relations. To change the fundamental values that the work policy is based on is often more difficult than changing the entire production apparatus. But even if most companies are characterized by strong values and traditions, the work political initiatives and their effects are overwhelmingly unpredictable. Just think of the the sausage factory which skipped the whole change project and returned to the original situation, and the production company Olsen which tried several times without any success to implement BPR. Most companies start projects with regular intervals that aim at changing the nature of the work. Most often, these projects, however, become something quite different from the original intention. This may be due to the fact that the company's work policy is based on many concurrent political constellations that interact in an unpredictable pattern (cf. Chapter 3). In addition, the unpredictability is caused by the fact that the work policy is very often influenced in quite unpredictable ways by external conditions. Suddenly there is growth in one production area and negative growth rates in another area; the manager is replaced; the company is bought by another; part of the production is outsourced; environmental demands require total restructuring; a strike knocks down the established order, etc. This unpredictability means that 'the good case' where a special effort has been made to involve the employees in development and improvement of the work environment rarely can be maintained as a 'good case' in the long run. Nonetheless, any experience (good as well as bad) can influence the work policy of the future, inside and outside the individual workplace. The experiences will spread through the people, who are involved in the particular case.

The work policy, that looks coincidental and chaotic at the individual workplace, may be influenced in a certain direction by institutions outside the company. In the following, we shall point to seven political factors that can induce the companies to establish a development of the human resources which improves the work environment and reduces the exclusion of employees. None of these initiatives have much effect on their own. But together, supporting one another, they can make a difference.

The Danish experience demonstrates first and foremost that a work policy with a broad break-through in society and in the companies must be developed over many years. It takes a long time before the various actors not only see the opportunities in such a policy but also learn how to actively use the policy. The employers must dare to pass a significant amount of power and influence on to the employees, and the employees must feel convinced that the offer to share influence is for real and will offer them new positive opportunities. There is no single solution as to how one overcomes these barriers. The companies are very different and the solution may come from many places. A constructive work policy must thus be based on a multiplicity of activities that together create a profusion of possibilities at company level.

In Denmark, the following seven instruments have been focal points for the work policy area over the past 10 years:

1. Campaign and Attention
   Trade journals and unions, business organizations, public authorities, and other agents may have the possibility of creating attention to employee inclusion and the work environment through campaign activities. This attention may very well result in companies adopting new words and concepts. In Denmark, 'psychosocial work environment', 'appraisal interview', 'social responsibility', and 'competence development' are examples of this happening over the past 10 years. Often, the new concepts are adopted, but the new concepts do not by themselves create big changes. In some cases, a new name has been given to activities that have been carried out all along, although not much new happens in practice. What was previously called 'post-education' is now called 'competence development'. In other cases, the campaign gives rise to new activities, but they are carefully placed on a sidetrack, so that they do not have any significant influence on the company. This may be the case, when 'the psychosocial work environment' is placed in a safety organization that gets no managerial attention. Campaigns may nevertheless be useful, as long as they do not stand by themselves.

2. Rewarding Companies that Act
   To put more force behind a campaign, the state or the parties of the labour market may earmark certain funds to be spent on rewarding companies that make a special effort. Over the past 10 years a great many allocations of funds and subsidies have been established in Denmark with the goal of promoting employee involvement, employee development, competence development, and work environment in the companies (Hvid 2001). A campaign is more successful when it is linked to economic funds. A possibility exists, however, that the companies through such arrangements apply for and obtain a subsidy for activities that they would have undertaken anyway, but which they would just have given a different name if they had financed the activity themselves. The evaluations that have been made of such subsidies seem to show that there is an element of 'The Emperor's New Clothes' in such activities, but that the subsidies also do contribute to real changes. The layer of consultants, counselors, and educators plays a significant role.

3. Support in Terms of Training, Consulting Assistance, and Similar
   When companies are to do things differently and break with the status quo, it is often necessary to get inspiration, counseling, and assistance from the outside. Most commercial consultants have only the top management as the addressee of their activities. The top management is typically involved in recruiting the consultants, and the consultants must be able see things from the same perspective as that of the top management in order to do their work (Hagedorn-Rasmussen 2000). Of course, this does not mean that work environment and employee involvement tends to just be seen as a means to the company's development in direct correspondence with the perspective of the top management. However, there are also consultants that to some extent use the employees and the mid-level managers as an entrance to the company. Here the consultants are primarily anchored in state legislature, collaboration between

the labour market's parties, and collective bargaining. Over the past 10 years, this type of consultant has grown strongly in Denmark. This employee-oriented type of consultant is, among others, to be found in the occupational health service. This service has grown over the past decade and it performs increasingly more consulting tasks that are linked to organizational development and work environment (Limborg 2001a). This is also true for the public and semi-public institutions that offer post-graduate training to the companies. They play an active role in the companies' personnel policy regarding competence development and by establishing a link between employee development and organizational redesign. The labour movement has made an attempt to contribute to the development of organisation and work in the companies, by developing employee-involving tools that can be used in this context. Finally, a number of private consulting firms have been established that get access to the companies, primarily by winning the trust of the employees. The labour movement owns some of these consulting firms.

This layer of consultants and educational institutions who make their way on an employee and working life perspective in their activities, has played a big role in the formation of the concrete work policy in Denmark over the past 10 years.

4. Political Involvement on the Part of the Labour Market's Parties
Involvement on the part of the labour market's parties in an employee involving and work environment-oriented development is extremely important, because the parties can create legitimization and support for such a policy in the companies and create the political platform for the state to get involved in the development. The parties have been supportive of this policy through their many political statements. The labour movement has made an attempt to assist the development by changing the shop steward training courses, so that the shop stewards become qualified to partake in change processes in the companies, and the professional organizations have developed a number of instruments that can be used in this context. The employer's organizations have approached the case differently. Here the promotion of 'The Learning Organization' has been a pivotal initiative. Together, the parties have contributed to breaking down the barriers for employee involvement and flexibility by carrying out an 'organised decentralization' (Hyman & Ferner 1995 and Crouch & Traxler 1998). More opportunity is given here for the companies themselves to arrange salary and work conditions in accordance with the special conditions, while respecting centrally negotiated framework agreements. An example of a joint activity by the labour unions and the employers association has been the action plan against repetitive work. The goal was to reduce hazardous repetitive work by 50% over a seven-year period. Although the goal was not completely fulfilled the plan resulted in consirable reduction of this type of strongly Taylorized work among unskilled workers (Hasle & Møller 2001).

5. Legislative Requirements to the Quality of Working Life
   Making opportunities available is not enough to get companies to orient themselves towards employee involvement and work environment. For most companies it takes more to change them. Legislation may therefore be a necessary and useful means to create change. It may be legislation that sets threshold limit values for the work environment in the company and that regulates working hours, dismissal notifications etc., (material rules). It may be legislation that imposes activities to improvement of the quality of working life on the companies such as establishment of a mandatory safety committee (procedure-oriented rules). And finally, it may be legislature that holds the companies responsible for the costs in case the quality of working life is poor, for instance in the form of costs related to sickness, dismissals etc., (dues). Almost all national States have rules in these areas. A legislative example can illustrate the Danish approach which is aimed at the companies' own attempt to improve their work environment and with a strong degree of employee participation. Based on the EU framework directive 89/391 (EEC 1989) Denmark has issued mandatory requirements for all companies to carry out a work place assessment of the risks in the workplace. The companies are free to select the workplace assessment method, but it is required to involve the employees and to complete the circle from identification over preparation of action plan to implementation of pre-ventive measures (Jensen 2002).

6. Development of Rights at Company Level
   Employee involvement and work environmental development of the company takes goodwill on the part of the management as well as the employees. But goodwill is rarely enough. In order to maintain the work environment perspectives, formal employee rights are pivotal. This is true for salary and employment conditions, for the right to know, and for participation and co-determination. In most European countries, there have not been any major improvements in the employees' rights to share influence since the middle of the 1970s (Knudsen 1995), and there are no immediate signs of a break-through in this area. There are, nevertheless, still huge opportunities for better utilization of the formal channels that the employees already have access to. In this sense, the labour unions play a major role.

7. Relating the Work Policy to Societal Policy – to Social Policy, Environmental Policy and Industrial Policy
   Work policy is increasingly being related to other policy areas. Social policy is oriented towards workfare – putting people to work must solve the social problems. This makes demands on inclusion of the labour force and social responsibility of the companies. A link has been created between work policy and environmental policy, because the environmental policy is increasingly getting involved in organizational and technological development and environmental learning in this connection. The industrial policy has abandoned the general subsidies and has instead emphasized stimulating the companies in their development. Innovation, competence development, creation of networks, and consulting assistance become central elements in the industrial policy,

which also comes in close contact with the work policy. The work policy can therefore gain strength and support in the social, the environmental, as well as the industrial policy areas. By formulating a policy for the sustainable work, (Hans Böckler Stiftung 2001, LO 2001a, Lund 2001, Lund 2002) a connection is created between employee involvement, work environment, social responsibility, environmental improvements, and productivity development.

The Role of the Players

The labour movement is a central player in the development of work policy. The Danish labour movement has, over the past decade, gradually shifted its focus on the market relationship between employee and employer towards focusing on work and its development. The strategy of Developmental Work has been an important part of this. While salary and working hours still play an important role in labour union policy, the agreements in this area have, to a great extent, become decentralized. The labour unions have increased their resources to improve the work environment, competence development, and mobilizing the members to participate in change and development. At workplace level, the shop stewards have increasingly been included in the managers' circle by involvement in discussion of the strategic development of the company. The solidaristic wage policy has gradually been given a lower priority to the benefit of a solidaristic work policy, where the goal is that everyone must be given developmental opportunities and therefore also the opportunity to maintain salary and employment.

So far, the labour movement seems to have difficulties recreating the same break-through in the workplaces for the trade union-based solidaristic work policy as happened for the solidaristic wage policy 50 years earlier. The solidaristic policy was a cornerstone in the post war development of the Scandinatian welfare societies (Mahon 1991), first of all launched by the two Swedish economists Rehn and Meiner (Silverman 1998). The idea in the solidaristic wage policy was that the stronger groups at the labour market should use part of their strength to raise the wages of the weaker groups. That would create a structural rationalization where low productive companies and sectors would collapse because of high wages. An active labour market policy and a Keynes inspired macro economic policy should secure new more productive jobs to those who would lose there jobs in the low productive sector. In the solidaristic wage policy, there was a direct connection between the centrally negotiated collective agreements and the local defense for meeting the agreements. And conversely, the good negotiation results at the local level could give leverage to new and improved collective agreements at the central level. An equally strong link between the central and the local level is not established at work policy level. The core part of the labour movement is strongly into work political issues, but the effort is very much addressed upwards and towards the outside; it is only slightly addressed downwards. The key union officers are involved in a myriad of councils, committees, and boards. They are part of the state policy in this area. They develop campaign material and create educational curricula. The local trade unions have so far only to a limited extent incorporated work policy issues into their agenda. When the employees in companies that have carried out Developmental Work projects are asked about union involvement, they most often say that the trade unions have not played any significant role – even though Developmental Work at its starting point was trade union policy. In many cases, not even the local shop steward has been a central player in the process. If the strong ties between employees in the companies, the local trade unions, and the central trade union associations are to be maintained, the union based work policy must be developed, so that it becomes relevant at all levels, and so that the activities at every level are interconnected.

Even though the labour union policy needs a major development, it is also obvious that the trade unions are in no way in a crisis in Denmark. The degree of unionization has been held at a high level – about 80% of the wage earners – and the part of the labour market that is covered by collective agreements has increased over this period. This has happened at a time when the service economy has been growing and the employment rate has gone up. The renewal of the union policy that has occurred, with more focus placed on the quality of the work, must be considered very conducive to this success.

The State is, of course, also an important motivating power for the development of a work policy, and the chances are good that the State becomes a stronger part in this development. The decline of the national economies as a result of internationalization and globalization weakens the state's macro-economic instruments and renders planned economical initiatives impossible. This makes human resource based strategies for development of competitiveness much more topical. The Nation cannot succeed just by employing smart macro-economic initiatives. It must arm itself with a work force of highly qualified and specific competencies and great innovative abilities. Social and labour market policy can be tied to it – social problems must be solved through employment. The educational policy is made more business-oriented. Even the cultural policy is transformed to become a motor for the innovative abilities of economic life (cf. Chapter 1).

What we see here is clearly a market orientation of state policy areas that previously were outside the market and, to a certain extent, were in opposition to the market. The humanistically centered state policies are developing towards a commodity for the market. But at the same time, the possibility exists that a humanization of the market will take place, because expectations that the market and the companies will act humanely are introduced, with the integration of the humane policies into the market place. However, this does not take place by itself. It presupposes a political pressure – from labour unions, environmental organizations and grass root organizations, among others. There are many examples to show that companies adopt social and environmental goals that go beyond their immediate market interests. The danger is great, however, that the companies will not 'walk the walk'. It is therefore both important and necessary that the humanization of the market is not left to the companies alone, but is supplemented with legal requirements – requirements concerning the environment and to the work environment; requirements as to learning and development; requirements on integration etc.

The employers' associations do not, at the formal level play a big role in the development of the work policy. The employers' associations tend to work as a wheelbarrow on these issues – they move as far as they are being pushed. This is very much caused by the fact that they function as the common denominator for all the employers and therefore oppose any restriction of the employers' right to command. This does not imply that the employer side does not play an active role in the development of the work policy. On the contrary, many new work political departures have happened after employer initiatives have been taken at the individual company. A company converts its organization to a 'spaghetti organization', where the employees 'own' the work organization to an extent never seen before. Another company creates a work environmental organization that is closely linked to the operation and that is anchored in the top management, but with inclusion of employee representatives. A number of companies use 'forum theater', as a means to create new open and responsible forms of dialogue in the companies. Here we see three new departures that have given content to the three core concepts in Developmental Work: the employee-owned work organization, the multi-dimensional interest protection, and the supremacy-free dialogue. Experiences from such new departures spread in the network of business leaders that the employers' associations and trade organizations encompass. These networks are therefore important elements in the development of a work policy.

Finally, more general developmental features play an important role for the work policy's development. In a Danish context, one can certainly call two important issues to attention: The development of attitudes and values in the population and development of the supply/demand relationship in the labour market.

The Western World at large is undergoing a shift of values, where more emphasis is placed on individual development, individual attitude, individual arrangement of one's own life (Inglehart 1997). This individualization is not just tied to individual gain, but also to individual attitudes towards ethical and social issues. It has, therefore, in a Danish context been possible to establish a connection between demands of individual development, demands of basic social rights, and ethically founded demands to the local and global development. This value-based development may interact well with a work policy that intends to make developmental opportunities accessible to all and that is based on an active attitude towards what is being produced and how.

It is easy to keep the work policy on the agenda when the economy is doing well. Over the last 10 years where the work policy has gained ground in Denmark, the employment rate has gone up and unemployment has declined. This makes it easier for the individual as well as society to say 'no thanks' to the most miserable jobs.

An Active Work Policy – Does it Work?

Have the many work-political institutions and initiatives any effect on the ordinary day at the ordinary workplace? And if so, what? This is a very crucial question, which is, however, also very difficult to answer.

One may find a clue in the study 'Work Environment in Denmark' (AMI 2002) which compares three comprehensive surveys of the Danes' work environment carried out over a period of 10 years: In 1990, 1995, and 2000. The study seems to show that significant improvements towards a Developmental Work has taken place in the course of this 10–year period. A few results can illustrate the development.

The share of wage earners claiming that they 'lack the possibility of arranging their own work' has fallen from 17% to 13%. The share of wage earners 'missing information on the work' has declined from 17% to 10%. The share 'lacking the possibility of speaking with work colleagues during the work' has declined from 21% to 17%. The share 'feeling great job insecurity' has declined from 26% to 16%. But these developments also have a price. The same data shows that the work has been much more demanding in the period. 42% of the respondents stated in 1990 that the work demands their attention at all times. In 2000, this share had gone up to 61%.

These survey data are the best accessible data regarding the development in work in general. They must however be subject to certain reservations, for two reasons: the data cover very different sectors and industries and may therefore cover very different developments and possibly shifts in sectors. The other problem regarding this type of data is that it is not the actual work conditions but the wage earners' estimate of the work conditions that are being measured. These estimates depend on attitudes, values, and expectations that may very well change over a 10–year period.

Case studies seem, however, to a great extent to confirm the results of the survey studies. The Danish Ministry of Labour supported in the period 1996 to 2000, 228 companies in their attempt to generate a development of work and organization that would give the employees more autonomy, influence, and a better work environment, as well as give the companies a higher income. A research team followed the many company projects. In 2001, the team concluded that the attempt to create developmental projects that gave more autonomy, better work environment, and higher income opportunities, had been highly successful. The success was greatest where the employee influence had been greatest. Most workers perceived that the workload had increased with the development of the work.

The SARA project's case studies show similar results. SARA has studied ten companies who have tried to implement Developmental Work, and who have been intensively monitored for a number of years. Here, we shall briefly make a broad outline of the conclusions. The reality is significantly more complex than this description can convey. In Chapter 4, a more detailed analysis of the companies' experience with Developmental Work was presented.

- A change has taken place in the role of ordinary wage earners as producers. He or she must to a higher degree than before, use his or her experiences, and plan and make decisions. It is necessary to have cooperative skills, to independently distribute tasks in the work group, and to be aware of what the purpose of one's work is, as viewed from the point of view of the customer or the client.
- The employees are made accountable. The employees gain more knowledge and understanding of their own effort in relation to customers or clients. Customer contact and greater knowledge of quality and care render meaning to the work and become motivating factors for development and improvements.
- The employees are active in shaping ideas and plans for new ways of working together. Development and change are, to a great extent, based on the employees' experience, and thus it is a bottom-up process.

- Many of the change processes have broken with the basic idea of Taylorism: that the worker is a weak-minded and dependent instrument, in the daily work as well as in changes of the work.
- Developmental Work change processes are difficult and contradictory. However, in most cases, completing the implementation process has been successful. The cases where cooperation worked well are also the case, where the results have been most satisfactory.
- This does not mean that the successful implementation processes have taken place without any conflicts. On the contrary, there has been an understanding that mutual recognition of opposing interests and the recognition of mutual interest form the cornerstone of cooperation and for development of the work.
- One may notice that in connection with the implementation processes, a change in culture and values in the companies has taken place. A change in values and attitudes related to the work has happened in continuation of the development towards accountability and autonomy. The work is, to an increasing degree, viewed as valuable in and of itself and the employees feel to a greater extent loyal to 'their company'.
- The old wage-earner culture with its division of 'us' (the workers) and 'them' (the managers) has, along with the many norms for behaviour aimed at drawing a boundary between employees and managers, been broken down. There is clear indication that the local solidarity among the employees has been maintained, while the relations to the company and managers have been 'softened'. Customers and clients have moved closer to the workers.
- We consider that the independent and accountable producer role represent a significant improvement of the employees' working life and their power status in the company and in the labour market, but Developmental Work does not automatically bring about better health and an improved work environment. To achieve this, an active effort to improve the work environment is needed.

However, There Are Also Risks

The development of flexibility and the development of the human resources in work carry along a risk of exclusion. A study of exclusion risks for unskilled workers has shown examples of how work organizational and management changes can lead to dismissals, for instance of older employees, who do not want to participate in self-managing groups (Danish Technological Institute 1998).

Another study has focused directly on the risk for exclusion and polarization in connection with development of the work, and it has distinguished between change processes with Developmental Work elements on the one hand, and change processes unilaterally run by management, on the other. The study has confirmed that the development of the human resources is associated with exclusion and increased polarization of the employees. The study has, however, also shown that if the companies utilize principles corresponding to the Developmental Work, the risk of exclusion and polarization is considerably reduced (Danish Technological Institute 1998).

Developmental Work may contribute to solving work environmental problems, related to the Tayloristic production philosophy, but Developmental Work also involves work environmental hazards: limitless work, work without adequate competency, constant demands to be flexible, and problems in collegiate cooperation. We are only vaguely beginning to discern these problems, and it will probably be a while, before they will appear more clearly.

Developmental Work has not functioned optimally as a political strategy. Creating a visible link between the Developmental Work activities in the companies and Developmental Work as an overall strategy for the labour movement has not been successful, although the Danish TUC has spent many resources on developing an impressive range of campaigns, materials, and courses (LO 2001).

Finally, we must conclude that the broad vision of the Developmental Work strategy has not been implemented. We have not found examples of Developmental Work projects that include societal considerations, as an integrated part of the work and thus exemplify an extended company democracy.

So even though it is a difficult task to determine precisely how a Developmental Work-oriented policy actually works, there is hardly any doubt that it makes a difference.

The Danish Experience in an International context

The Danish experience with work policy has similarities with the other Scandinavian countries, but it may be quite different from the situation in most other industrialized countries. The high degree of unionization; collective agreements (supported by legislation) as the dominating regulation of the labour market; a relatively high employee influence secured by both agreements and legislation; and a general expectation from both management and employees of participation as an element of all aspects of work are conditions not easily found outside Scandinavia.

Can the Danish experience be used then? We strongly believe that it can. Most industrialized countries are facing shortage of labour in the near future, companies are realizing that the human factor is the crucial point for further development, and unions strive to define a new platform after years of declining membership. These challenges must, from our point of view, open the interest for the Danish case. Not as a copycat experience, but as an inspiration for the development of national work policies fitted to the specific context in each country. The European Union is already pointing in this direction. The Luxembourg process for development of a European employment policy is very much focussed on adapting modern work organizations to human needs and thereby creating a competitive edge.

The Danish case also tells, however, that a work policy based on the employees is not developed and realized through nice words. It is a long time development which is often tedious and contradictory, but it could be one of the most valuable experiences from Denmark, that employee based development is something to abandon when the first problems pop up. This is important for the development in the companies as well as the more general political development in the society.

Developmental Work Policy in a New Political Situation

Like most of Europe, Denmark has been dominated by center-left governments in the 1990s – the period where Developmental Work has had an impact on Denmark and where a number of similar European initiatives have been taken. Now it seems, however, as if the political climate is changing. A new protest-oriented conservative wave is building. A wave that may well lend support to forces that to a higher degree, want de-regulation and a freer market.

This, however, does not render the Developmental Work policy less interesting or important for the following reasons:

- Because such a policy may be said to hold the answer to some of the problems that have given rise to the conservative wave.
- Because a continued insistence on influencing the work's content will make it possible to maintain and strengthen the legitimacy of the labour movement and the labour market institutions.
- Because there are forces presently at work in the business community that make it possible to create alliances between Developmental Work policy and parts of business.

There are many explanations for the new protest-oriented conservative wave. Among several plausible explanations, one is that the people who support the new far right are those who have not gained access to the new globally oriented 'Knowledge Economy'. They feel pushed aside and insecure – with good reason, because they are the group that runs the highest risk of becoming marginalized and excluded from the labour market. This group really needs a Developmental Work-oriented work policy that can create a safe platform for a gradual transition from traditional jobs towards more development-oriented jobs. This presupposes, however, that the work policy is not presented as an elite strategy with references to the most modern global companies, but takes its starting point in ordinary work places with ordinary people.

The labour movement and many of the established labour market institutions are often presented as pre-historic dinosaurs that are kept artificially alive in a world where there is no need for them whatsoever. Many research results show, however, that the new flexible work contains a long range of social risks that justifies trade union influence. The legitimacy of this view gains support when it can be demonstrated that organized employee influence has a positive effect, not just on the work conditions, but also on the companies' business opportunities. This has already been shown in a number of concrete cases, but the message has not yet reached all places.

In the business world, a wave is rising that may become as wide-spread as the Quality Wave became in the 1980s. The wave is called Sustainability or Social Responsibility. The fact that the companies' long-term developmental interests are best secured through a high degree of environmental and social responsibility is emphasized here. The fact that maintaining a good relation to shareholders holds a decisive strategic advantage for the company, and that the company succeeds better by building partnerships with institutions and NGOs outside the company is also given high priority. Here, the institutions and organizations promoting Developmental Work-oriented work policy can offer partnership in a sustainable business development.

There are therefore good opportunities to maintain and develop the recent decades' work of political involvement. The challenge is to make it more popular and, at the same time, make it more business-oriented. The perspective is to humanize and democratize economic life.

Bibliography

Abel, E. & Nelson, M. (1990), 'Circles of Care: An Introductory Essay', in Abel & Nelson (eds.), *Circles of Care, Work and Identity in Women's Lives*, State University of New York Press.

Abrahamson, E. (1996), 'Management Fashion', *Academy of Management Review* **21**(1), pp. 254–85.

Agersnap, F. (1973), *Samarbejdsforsøg i jernindustrien*, Business School of Copenhagen.

AMI (2002), '*Arbejdsmiljø i Danmark*', The Danish Institute of Occupational Health, Copenhagen.

Appelbaum E. et al. (2000), '*Manufacturing Advantage: Why High–Performance Work Systems Pay Off*', ILR Press.

Arbejdsmarkedsstyrelsen (2001a), '*Evaluering af puljen til fremme af et bedre arbejdsliv og øget vækst. Hovedrapport*', Copenhagen, Denmark.

Arbejdsmarkedsstyrelsen (2001b), '*Evaluering af puljen til fremme af bedre arbejdsliv og øget vækst: Delrapport 2: Resultater af projekternes selvevalueringer*', Arbejdsmarkedsstyrelsen, Copenhagen.

Arbejdstilsynet (2000), '*AT–vejledning: Kortlægning af psykisk arbejdsmiljø*', Arbejdstilsynet, Copenhagen.

Atkinson, J. (1984), 'Manpower Strategies for Flexible Organizations', *Personnel Management*, August 1984.

Bailey, D.E. & Adiga, S. (1997), 'Measuring Manufacturing Work Group Autonomy', *IEEE Transactions on Semiconductor Manufacturing*, **2**.

Bauman, Z. (1998), *Globalization – The Human Consequences*, Polity Press, Cambridge.

Benders, J. & van Bijsterveld, M. (2000), 'Leaning on Lean; The Reception of a Management Fashion in Germany', *New Technology, Work and Employment*, **15** (1), pp. 50–64.

Berggren, C. (1993), *The Volvo Experience: Alternatives to Lean Production in the Swedish Auto Industry*, MacMillan.

Bilfeldt, A. (2000), 'Struktureret familieliv og engagement i arbejdet – Kvinder i industriens monotone arbejde', in: Bjerring, B. (ed.), *Hvor går grænsen*, Samfundslitteratur, pp. 198–218.

Bilfeldt, A. & Hofmeister, E. (2001), '*Evaluering af Projekt Fravær og Nærvær*', Roskilde Universitetscenter, Tek.Sam Forlaget, Denmark.

Björkman, T. & Lundqvist K. (1981), *Från MAX till PIA – reformstrategier inom arbetsmiljöområdet*, Arkiv Avhandlingsserie 12, Malmø.

Borg, W. & Burr, H. (2002), *Psykosocialt Arbejdsmiljø, Arbejdsmiljø i Danmark 2000*, Arbejdsmiljøinstituttet, Copenhagen.

British Standard (1999), '*Occupational Health and Safety Management Systems*'.

Brod, C. (1984), '*Technostress – The Human Cost of the Computer Revolution*', Addison–Wesley Publishing Company, Reading, Massachusetts.

Brulin, G. (1989), 'Från den svenska modellen til företagskorporatism? Facket och den nya företagsledningsstrategin', *Arkiv avhandlingsserie* **31**, Lund, Sweden.

Buhl, H. (2000), '*Hvor vildt kan det blive*?', DTU, ITS.

Buhl, H., Hansen, H. and Koch, C. (2001), '*Nye styrings– og forandringsværktøjer i industrien*', Roskilde Højskole.

Bullinger, H.–J. (2000), 'The Changing World of Work: Prospects and Challenges for Health and Safety', In *The Changing World of Work – Magazine of the European Agency for Safety and Health at Work*, Luxembourg.

Burke, G. & Peppard, J. (eds.) (1995), '*Examining Business Process Re–engineering*', London, Kogan Page.

Børsting, H. & Bruvik–Hansen, A. (1999), 'Uddannelse og Udvikling', in Clematide, B. and Lassen, M., *Virksomheden og Det Udviklende Arbejde – et kritisk blik*, Samfundslitteratur, Copenhagen, Denmark.

Callon M. (1987), 'Society in the Making: The Study of Technology, as a Tool for Sociological Analysis', in Bijker, W. et al., '*The Social Construction of Technological Systems*', Cambridge, MIT Press.

Callon, M. (1991), 'Techno Economic Networks and Irreversibility', in Law J. (ed.), '*A Sociology of Monsters: Essays on Power, Technology and Domination*', London, Routledge.

Casey, C. (1995), 'Work, Self and Society – after Industrialism', Routledge, London & New York.

Champy, J. (1995), '*Re–engineering Management. The Mandate for New Leadership*', London, Harper Collins.

Champy, J. & Hammer, M. (1993), *Reengineering the Corporation. A Manifesto for Business Revolution*, Harper Collins, New York.

Champy, J. & Hammer, M. (1994), '*Omstrukturering af virksomheden*', Borgen, København.

Christensen P. (1998), '*Medarbejderdeltagelse – en ressource ved miljøstyring*', LO, Denmark.

Christensen P., Holm. E. and Remmen, A. (1997), '*Miljøstyring og miljørevision i danske virksomheder*', Miljøstyrelsen.

Christensen, S. & Westenholz, A. (1997), 'The Social/Behavioral Construction of Employees as Strategic Actors on Company Boards of directors', *American Behavioral Scientist*, **40**(4), pp. 490–501.

Christensen, S. & Westenholz, A. (1999), *Medarbejdervalgte i danske virksomheder*, Copenhagen Business School Press, Copenhagen.

Clausen, C. & Broberg, O. (eds.) (2001), '*Arbejdsmiljø og teknologisk udvikling –Nye strategier og perspektiver*', Arbejdsmiljøets Service Center, København.

Clifton, R. (2000), 'The Consequences of New Enterprise Structures'. In *The Changing World of Work' – Magazine of the European Agency for Safety and Health at Work*, Luxembourg.

Crouch, C. & Traxler, F. (1998), '*Organized Industrial Relations in Europe: What Future?*', Aldershot, Avebury.

Csonka, A. (2000), 'Flexible Management and Empowered Work – Myth or Reality?' *Ledelse og arbejde under forandring*, **6**, Danish National Institute for Social Resarch, Copenhagen.

Csonka, A. (1999), *Fleksible virksomheder?*, SFI, Copenhagen.

Dahl, P. Nørgard (1999), 'Medarbejderinvolvering i ord og gerning – en kritisk diskursanalyse', *Dansk Sociologi*, **10**(3), pp. 47–68.

Danish Technological Institute (1998), '*Mellem udvikling og udstødning – fokus på de ufaglærte*', Danish Technological Institute, Denmark.

Davenport, T. (1993a), 'The Business Change and Re–engineering', interview with Tom Davenport by Watts, J. & Marwick, P., *Business Change & Re–engineering*, **2**(1).

Davenport, T. (1993b), '*Process Innovation. Re–engineering Work through Information Technology*', Boston, Harvard Business School Press.

Davenport, T. & Short, J. (1990), 'The New Industrial Engineering: Information Technology and Business Process Redesign', *Sloan Management Review* **31**(4).

Dawson, P., Clausen C. and Nielsen, K.T. (2000), 'Political Processes in Management, Organization, and the Social Shaping of Technology', *Technology Analyses & Strategic Management*, **12**(1).

Digrius, B. (1995), '*BPR consultants part 1–3*', Gartner Group Research note M–800–044.

Due, J. et al. (1993), *Den danske model: en historisk sociologisk analyse af det kollektive aftalesystem*, Jurist– og Økonomforbundets Forlag, Copenhagen.

Due, J. et al. (1994), *The survival of the Danish model: a historical sociological analysis of the Danish system of collective bargaining*, Jurist– og økonomforbundets forlag, Copenhagen.

Due, J., Madsen, J. S. and Strøby Jensen, C. (1993), *Labour Market Consensus: the Main Pillar of the Danish Model*, Danish Ministry of Labour, Copenhagen.

Earl, M. et al. (1994), 'How New is Business Process Redesign', *European Management Journal*, **12**(1).

Edling C. & Sandberg Å. (1997), 'Nya ledningsstrategier i Sverige', in: Å. Sandberg (ed.), *Ledning för alle? – Om perspektivbrytningar i företagsledning.*, SNS förlag, Stockholm.

EEC (1989), 'Directive on the Introduction of Measures to Encourage Improvements on the Safety and Health of Workers at Work', *EEC–Directive* 89/391, Brussels.

Eliasson–Lappalainen, R. & Szebehely, M. (1998), 'Omsorgskvalitet i svensk hemtjänst – hotad eller säkrad av att mätas?', in: Lappalainen, R. and Szebehely, M. (eds.), *Vad förgår och vad består? En antologi om äldreomsorg, kvinnosyn och socialpolitik*, Sweden.

Emery, F. E. (1976), *Democracy at Work: The Report of the Norwegian Industrial Democracy Program 1976*, International Series on the Quality of Working Life 2, Nijhoff.

Emery, F. E., & Thorsrud, E. (1976), *Democracy at work – The report of the Norwegian industrial democracy programme*, Martinus Jujhoff, Leiden, The Netherlands.

EPOC Research Group (1997), '*New forms of work organisation – Can Europe realise its potential? Results of a survey of direct employee participation in Europe*', European Foundation for the Improvement of Living and Working Conditions, Dublin, Ireland.

European Commission (1997), '*Green Paper: Partnership for a new organisation of work*', European Commission, Brussels.

European Commission (2001), 'Employment and social policies: a framework for investing in quality', *COM*(2201), 313, Brussels.

European Fondation of Social Quality, (2002), '*Social Quality and the Policy Domain of Employment*', Chapter 7, Amsterdam.

Finansministeriet (1994), *Medarbejder i staten: ansvar og udvikling*, Copenhagen.

Fisher, B. and Tronto, J. (1990), 'Towards a Feminist Theory of Caring', in: Abel & Nelson (eds.), *Circles of Care, Work and Identity in Women's Lives*, State University of New York Press.

Furusten, S. (1999), '*Popular Management Books; How They are Made and What They Mean for Organizations*', Routledge, London/New York.

Gardell, B. (1977), 'Autonomy and participation at work', *Human Relations*, **30**, pp. 515–533.

Gardell, B. (1991), 'Worker partipation and autonomy: A multilevel approach at the workplace', in: Johnson, J. V. & Johansson, G. (eds.), *The psychosocial work environment: Work organization, democratisation and health*, Baywood Publishing Company, Amity, pp. 193–223.

Gorz, A. (1999), '*Reclaiming Work: Beyond the Wage–Based Society*', Polity Press, Cambridge.

Gowler D., Legge, K. & Clegg, C. (1993), '*Case Studies in Organizational Behaviour and Human Resource Management*', 2nd ed, Paul Chapman Publishing Ltd, London.

Grint, K. (1995), '*Management – A Sociological introduction*', Cambridge, Polity Press.

Gustavsen, B. (1990), '*Vägen till bättre arbetsliv – Strategier och arbetsformer i ett okalt utvecklingsarbete*', Arbejdslivscentrum, Stockholm, Sweden.

Gustavsen, B. (1992), *Dialogue and Development*, Van Gorcum, Assen. Mastricht.

Gustavsen, B., Colbjørnsen, T. and Pålshaugen, Ø. (2000), *Development Coalitions in Working Life. The 'Enterprise Development 2000' Program in Norway.*

Gustavsen, B. et al. (1996), *Concept–Driven Development and the Organization of the Process of Change – An Evaluation of the Swedish Working Life Fund*, John Benjamin's Publishing Company, Amsterdam/Philadelphia.

Hagedorn–Rasmussen, P. (2000), '*Ledelseskoncepter fra idé til social dynamik – politiske processer på tværs af organisatoriske grænser, En analyse om sammenhænge mellem koncepter, forandringer og arbejdsforhold*', Ph.D. afhandling. RUC.

Hagedorn–Rasmussen, P. and Hvid, H. (1997), 'Management Concepts and Work Conditions – in a Danish Context', in Nielsen et al. (ed.), '*Work Environment and Technological Development – Positions and Perspectives*', Working paper, no. 3, Roskilde, Lyngby and Ålborg.

Hajer, M. A. (1995), '*The Politics of Environmental Discourse – Ecological Modernisation and the Policy Process*', Oxford University Press, Great Britain.

Hammer, M. (1990), 'Re–engineering Work: Don't Automate, Obliterate', *Harvard Business Review*, July–August.

Hammer, M. (1995), '*The Re–engineering Revolution*', London. Harper Collins.

Hans Böckler Stiftung (2001), '*Pathway to a Sustainable Future – Results from the Work & Environment Interdisciplinary project*', Hans Böckler Stiftung, Düsseldorf, Germany.

Hasle, P. & Møller, M. (2001), 'The Action Plan Against Repetitive Work – An Industrial Relation Strategy for Improving the Work Environment', in: *Human Factors and Ergonomics in Manufacturing*. **2**.

Hentze, S. (1992), '*Virksomhedens indførelse af kvalitetsstyring efter ISO 9000–serien og dens betydning for virksomhedens arbejdsforhold*', Institut for Arbejdsmiljø, Danmarks Tekniske Højskole, Denmark.

Heusinkveld, S., Benders, J. and Koch, C. (2000), '*Dispersed discourse? Defining the Shape of BPR in Denmark and The Netherlands*', Paper presented at the 16th EGOS Colloquium Helsinki.

Hirst, P. & Thompson, Grahame (1996), *Globalization in Question*, Polity Press, Cambridge.

Hochschild, A. R. (1997), '*The Time Bind – When Work becomes Home and Home becomes Work*', Metropolitan Books, New York.

Hofstede, G. (1994), *Cultures and Organizations: Software of the Mind*, McGraw–Hill, London.

Holt, H (2001), '*Evaluering af puljen til fremme af bedre arbejdsliv og øget vækst : Delrapport 1: 10 casebeskrivelser*', Arbejdsmarkedsstyrelsen, Copenhagen.

Hvenegaard, H. & Jessen, H. (2001), '*Stress og arbejdsglæde – om gruppeorganiseret arbejde*', CASA, Copenhagen.

Hvenegaard, H., Limborg, H.J. and Mathiesen, K. (1999), *Erfaringer fra forsøg med Det Udviklende Arbejde i 9 statsinstitutioner*, Centralrådet for statens samarbejdsudvalg, Copenhagen.

Hvid, H. (1990), *Det gode arbejde*. Fremad, Copenhagen.

Hvid, H. (2001), 'Dansk arbejdspolitiks gyldne tiår', in *Tidsskrift for arbejdsliv*, **4**.

Hvid, H. & Møller, N. (1992): *Det udviklende arbejde : mennesket i arbejdet – virksomheden i samfundet*, Fremad, Copenhagen.

Hvid, H. & Møller, N. (2001), 'The Developmental Work', *Human Factors and Ergonomics in Manufacturing*, **11**(2) pp. 89–101.

Hyman, R. & Ferner, A. (eds.) (1995), '*New Frontiers in European Industrial Relations*', Oxford: Blackwell, England.

Ibsen, F. (1999), 'Er det rationelt for virksomhederne at påtage sit et socialt ansvar?', *Tidsskrift for Arbejdsliv*, **1**(2), pp. 35–44.

Inglehart, R. (1997), '*Modernization and Postmodernization: Cultural, Economic, and Political Change in 43 Societies*', Princeton University Press, Princeton, N.J., USA.

Inglehart, R., Basanez, M, and Aljeandro, M. (1998), *Human Values and Beliefs: A Cross–Cultural Sourcebook.*

Isaksen, J. (2000), 'Constructing Meaning Despite the Drudgery of Repetitive Work', *Journal of Humanistic Psychology*, **40**(3) pp. 84–107.

Jackson, B. (2001), *Management gurus and management fashions*, Routledge, London and New York.

Jensen, P. L. (2002), 'Assessing Assessment: The Danish Experience of Worker Participation in Risk Assessment', *Economic and Industrial Democracy*, **2**, pp. 201–27.

Jessen, H. & Hvenegaard, H. (2001), '*Arbejdsmiljøfaktorer i gruppeorganiseret arbejde – litteraturstudie: Dokumentationsrapport Del 2*', CASA, Copenhagen.

Jessop, B. (1990), *State theory: putting the capitalist state in its place*, Polity Press, Cambridge.

Johnson, J. V. & Johansson, G. (eds.) (1991), *The Psycho–Social Work Environment: Work Organization, Democratization, and Health, Essays in Memory of Bertill Gardell*, Amityville, Baywood Publishing Company, N.Y.

Jørgensen, H. et al. (1992), '*Medlemmer og meninger – Rapport over en spørgeskemaundersøgelse blandt medlemmer af LO–forbundene*', APL–undersøgelsen, A–pressens trykkerier, LO and CARMA, Denmark.

Jørgensen, H. et al. (1993), *Medlemmer og meninger – Arbejdsliv og politik set i et lønmodtagerperspektiv*, LO and Karma, Aalborg.

Karasek, R. A. (1979), 'Job demands, job decision latitude, and mental strain: Implications for job redesign', *Administrative Science Quarterly* 24, 285–307.

Karasek, R. & Theorell, T. (1990), *Healthy Work. Stress, Productivity, and the Reconstruction of Working Life*, Basic Books, New York.

Kjellberg, A. (2001), *Fackliga organisationer och medlemmar i dagens Sverige*, Arkiv Förlag, Lund.

Kleinberg, K. (1996), '*BPR Tool Market: Mid 1996 Update part 1*', Gartner Group Research note.

Kleiner, A. (1995), 'The Battle For the Soul of Corporate America', *Wired*, Aug.

Knights, D. & Murray, F. (1994) '*Managers divided – Organizational Politics and Information Technology Management*', Chichester, Wiley.

Knudsen, H. (1995), '*Employee Participation in Europe*', Sage, London, England.

Koch, C. (2000a), '*The Uptake of Variants of BPR and Redesign in the Region of Denmark, internal paper*', The PRECEPT Project, Department of Technology and Society, Technical University of Denmark.

Koch, C. (2000b), '*Management Fads and Concepts: Knowledge Transfer, Isomorphism or Social Shaping – Conceptualizing the Danish Transformation of Business Process Re–engineering*', Paper prepared for the 4S/ EASST conference 'Worlds in Transition'. Wien.

Koch, C., Manske, F. and Vogelius, P (1997), '*The Battle for the Soul of Management Denmark –The Shaping of the Danish Versions of Business Process Re–engineering. Proceedings Management at a Crossroad*', University of Groningen.

Kompetencerådet (2000), *Kompetencerådets rapport 2000*, Huset Mandag Morgen, Copenhagen.

Korremann, G. (1987), '*Kvinder, mænd og omsor*gsarbejde', AKFs forlag, Copenhagen, Denmark.

Kristensen, T. S. (1996), 'Job Stress and Cardiovascular Disease: A Theoretic Critical Review', *Journal of Occupational Health Psychology* **3**, pp. 246–60.

Kristensen, T. S. (1999), 'Challenges for research and prevention in relation to work and cardiovascular diseases', *Scandinavian Journal of Work, Environment & Health* **25**, pp. 550–57.

Larsson, A. (1999), 'What Can We Learn From Denmark' in G. Schmid, and K. Schömann: '*Learning from Denmark*', Wissenschaftzentrum, Berlin.

Latour, B.(1987), '*Science in Action*', Open University Press, Milton Keynes.

Le Blansch, K. & Lorentzen, B. (1996), 'Do Workers and Trade Unions Have a Role to Play in Environmental Protection?', *Transfer* **3**.

Legge, K. (1995), *Human resource management – Rhetorics and realities*, Macmillan Business, London.

Limborg, H. J. (2001a), 'The Professional Working Environment Consultant – A New Actor on the Health and Safety Arena', *Human Factors and Ergonomics in Manufacturing*, **2**.

Limborg, H. J. (2001b), '*Den risikable fleksibilitet*', Ph.D..Afhandling, Forlaget Frydenlund, København.

LO (1991a), *Det udviklende arbejde – et idéoplæg*, Copenhagen

LO (1991b), *Det utvecklande arbetet. Människor och möjligheter*, Stockholm.

LO (2001a), '*The Developing Workplace Sample Kit. Copenhagen*', Located at: http://www.lo.dk/smcms/English_version/The_Developing/Index.htm?ID=2978.

LO (2001b), '*Danmarks strategi for bæredygtig udvikling – LO's holdninger og anbefalinger*', LO, København.

Lorentzen, B. et al. (1997), 'Medarbejderdeltagelse ved indførelse af renere teknologi', *Miljøprojekt* no. **354**, Miljøstyrelsen, Denmark.

Lund, H. (2001), '*Vejen mod en bæredygtig arbejdsplads – et medarbejderejet ledelsesprojekt*', Specialerapport, Institut for Miljø, Teknologi og Samfund, Roskilde Universitets Center, Roskilde.

Lund, H. (2002), 'Integrerede ledelsessystemer og arbejdspladsdemokrati i et bæredygtighedsperspektiv', *Tidsskrift for arbejdsliv*, **4**.

Lysgaard, S. (1967), '*Arbeiderkollektivet*', Universitetsforlaget, Oslo.

Madsen, M. (1997), 'Demokrati og individualisering – Udfordringer til det organisationsinterne demokrati i fagforeninger set i et medlemsperspektiv', *Licentiatserien* **5**, Institut for Statskundskab, Københavns Universitet.

Mahon, R. (1991), 'From Solidaristic Wages to Solidaristic Work: A Post–Fordist Historical Compromise for Sweden?', *Economic and Industrial Democracy*, **12**(3), pp. 295–326.

Marmot, M. G. et al. (1991), 'Health inequalities among British civil servants: the Whitehall II study', *The Lancet* **337**, 1387–93.

Mathiesen, K, et al. (1998), '*Udvidet medarbejderindflydelse i staten (MIO)*', Finansministeriet and Centralorganisationerne, Copenhagen.

Mathiesen, K. & Hvenegaard, H., (1999), 'Nye samarbejdsformer mellem ledelse og medarbejdere i staten', in: *Arbejdsliv*, **3**.

Mathiesen, K. & Hvenegaard, H. (2001), 'New Work Councils: Expanded Cooperation in the Public Sector in Denmark', in: *Human Factors and Ergonomics in Manufacturing*, **2**, pp. 145–57.

Metal (1994), '*KAM–projekt: Konkurrenceevne, miljø og arbejdsmiljø*', København, Metal.

Metallindustriarbetareförbundet (1985), *Det goda arbetet*, Tiba Tryck. Stockholm.

Metallindustriearbetarförbundet (1989), *Solidarisk arbetspolitik för det goda arbetet*, Gotab, Stockholm.

Miljøstyrelsen (1999), 'Erfaringer med miljøledelse i danske virksomheder', *Miljøprojekt* , **486**, Miljø– og Energiministeriet, Miljøstyrelsen, Denmark.

Navrbjerg, S. (1999), '*Nye arbejdsorganiseringer fleksibilitet og decentraliering – et sociologisk casestudie af fem industrivirksomheders organisering og samarbejdsforhold*', Jurist og Økonomforbundets Forlag, Copenhagen.

Nicky, J. (1992), 'Care = Organisation + Physical Labour + Emotional Labour', in: *Sociology of Health and Illness*, **4**, pp. 488–509.

Nielsen, K. (2000), 'Welfare, workfare and the good society: reflections on the offensive, neo–statist workfare strategy in Denmark'. In Greve, B. (2000), *What constitutes a good society?*, Macmillan, Basingstoke.

Pålshaugen, Ø. (1999), *The End of Organization Theory?*, John Benjamin's Publishing Company, Amsterdam/Philadelphia.

Paoli, P. & Merllie, D. (2001): *Third European survey on working conditions 2000*, European Foundation for the Improvement of Living and Working Conditions, Dublin.

Pettigrew, A.M. (1973), '*The Politics of Organizational Decision Making*', London, Tavistock.

Pfeffer, J. (1981), '*Power in Organizations*', Marshfield Mass, Pittman Publishing Inc.

Powell, W. & Dimaggio, P. (1991), '*The New Institutionalism in Organizational Analysis*', *Chicago*, Chicago University Press.

Sandberg, Å. (1992), *Technological Change and Co–Determination in Sweden*, Temple University Press, Philadelphia.

Sandberg, Å.(1997), '*Ledning för alla? Om perspektivbrytning i företagsledning*', SNS Förlag. Stockholm.

Sant, K. & Hviid, J. (1994), *Business Process Re–engineering*, København. Børsen Bøger.

Schmid, H. (1999), 'Velfærdsydelser som produktion', in: Eriksen T. R. et al. (eds.), *Spor i tiden. Kvalifikationer, definitioner, ord eller relationer mellem mennesker*, Munksgaard, Denmark.

Schnall, P. L., Landsbergis, P. A., and Baker, D. (1994), 'Job strain and cardiovascular disease', *Annual Review of Public Health* 15, 381–411.

Sennett, R. (1998), '*The Corrosion of Character: the Personal Consequences of Work in the New Capitalism*', W.W. Norton & Company, New York & London.

Setterlind, S. & Larsson, G. (1995), 'The Stress Profile: A psychosocial approach to measuring stress', *Stress Medicine* **11**, pp. 85–92.

Silverman, B. (1998), '*The rise and fall of the Swedish model*', interview with Swedish economist Rudolf Meidner, located at http://www.findarticles.com/cf_0/m1093/n1_v41/20485334/p1/article.jhtml.

Skorstad, E. J. (1999), *Produktionsformer i det tyvende århundrede – organisering, arbeidsvilkår og produktivitet*, Ad Notam Gyldendal, Oslo.

Storey, J. (1995), '*Human Resource Management – a Critical Text*', Routledge, London & New York.

Storey, J. (1992), '*Developments in the Management of Human Resources*', Blackwell.

Streck, W. (1999), *Competitive Solidarity: Rethinking the European Social Model*, Working paper, Max Planck Institute.

Svensson, L. (1983), '*Självstyrande grupper*', Arbetslivscentrum, Stockholm, Sweden.

Szebehely, M. (1995), '*Vardagens organisering. Om Vårdbiträden och gamla i hemtjänsten*', Lund Arkiv Förlag, Sweden.

Szebehely, M. (1996), 'Om omsorg og omsorgsforskning', in Rosmari Eliasson (ed.) Omsorgens skiftninger, Studentlitteratur, Lund, Sweden.

Szebehely, M. (1999), 'Changing divisions of carework: Caring for children and frail elderly people in Sweden', in Lewis, Jane, '*Gender, social and welfare state restructuring in Europe*', Ashgate, Aldershot.

Teknik&Data (1996), 'BPR har ikke fået sit danske gennembrud', *Techworld* **1**.

Teknologisk Institut (2000), '*Organisationsudvikling og udvikling af arbejdet – en analyse af perspektiver, muligheder og potentielle risici for polarisering og udstødning*', udarbejdet for LO, Denmark.

Thorsrud, E. (1970), *Mod nye samarbejdsformer : eksperimenter i industrielt demokrati.*, Hasselbalch, Management serien, Oslo.

Toulmin, S. and Gustavsen. B. (1996), '*Beyond Theory*', John Benjamin Publishing Company, Amsterdam.

Ullmark, P., Steen, J. & Holmgren, A. (1986), '*Det matnyttiga arbetet*', Tiden, Sweden.

Van Veen, K. & Sanders (1997), '*From Function to Fad: A Model to Understand The Emergence Diffusion and Decline of Management Concepts. Proceedings Management at a Crossroads*', University of Groningen.

Wærness, K. (1982), '*Kvinnoperspektiver på socialpolitikken*', Universitetsforlaget, Oslo, Norway.

Wærness, K. (1983), '*Kvinnor och omsorgsarbete*', Stockholm, Sweden.

Wærness, K. (1985), 'Den nye "Community" –ideologin – en utfordring for sociologisk forskning', *Sociologisk forskning* **2–3**, pp. 21–36.

Wærness, K. (1990), 'Informal and Formal Care in Old Age: What is Wrong With the New Ideology in Scandinavia Today?', in Ungerson, C. (ed.) '*Gender and Caring*', Harvester Wheat Sheaf.

Wærness K. (1992), 'Privat og offentlig eldreomsorg' in Daatland, S.O. and Solem, P.E. (eds.), '*Og du skal leve længe i landet*', Universitetsforlaget, Oslo, Norway.

Wærness, K. (1996), 'Omsorgsrationalitet' in Eliasson, R. (ed.) 'Omsorgens skiftningar. Begreppet, vardagen, politiken, forskningen', Studentlitteratur, Lund, Sweden.

Wærness, K. (1999). 'The changing "welfare mix" in childcare and care for the frail elderly in Norway', in Lewis, J. '*Gender, social and welfare state restructuring in Europe*', Ashgate, Aldershot.

Ware, J. E. et al. (1993), *SF–36 health survey. Manual and interpretation guide*. The Health Institute, New England Medical Center, Boston.

Wilkinson, A. & Willmott, H. (eds.), (1995), '*Making Quality Critical*', New Perspectives on Organizational Change, Routledge.

Wobbe, W. (1992), '*What are anthropocentric production systems? Why are they a strategic issue for Europe?*', Brussels.

www.arbejdsliv.dk.

www.saraweb.dk.

Index

Page numbers in *italics* refer to figures and tables